BOOTH GIRLS

BOOTH GIRLS

Pregnancy, Adoption,
and the Secrets We Kept

KIM HEIKKILA

MINNESOTA
HISTORICAL
SOCIETY PRESS

CLEAN
WATER
LAND &
LEGACY
AMENDMENT

Portions of this story have been told in the following publications:

Kim Heikkila, "'Brighter and Better for Every Person': Building the New Salvation Army Rescue Home of St. Paul, 1913," *Ramsey County History* (Spring 2016): 3–11.

Kim Heikkila, "A Child's Sorrow," in *Inside and Out: Women's Truths, Women's Stories: Essays from the Story Circle Network* (Georgetown, TX: Story Circle Network, 2017), 106-9.

Kim Heikkila, "'Everybody Thinks It's Right to Give the Child Away': Unwed Mothers at Booth Memorial Hospital, 1961–1963," *Minnesota History* 65, no. 6 (Summer 2017): 229–41.

Kim Heikkila, "Insomnia," *Under the Gum Tree* (October 2016): 20–31.

Kim Heikkila, "My Mother 'Got in Trouble' in 1960s Minnesota," *Minneapolis Star Tribune*, April 30, 2016.

Kim Heikkila, "Sparring with Infertility," Broad! eZine (Summer 2014), https://issuu.com /broadzine/docs/mothers.

mnhspress.org

The Minnesota Historical Society Press is a member of the Association of University Presses.

Manufactured in the United States of America

10 9 8 7 6 5 4 3 2 1

∞ The paper used in this publication meets the minimum requirements of the American National Standard for Information Sciences—Permanence for Printed Library Materials, ANSI Z39.48–1984.

International Standard Book Number
ISBN: 978-1-68134-190-3 (paper)
ISBN: 978-1-68134-191-0 (e-book)

Library of Congress Control Number: 2020950675
This and other MNHS Press books are available from popular e-book vendors.

To all the mothers whose children

have been raised by others

CONTENTS

A NOTE ABOUT LANGUAGE

THE TERMS USED TO DESCRIBE ADOPTION and the people whose lives it most directly affects are as fraught as the practice itself, conveying different sympathies and stigmas depending on who is speaking to whom and when. Adoption language, like adoption itself, has a history. When my husband and I went through training at our adoption agency in 2005–06, we were taught to use positive (or respectful) adoption language (PAL or RAL), a concept first advanced by adoption social worker Marietta Spencer of Children's Home Society of Minnesota in 1978–79. We and the other trainees were going to be "parents" of a child whose "birth mother" had "made an adoption plan" for her child, in the case of "domestic infant adoption," or who was "awaiting placement" for "international adoption." Such words, we were told, did away with outdated, hurtful terms that described "natural" or "real" parents or "unwed mothers" who "put up," "gave up," "surrendered," or "abandoned" for adoption an "illegitimate" child to be raised by "adoptive parents." We were also warned that insensitive people would ask us how much we had paid for our children and were advised to explain that we paid for services provided by social workers and adoption agencies, much like biological parents paid for services provided by doctors and hospitals. Children were not commodities bought and sold in an adoption market. Still, the language of the market has been widely used for decades, whether by social welfare officials who distinguished adoptions effected by licensed agencies from those that occurred in the "black" or "gray" markets, by scholars who applied the laws of supply and demand to their analysis of the transfer of children from one set of parents to another, or by critics who deplore the economic factors that force one woman to "transfer" her child to another.[1]

In 1978, Concerned United Birthparents (CUB), a support and advocacy group founded by birthmothers, issued its own guidelines on proper word usage. CUB argued that "birthparent/birthmother" (versus Spencer's proposed "biological parent") was "both accurate and sensitive to our place in the child's existence" and that "surrender" most accurately depicted its members' experience of having released their children for adoption under pressure and in the absence of genuine alternatives. By the 2010s, language has shifted again. Many women who carry and deliver a child who is then raised by others now take umbrage when their status as mothers is qualified by the term "birth," believing it to be a dehumanizing term that reduces them to breeders or incubators for wealthy couples searching for a baby in the adoption market. Instead, building on CUB's logic, they propose the use of honest adoption language (HAL) that recognizes their enduring relationship to their children.[2]

In this book, I use many of these terms interchangeably, depending on the context in which I am writing and what I am describing. Since most of the book focuses on my mother's experience of her first pregnancy in 1960–61, I frequently rely on the terminology in vogue at the time, even if—or precisely because—it carried negative connotations (e.g., "unwed mother," "unmarried mother," "out of wedlock," "illegitimate," "relinquish"). "Single pregnant women" is a more contemporary phrase intended to be more neutrally descriptive. I follow CUB's lead (at least from the late 1970s) in referring to the "surrender" of a child; nowhere do I describe Mom or other Booth girls as having made an "adoption plan." I use the term "illegitimate" without quotation marks when describing ideas about behavior, but never to refer to children. Though the term was widely used at the time, and therefore is important to understanding the world in which Mom lived, I always put it in quotation marks to call attention to its contested nature. I use "adoption market" deliberately to refer to the economic forces underlying adoption and the inequitable position in which they place birth mothers relative to adoptive mothers. Finally, I adhere to CUB's 1978 guidance to use the term "birthmother"—one word—understanding that it, too, is troubling to many. But CUB used it as a self-identifying term of empowerment in the 1970s, and I retain it as such here. When referring to my son's mother, however, I call her his "Vietnam mama/mother," only to distinguish her from me in the most basic, literal sense. She is there, I am here, and we are both his mother, though we occupy very different places in the hierarchy of power on which adoption is built. I refer to myself most often, though not only, as an "adoptive mother" because I believe that my route to motherhood through adoption is salient to the issues under discussion here.

BOOTH GIRLS

ORIGINS

I AM NOT A BOOTH GIRL. My mother, Sharon Lee Moore Wikstrom, was.

I first learned I had a sister in July 1994, over burgers and fries at the Ground Round in Crystal.

It was just me and Mom that night. We slid into a booth, peanut shells crunching beneath our feet. I didn't notice Mom's nervousness as we snacked on salty yellow popcorn, how she barely touched her food once it arrived. I was twenty-six, married, working as an assistant probation officer, and full of myself in the way that even adult children can be with their parents. I waxed on about my unhappiness at work and frustrations at home, oblivious to Mom's unease. Then, finally, she took advantage of a pause in my diatribe as I bit into my burger.

"Kim, there's something I have to tell you."

"Mm hmm?" I mumbled with my mouth full.

She took a breath, then the words came tumbling out:

"When I was twenty before I met your dad I got pregnant and had a baby that I gave up for adoption you have a sister."

She paused, looking at me expectantly. I finished chewing, swallowed, and said:

"Wow."

"It was a different time then. I made a mistake and handled it the best way I could."

"Wow."

"I hope you're not angry or disappointed. I hope you can forgive me."

"Forgive you? For what?" I saw her shoulders relax. "It didn't have anything to do with me. I wasn't even around. Wow. I have a sister."

"Yes, you do." She took another breath. "And I've been in touch with her. In fact, I just met her. She and her husband live in Michigan, but they were driving through town on their way to visit family up north, so she stopped in and we spent the day together. She's coming back at the end of the month to meet you and Eric and everyone else."

"Wow. Okay, cool. Wow."

This time, Mom took a bite of her burger.

"Oh, and by the way? Her name is Kim."

I spent the rest of that dinner listening to Mom tell her story: how she had gotten pregnant in 1960 while she was a student at the University of Minnesota; how her boyfriend—a man I'll call Jack—had left her to deal with the situation alone; how her parents had hidden her in an upstairs bedroom for months; how she had spent the last weeks of her pregnancy at the Salvation Army Booth Memorial Hospital in St. Paul; how she had delivered a baby girl on January 16, 1961, and surrendered her for adoption for the good of everyone involved; how she had told no one but my father about her secret and how they had both kept it for the next thirty-three years.

I wasn't angry or disappointed, as Mom had feared my brother, Eric, and I would be. Mostly I was shocked. Shocked that I had a sister, shocked that my mother had lived with such a secret in such silence for so long, shocked that she had never let it slip, not once in my twenty-six years. But, more than all of this, I was shocked to realize that my mother's life had a trajectory of its own, determined in equal parts by history, circumstance, choice, and luck; it hadn't always and only been steaming ahead toward the destination that was me. It's embarrassing to admit my self-centeredness now, as an adult and a mother myself. Of course mothers are more than a status defined by their children. Part of my surprise, then, stemmed from an understanding of how myopic a view I had of the woman who had borne and raised me. How well did I really know my mother? What did I know of her past, really, beyond the stories of the "olden days" that she had shared with me when I was a child? Who was this woman I called Mom?

I wish I had taken the opportunity to ask Mom about the details of her first pregnancy when I had the chance. Just after I met my sister, I returned to graduate school to study US history and feminist theory. After completing my doctorate in 2002, I taught women's history and oral history methods at a women's college, helping students interview their mothers and grand-mothers. Somehow, though, I never asked my own mother to tell her story. There had been plenty of time, numerous opportunities. I had been aware of her once-secret past for fifteen years by the time she died in February 2009. Though we had not consciously avoided such discussions, neither had we intentionally sought them. Our rather matter-of-fact discussions of Mom's experience and Kim's new presence in our lives were in keeping with our style of family communication. Scandinavian stoics, we preferred to deal with pragmatics rather than emotions, and the most obvious fact was that there was a new member of the family. It was only in the years after her death, as I struggled with my own experience of motherhood, that I began wondering about the long-term effects of Mom's experiences as a Booth girl. Because I had not taken the most direct path toward the understanding I sought, I was left to wend my way along a circuitous trail, through the thickets of memory and history and imagination, toward the destination of knowing my mother better. This book is the story of that journey.

I met my sister* Kim for the first time just a few weeks after having learned of her existence. She returned to Minnesota in late July 1994 to meet me and Eric and her biological maternal aunts, uncles, and cousins. She looked like Eric and my mother's youngest siblings, the fair-haired, blue-eyed standouts in a family full of dark hair and eyes. I watched Mom and Kim together, their interaction a blend of deep communion and awkward newness. We all joked about my brother having two sisters named Kim (her adoptive parents had chosen the name) and dusted off old family photo albums to give Kim a chance, for the first time, to see herself reflected in the cracked and blurry images of her forebears. She must have been studying all of us, searching for missing links in her family history or explanations for quirky habits or physical features—her deep-set dimples and long legs weren't just flukes of nature; they came from somewhere, from someone. At that family picnic at

---

*Technically, Kim is my half-sister, as we share only a maternal genetic heritage. To describe her as such feels pedantic and parsimonious, however, so I most often refer to her merely as "my sister."

Lake Harriet in the summer of 1994, she was surrounded by a bunch of those someones.

But Kim trained most of her attention on me, Eric, and Mom, searching for threads that would bind us together. Having been raised an only child, she was excited at the idea of having siblings for the first time in her life. The three of us studied her, too. We looked for the effects of nature but noted the impact of nurture. Kim was a cat person; we loved dogs. Kim found a creative outlet in serious scrapbooking, while Eric shared Mom's musical talents and I her love of writing. Kim liked to shop; I hated it.

The four of us shared a great deal, too, from handwriting styles to a tendency toward introversion. We also had in common a certain cool regard toward children. It wasn't that we didn't like them, but none of us was, as they say, a "baby person." Mom had had three children, raised two of them, and played an active role in the lives of her nieces and nephews, but she viewed women who had a single-minded focus on children and babies with wonder and a hint of disapproval. In 1994, Kim was thirty-three, childless, and happily married to her second husband, and I had rebuffed my husband's overtures toward starting a family for the four years of our marriage. (Eric was twenty-four, single, and a man, so the question hardly seemed relevant to him at the time.) When Kim and I both eventually became mothers to only-children boys—she within a year of her reunion with us and me eleven years after that—we found new common ground; we loved our boys, but naturally nurturing mothers we were not.

Looking back on it now, it hardly seems surprising that the three of us might share a legacy of uneasy maternal nurturing, given the disruptions surrounding Mom's first pregnancy. In the mid-1990s, though, I was in graduate school, with motherhood a distant speck on the horizon, so I didn't give this family inheritance much thought. I did, however, get a glimpse of the profound impact Mom's first pregnancy had made on her life when, in the late 1990s, I visited Kim and her family while I was in Detroit for a conference. One day, as we sat in her living room, Kim asked if I'd read the story Mom had written about fleeing to California after she learned she was pregnant. I had not; I had not even heard about the story. Kim dug through some papers in a desk drawer, found the essay, titled "Greyhound," and gave it to me to read. I sat on Kim's couch and, for the first time, "listened" to my mother describe the painful experience of hiding her illicit pregnancy and surrendering her "illegitimate" baby for adoption. I was flabbergasted at the emotionality of the piece, moved almost to tears. Kim offered to make a copy of it for me, but I hesitated, feeling as if I had intruded on a private moment between Mom and Kim. Mom had given it to Kim, not me. I didn't feel hurt or excluded, but I was surprised at the depth of their relationship. I handed the essay back to Kim and never mentioned to Mom that I had read it.

Several years later, in 2006, Ann Fessler published her influential book, *The Girls Who Went Away: The Hidden History of Women Who Surrendered Children for Adoption in the Decades Before* Roe v. Wade. Herself an adoptee, Fessler interviewed numerous women whose lives had been profoundly altered by the shame, silence, and stigma surrounding premarital pregnancy in the post–World War II United States. Her book helped me understand that Mom's invisible experience of unwed motherhood had likely shaped her subsequent experience of married motherhood.

The publication of *The Girls Who Went Away* would seem to have provided another opening to talk about Mom's Booth story—Mom and I both read the book—but in 2006, I was consumed by events in my own life. My husband, Steve, and I spent that year immersed in the process of becoming adoptive parents. On December 13, in a small room in a government office in the sweltering heat of southern Vietnam, we became parents to another woman's son.

Mom stood by, cheering us on, throughout this whole process. I gave Mom updates about our adoption status, conveyed information we learned in our adoption training, shared my reading list of books about transracial and transnational adoption. We both read Jane Jeong Trenka's *The Language of Blood* and Cheri Register's *Beyond Good Intentions.* I remember discussing these books with her, talking about how race and power and privilege would shape the family we were going to be. I do not remember asking how she felt about all of this as a woman whose first experience of motherhood was also, if differently, disenfranchised.[1]

Once we brought our son, Tu, home with us, in late December 2006, I was swallowed up once again by a situation that felt all-consuming and alienating. And, once again, Mom was there. For the brief time that her life intertwined with Tu's, she was his biggest fan and my biggest supporter. Motherhood did not come easily to me, but Mom's delighted infatuation with Tu, her genuine enthusiasm to help—along with Steve's patience and good humor—helped me survive early motherhood's darkest moments. When she died in 2009, I lost not only the woman who had raised me for forty years, but the woman who had helped me raise my son for two.

And so here I am, more than a decade later, trying to weave together the strands of Mom's life and mine, both of us having mothered through the gains and losses of adoption.

This book is many things, but it is first and foremost my attempt to come to a better understanding of my mother, in her absence, by learning about a formative experience from her life before I entered it. To comprehend that experience, I needed to study the context in which it had occurred, to see the ways in which it had not been hers alone. Though she is the "Booth girl" at the center of this story, she was but one of thousands whose paths crossed with Booth Memorial Hospital in St. Paul between 1898 and 1973, one of tens of thousands who hid their pregnancies in the nationwide network of maternity homes run by the Salvation Army in the first half of the twentieth century, one of hundreds of thousands who surrendered their babies in the post–World War II era, when adoption was heralded as the "best solution" to the problems of "illegitimacy" and infertility. In making a historical study of Mom's past, then, her individual story takes its place in a collective narrative about how mothering is practiced in our most intimate relationships and enacted through our most public debates.[2]

Though I draw on my training as a historian and rely on traditional historical sources and research methods, I do not intend this book to be a traditional work of historical scholarship. Instead, I blend more explicitly the various habits of mind, lines of inquiry, and styles of expression that define, but are not limited to, all good works of history. I give equal space to documents preserved in archives and notebooks moldering in musty basements, to polished analyses disseminated in scholarly circles and halting reflections shared across a kitchen table, to firsthand rememberings of one's own past and secondhand imaginings of another's. More specifically, I draw on five kinds of sources that shape the content, structure, and style of the book.

My mother was a prolific writer. In her first attempt at college—from 1957 to 1960, when her surprise pregnancy derailed her education—she studied journalism. Though she wouldn't complete her degree for almost four decades, she made a career out of writing, mostly in the marketing department at Carlson Companies and eventually for the University of Minnesota Foundation. She also kept a daily journal and wrote prose and poetry and plays. When she returned to the university in the late 1990s, she earned a degree in English and creative writing. It was as part of her coursework that she wrote "Greyhound," the essay she shared with Kim and Kim with me. Sometime prior to this, she wrote another essay about her first pregnancy, titled "Birth Rite." These two pieces provide the fullest account of Mom's experience as an "unwed mother," including her time at Booth Memorial Hospital and relinquishment of and reunion with Kim.

Excerpts from these writings—the bulk of them from "Greyhound"—open each chapter, allowing Mom to "speak" in her own, first-person voice and guide the narrative that unfolds. Other selections appear where her voice tells the story most powerfully. As such, these essays provide the primary framework for this book.

But Mom's accounts evoke additional questions as well, some that she may have been able to answer had I put them to her, others that require stepping beyond the confines of personal recall to address. Most of each chapter is thus my attempt to ask and answer these questions by turning to the historical record, the second source that drives this narrative. Both published scholarship and archival collections help us understand Mom's experience as part of a collective past. Some of her most intimate experiences sit squarely within public debates occurring across the nation and within Minnesota about premarital sex, sex education, birth control, and abortion. Historians have produced excellent scholarly work on the gendered sexual culture of the post–World War II United States as well as analyses of single pregnancy, adoption, and reunion, all of which illuminate the choices that were—and were not—available to Mom as she made plans for her baby and lived with their consequences. Records from organizations such as the Salvation Army, Planned Parenthood of Minnesota, Concerned United Birthparents of Minnesota, the University of Minnesota, state health and welfare departments, and other social welfare agencies reveal the ways in which national trends described in published scholarship played out in Minneapolis, St. Paul, and the state of Minnesota.

If scholarly studies and archival collections help us see that Mom's experiences were defined by the historical forces of her time, the third source on which I rely brings us back into the realm of lived experience. With the support of the Minnesota Independent Scholars Forum and funding from the Minnesota Arts and Cultural Heritage Fund, I was able to conduct oral history interviews with nine women who had connections to Booth Memorial Hospital in St. Paul (Booth St. Paul): a former labor and delivery nurse who had worked at the home for five years, a former Ramsey County caseworker who had counseled Booth girls for two years, and seven women who had delivered babies at (or under the auspices of) Booth St. Paul between 1957 and 1965. I found some of these women through contact with the local chapter of Concerned United Birthparents (CUB) and with the former Booth Memorial

Hospital, now the Salvation Army Booth Brown House; others reached out to me after reading articles I had published about Mom and my research. One woman introduced herself during a talk I gave at St. Catherine University. I told these women about Mom and the goals of my project, that I was an adoptive mother searching for answers in my own mother's past. All of them agreed without hesitation to share their memories of what, for the former Booth girls at least, had been one of the most difficult experiences of their lives.[3]

Their stories provide another organizing structure for the book. I retell one Booth girl's story near the end of each of seven chapters, their experiences echoing Mom's own, their voices giving flesh and blood to researchers' statistics and experts' theories and historians' analyses. Although the nurse's and caseworker's stories are not highlighted in the same way as the Booth girls', they provide important, humanizing insight into the professionals tasked with caring for and counseling unmarried mothers-to-be.[4]

These nine interviewees constitute a tiny sample of Booth's overall population, and their accounts should not be taken as a statistically significant representation thereof. My goal was not to conduct a comprehensive, generalize-able study of Booth St. Paul's onetime residents or staff, but to talk to women who might serve as proxies for Mom, to see if, in listening to their stories, I might come closer to understanding what it had felt like to be a Booth girl. Another way I attempt to do this is through imagination, the fourth source on which I draw. Though some historians might balk at the idea of projecting themselves into another person's life, I believe that, in many ways, this empathy is at the very heart of our enterprise. We ask our questions, gather our evidence, and listen to what it tells us so that we might feel what it was like to live in those times in those circumstances, understand how something amazing or horrible or seemingly incomprehensible or frighteningly mundane might have occurred. Imagining another's life is not the same as appropriating it or searching for false camaraderie or proclaiming an impossible universal human experience. There are often real and important differences in power—racial, economic, institutional— between the historian and the people she studies, not least that the historian can choose if, when, and how to engage with the world in which her "subjects" live their daily lives. But abandoning even the possibility of imagining, however briefly and imperfectly, the taste of sweetness or bitterness on someone else's tongue seems to me to lead to a dead end of intractably sealed silos.

Brief sections in which I depict scenes from Mom's life in the third person are woven into each chapter and highlighted typographically. Though they are rendered imaginatively, I have not created them out of whole cloth. They are based on actual occurrences Mom and others described, sometimes at length, sometimes in passing. If details in one source were lacking, I filled them in with details from another or from my knowledge of Mom and the world in which she lived. A few of these sections draw heavily on Mom's own writing, but the creative act of translating her first-person account into my third-person depiction helped me inhabit some especially crucial incidents from her Booth girl story. The moment she felt the first twinges of pregnancy. The wakeful hours she spent listening to another Booth girl labor in the middle of the night. The day she received a life-changing telephone call from a woman named Sandy.

The final source that informs the content and structure of the book is my own experience of infertility and adoptive motherhood. Though these events cast only refracted light on Mom as she becomes a grandmother to another woman's adopted-away child, they are one of the primary motivations driving this entire project. I wanted to understand my mother better, yes, but I wanted to do so in part because I struggled so mightily in becoming a mother myself. That I did so through adoption, the same mechanism that had stripped Mom of her maternal identity, is too great an irony to have ignored.

And so I have indulged in the conceit of memoir, offering after the close of each chapter a brief account of a particularly important step in my path to becoming a mother, from losing a pregnancy and undergoing infertility treatments to traveling to Vietnam to adopt our son and starting life as a family back in Minnesota. I have chosen these moments not only because they are central to my mothering story but also because they are inverse reflections on Mom's. She confronted the pain of an unplanned pregnancy, of an "excess" of fertility; I mourned the loss of a pregnancy, a deficit of fertility. The private and state child welfare apparatus helped to separate her from her child, but it brought me mine. Her task was to make a fresh start of life without her baby; mine was to build a new life with a toddler. The upside-down parallels are not exact; the pain, privilege, and power not equivalent. Adoption bestows unequal gifts and inflicts unequal heartache on its mothers, yet even in its blessings lay hardship and in its difficulties a degree of comfort.

Theoretically, it would be possible to separate these five strands into their own complete stories, distinct in tone, style, and content. Others have done this, to good effect: birth and adoptive mothers have written memoirs, historians have published monographs, oral historians have compiled collections of interviews, writers have made artful fiction out of actual experience. My challenge has been to weave these threads together into an interlocking whole. Our lives don't unfold in the separate tracks suggested by academic discipline or literary genre. Instead, they emerge in the warp and woof of experience and knowledge, of emotion and intellect, of fact and imagination. Liberating myself from the constraints of any single approach allowed me to see Mom, to feel her, in fuller dimension. Sometimes, when I felt stuck in the historical analysis, overwhelmed by the mass of information and data, I put it aside and stepped into the realm of imagination. The words, the ideas, the understanding suddenly flowed differently. When I couldn't quite touch something Mom or the other Booth girls had experienced, the how and the why of it, I turned to the scholarship. I could feel a different region of my brain activate; you may hear my writing voice change. If I found myself questioning the entire enterprise of adoption, I reminded myself that I could not do so without examining how my life had been shaped by it, that its contradictions live inside the four walls of my house. If I were another person, I might have sought understanding through art or music or religion or psychology. But I am a daughter, a historian, a writer, an adoptive mother. These are the channels through which I conjure my mother.

Now, a few words about what this book is not. It is not an attempt to tell a complete story of adoption. Most obviously, it is not intended to represent the perspective or experiences of adoptees. I recount some of Kim's story in the final chapter, as Mom (and the rest of us) gets to know her an adult. I tell snippets of my son's story, but only through the lens of my becoming his mother. My focus is on *mothering* through adoption and, as such, addresses only two angles of what for many years was known as the "adoption triad"—birthmother/parents, adoptive mother/parents, and adoptee. In my role as Mom's daughter, however, I also speak from my position in what is now known as the "adoption constellation"—the much broader group of people whose lives are impacted by adoption, including birth siblings like me. Adopted people occupy a central and unique position in both of these configurations. As children, they have often been the subject of much public debate and policy maneuverings as others have attempted to act in their "best interest." As adults, they have spoken with powerful and diverse voices to reframe those discussions and reform those policies. Those voices have shaped my understanding of adoption and practice of mothering in profound ways, even if they are not given full attention here.

Some of the most compelling accounts and analyses of adoption have come from transnationally and transracially adopted people. That my family has been achieved by adopting a child away not just from his birthmother but from his birth culture, nation, language, and identity is one of the most significant distinctions between Mom's and my inverse relationship to adoption. The powerful forces that directed so many children of white single mothers to adoptive homes in the middle of the twentieth century are exaggerated by degree and kind in transnational, transracial adoption. This context is not the immediate subject of the story at hand, even if it is the defining factor in our family's adoption story. Though including the story of our son's adoption may elicit questions about it, and though I end the book with a brief discussion of transnational and transracial adoption, I leave a fuller exploration of these dynamics to future work as I concentrate here on searching for meaning in my mother's past.

In many ways, Mom's experiences and the history of single pregnancy and adoption are examples of the power of sexism and patriarchy to inflict pain on women. Single pregnant women were the targets of shame and intervention by public and private social welfare agencies, while their male partners could, and often did, evade similar consequences. But it is impossible to understand her experiences or this history solely in terms of gender. If race has been central to my becoming and being an adoptive mother, it was no less critical to Mom's as a relinquishing mother.

Black women were far more likely than white women to have babies outside of marriage, yet they were far less likely to land in a maternity home and to relinquish their children for adoption. In 1960, the year Mom got pregnant, nine of every one thousand unmarried white women gave birth to a child, compared to 98 of every one thousand unmarried Black women. In Minnesota that year, nearly 25 per one thousand white babies were born to unmarried women, while the rate was about 213 per one thousand for nonwhite women.** Yet 94 percent of Black babies born to single mothers across the country lived with their parents or relatives, while only 29 percent of white babies born to single mothers stayed with those women.[5]

**In 1960 Minnesota was 98.2 percent white, with the largest nonwhite groups being Black (0.7 percent) and Native American (0.5 percent). Thus the research on this era focuses on these two groups, as does the discussion that follows.

Mom's story is a white woman's story, not just because she happened to be white, but because her experiences were channeled through her whiteness. Single pregnant white women were viewed, understood, and treated in ways distinct from those in which single pregnant Black, Brown, and Indigenous women were viewed, understood, and treated. It is no accident that the majority of single women who hid their pregnancies in institutions such as Booth St. Paul were white. It is not mere coincidence that most of the women who surrendered babies for adoption, or that most babies who were formally adopted in the post–World War II United States, were white, despite the uneven numbers of "illegitimate" children born to white and nonwhite women. As historian Rickie Solinger has pointed out, race was the single most important factor in determining the fate of a single pregnant woman and her baby in this country at that time. It determined the professional, public, and private understanding of her premarital pregnancy, the resources and services devoted to addressing it, and the response to and outcome of it.[6]

Why was this so? Because race has always been intimately associated with reproduction, insofar as it has been defined in terms of lineage, biological inheritance, and kinship. "The core notion of common substance transmitted through heterosexual intercourse and birth underscores the gendered nature of the concept of race," historian Tessie Liu writes. "In a male-dominated society, this concept focuses particular attention on women's activities, on reproductive politics, and, more generally, on control over sexuality and sexual behavior." Maintaining racial hierarchy and the material benefits it confers on those at the top depends on controlling women's reproduction in race-specific ways. Policies and practices that seek to accomplish these ends do not merely respond to preexisting, naturally occurring, easily identifiable racial groups; instead, they help to create and perpetuate social, political, and economic differences that come to be associated with racial groups.[7]

Historians and legal scholars have traced the parallels between cultural beliefs and institutional policies regarding race and those regarding single pregnancy and adoption, most of them hinging on the economic interests of the state as well. The white-dominated public health and social welfare systems inflicted different pressures on single, economically insecure white, African American, and Native American women to control their sexual behavior and, once pregnant, to ensure that they and their children would not become dependent on public welfare funds. Policies and practices regarding contraceptives, sterilization, illegitimacy, infertility, and adoption depended on and reinforced ideas about race that viewed some women as, to use Solinger's language, "socially productive breeders" and others as "socially unproductive breeders."[8]

In this formulation, Mom and other white women who became pregnant outside of marriage threatened the nuclear family ideal and the ideas about gender on which it relied, but their babies were highly prized in the swelling adoption market. So she followed—or was directed down—a path that would ostensibly lead to her rehabilitation and her child's success in the loving care of deserving adoptive parents. The racist social welfare apparatus viewed Black and Indigenous unwed mothers, on the other hand, as acting out inherent and immutable biological or cultural defects and so beyond the reach of any redemptive intervention. Moreover, the thinking went, their children would inherit those same defects, be judged to have little value in the white-dominated adoption market, and, with their mothers, become drains on the public purse. Instead of being directed to maternity homes and the adoption option, they were left to the care of kin and community. Although African Americans and Native Americans may have been, for various reasons, more accepting of single motherhood than the white middle class and so less interested in sending their young women to far-off maternity homes, there were relatively few maternity homes and prospective adopters who would have accepted them and their children. Solinger points out that, in 1951, only seven homes across the country served Black women exclusively, a mere "handful of others" accepting them alongside their white counterparts, and that, in 1960, 70 percent of babies born to single white women but only 5 percent of babies born to single nonwhite women were adopted.[9]

Though white children have always made up the lion's share of formal adoptions in the United States, the numbers shifted throughout the 1960s as changes spurred by the civil rights movement, federal policy toward Indigenous peoples, and decreasing rates of surrender by white single mothers led to concerted efforts, in Minnesota and elsewhere, to place African American and Native American children in white adoptive families. This had an especially devastating effect on Indigenous families. According to historian Margaret Jacobs, Native children were nineteen times more likely than other children to be adopted away from their families. When foster care and boarding school placements are included in the tally, Native parents and children were separated at rates *seventy-four* times greater than white parents and children in some states. In Minnesota in 1971, when Native Americans constituted approximately 0.6 percent of the state's population, almost 25 percent of Native children less than a year old were placed for adoption.[10]

These bald statistics reflect the complicated history of race, single pregnancy, and adoption in the United States, one that varies by region and era
and the specific histories of specific racial groups. I cannot tell this story—
these stories—in their entirety here, though I will take note of how, when,
and why social welfare experts steered white women down a different course
than they did Black and Indigenous women, even as I stay focused on the
road my mother traveled.[11]

I have visited the former Booth Memorial Hospital on Como Avenue three
times, in 2012, 2015, and 2019. When Mom was there in 1961, it was one of
thirty-six maternity homes and hospitals run by the Salvation Army throughout the United States. The Army now operates the facility as the Booth
Brown House, a shelter and transitional housing program for young people.
The institution consists of two distinct wings: a bland utilitarian structure
on the east and the stately original building on the west. The latter has been
listed on the National Register of Historic Places since 1983, a tribute to its
architectural style and cultural significance. For sixty years, from 1913 to
1973, that two-and-a-half story Tudor Revival sheltered unmarried pregnant
women and girls from across the region as they waited to deliver their babies.
     When I first visited Booth in 2012, I wanted to see where Mom had spent
the last weeks of her pregnancy and my sister had made her entrance into
the world. I retraced the steps Mom and so many other young women had
taken over the decades. I climbed the marble staircase that had ushered them
into Booth's interior, away from their previous lives and toward their uncertain futures. In the wall of what is now a utility closet, I saw the outline of
what had been a spiral staircase leading from Salvation Army officers' quarters on the main floor to a hospital ward on the second and sleeping quarters
on the third. I stood in that hollowed-out third floor and gazed through its
dormer windows, imagining the giggles and nervous whispers and silent anxieties that once sifted between the stud walls as schoolgirls and secretaries
and waitresses and coeds waited out their pregnancies in collective isolation.
I pictured Mom there among the others, long before she was my mother,
trying to put on a brave face, smoking and playing cards in the light of day,
stomach churning with fear in the dark of night. I pondered how the two
weeks she spent inside these brick walls had shaped the rest of her life and,
by extension, my own.
     I may never arrive at a complete answer to that question, but this book is
my best attempt at doing so.

1

GOOD GIRL

I had fallen in love. It wasn't the first time. It was something I had done more than once since graduating from high school and discovering that there were, after all, men in the world who liked tall women. At 5'10," I had been anything but the five-foot-two, eyes-of-blue ideal date. High school had been a series of all-girl parties occasionally broken by an awkward two-some, invariably with a guy who was either shorter than me or brave enough to go out with a female who could look him in the eye.

Almost from the beginning, my days at the University of Minnesota had been different. I had lost some weight and gained some confidence, and the boys were paying attention. More attention, in fact, than I had ever had. This was a new sensation for me, and it was wonderful. I had even been selected for the "Miss Engineering Day" contest. When I came in second, ahead of the sorority girls, I started to believe that I wasn't a complete failure in the Big Beauty Contest of Life which I thought all women had to enter.[1]

MY MOTHER GRADUATED FROM Spring Lake Park High School in 1957, when she was just seventeen years old. In an essay she wrote decades later, she described herself as a shy young woman whose self-confidence existed in inverse proportion to her height and weight. As a child, though, she'd been a spunky tomboy, tagging along with her older brother, Earl, whenever she had the chance. In a photograph from the early 1940s, Earl, Mom, and their cousin Margo stand half grinning, half squinting into the sun. Margo's left hand is clasped in Earl's right, her blonde hair tied back neatly on one side with a ribbon, her dress and stockings neat and unsullied. Mom, then only three or four years old, stands to Earl's left, holding tightly to his hand with both of hers, dark hair mussed, knobby knees leading to socks turned black with mud from her rambunctious play. A few years later, when Earl and his friends tipped over outhouses as a Halloween prank in the small town where they were living in the late 1940s, Mom was right there with them, running down the sidewalk in furious glee. When Earl and Six-Toed LeRoy spied on Lester who lived next door, Mom's head ducked behind the bushes to evade detection just as theirs did. She snooped on teenagers necking at Lovers' Lane, eavesdropped on conversations on the telephone party line, and "generally got into trouble and was a nuisance to everyone."[2]

She told me these stories when, as a child myself, I asked her about the "olden days." I loved imagining my mother as a mischievous little girl and aspired to be just as much a tomboy as she had been. As I grew older and became a self-absorbed teen, however, my interest in my mother's past gave way to a focus on my present and the stories stopped, the image of my mother as a spirited young girl frozen in time. Only later did I learn about her flagging confidence as a high schooler, how the onset of puberty and the ability to imagine herself through others' eyes led to a self-consciousness and "low self-regard" that would follow her the rest of her life, despite her popularity and achievements. This awkward transition from child to adolescent, when bodies are changing and hormones are raging and the opinions of peers become the yardstick of self-measurement, has turned many a confident youngster into an insecure teen.

These dynamics surely impacted my mother as well. Still, I wonder if there's more to the story of how she transformed from a sassy child who ran with the boys

Mom at high school graduation, 1957.

to a self-conscious high schooler who rarely dated, then to a popular college coed who found herself "in trouble" at age twenty. How might the circumstances of her personal life have interacted with the culture in which she came of age to contribute to her surprise pregnancy? As a historian, I can see that my mother's most intimate experiences reflected the contours not just of her personal psyche but of a whole culture. Her story mirrored those of many other young white women whose sexual awakening occurred in the confounding and contradictory 1950s, a period characterized by a burdensome pressure to maintain appearances, to mask with a polished secrecy the difference between public image and private reality when the two did not accord. These forces shaped Mom's family and, as they did for so many other girls, formed the twin pillars of a stifling, dichotomous identity: she could be either a "good girl" or a "bad girl."

She started as one but ended up the other.

Sex in the Country, Sex in the City

My mother was born in Minneapolis on December 22, 1939, the second child and first daughter of Earl and Thelma Moore. She spent her earliest years in the suburbs surrounding the city, but by 1948 the Moore family had fallen on hard times, so my grandmother swallowed her pride and moved with her four children back to her hometown. Situated on the western Minnesota prairie midway between Redwood Falls and Granite Falls, Echo boasted a population of just under five hundred in town with roughly equal numbers inhabiting the surrounding farmlands. My grandmother and the kids lived in a trailer in my great-grandmother's yard, between the main house and the cornfields that stretched into the distance. My great-grandfather had died in 1947, and my grandfather spent the weekdays tending bar in Minneapolis, driving to Echo on the weekends to deliver gifts and good humor before heading back to the city on Monday morning. So it was that from age eight to age thirteen, my mother grew up in a family headed by women.

Though Mom wouldn't realize it until much later, these were tough times for my grandmother, a hardworking woman who chafed at the economic straits into which she had been cast as well as the small-town gossip that surrounded my good-time grandfather's comings and goings. For Mom, though, the Echo years were mostly happy, marred only by a longing for her absent father and a sense of "general disapproval that came wafting" from her mother. She didn't mind living in a trailer, happily viewing it as a measure of distinction from her friends in town. When the small space began to close in too tightly around the family, my grandmother sent Mom and her brother Earl to sleep in an upstairs bedroom in the main house. By 1950, my grandmother and the kids, then numbering five, had moved into a rented house of their own just down the street from my great-grandmother's. They would stay there until 1953, when they reunited with my grandfather in a home on Tyler Street in Blaine, a suburb adjoining Spring Lake Park in the northern Twin Cities metro area.[3]

It was in Echo that my mother had her first glimpse of childbirth and first stay in a maternity home. My great-grandmother, Carrie Iverson, was a midwife who delivered babies in her front parlor. She had opened the Iverson Maternity Home in 1943, tending to laboring women, most of them white Lutheran housewives, from across Echo and the surrounding towns of

My grandmother Thelma (Iverson) Moore on the left, my great-grandmother, the midwife Carrie (Waller) Iverson seated, in 1963.

Yellow Medicine County. Their husbands—farmers and clerks and laborers and mechanics—waited anxiously outside the room set up with two hospital beds, and the town doctor, a man, attended the births, but it was Carrie's calming assurance the women sought. Over the next fifteen years, more than three hundred babies took their first breath in the capable hands of my great-grandmother.[4]

When an expectant mother arrived at my great-grandmother's home, Mom and Earl would be shooed back into the trailer for a couple of nights. One time, however, Mom was sleeping by herself in the house when a husband and wife arrived unexpectedly, leaving no time for her to relocate. Mom later wrote about this, and I find my way into her experience with a reimagining.

1948

The screen door slams. Urgent voices drift up the stairs, stirring her from sleep. She recognizes her grandmother's calm, matter-of-fact tone as it weaves in and out of the man's queries and the woman's cries. The baby is coming, the man says. Ooohhhh, the woman wails. It will be all right, okay, her grandmother says as she shows the couple to the birthing room in the front of the house. You lie down here, her grandmother says to one. You help her, her grandmother says to the other.

She shivers under her bedcovers, eyes wide with fear, as she listens to the commotion below, the woman panting and cursing, quieting momentarily as her grandmother telephones the town doctor, then erupting into shrieks once again. The doctor arrives, takes command of the situation. Finally, the pained cries of the woman give way to the familiar cries of the baby. The doctor leaves. Her grandmother makes coffee.

The next day, everyone carries on as usual, her grandmother tending to mother and child as if nothing worth remarking upon has happened. ●

The baby whose arrival had so alarmed my mother, eight years old in 1948, was one of thirty-five to be born at the Iverson Maternity Home that year. My mother knew that her grandmother helped bring babies into the world. She had heard newborns' wails in the night and seen bloodied sheets soaking in the laundry tub. She took delight in the task of delivering birth announcements to the local paper. But on that night in 1948, she came closer than she'd have liked to the actual experience of childbirth. The new mother and child survived the ordeal in good health, but my mother was still so rattled the next morning that she allowed her younger sister the honor of delivering the birth announcement.

The events of that night made a lasting impression on Mom, not just for their instruction in the painful physical aspects of labor and delivery, but also for her grandmother's stoic handling of the situation. "Gramma never said a word about that night," Mom wrote many years later, "never acknowledged my uneasiness and fear, never gave a hint that anything unusual had occurred. Her silence told me that what had happened was a secret but necessary thing, a thing of darkness and torment to be sure, but an agony that strong women endured without frivolous, self-indulgent complaint." This lesson etched itself into my mother's consciousness and would resurface with new meaning some thirteen years later.[5]

If there had been no discussion of the bloody rituals of childbirth, neither was there talk about the passionate—and presumably marital—experience of sex that led to it, either at home or elsewhere. As an adolescent in Echo, Mom gleaned what little she knew of sex, romance, and dating from her spy missions to Lovers' Lane and, later, the giggling flirtations between her girlfriends and the "strutting" boys who gathered at the Hurry Back Inn after school. Mom was still young and ill at ease in her developing body, the boyish lankiness of her childhood giving way to soft pubescent curves and an unladylike growth spurt, so sexual adventures of her own seemed beyond contemplation. But certainly some of those other flirtations led to more than mere necking in the back seat of a car; researchers at the time and since have pointed out that country living offered no greater protection against teens' raging hormones than did city living.[6]

If any of those trysts resulted in surprise pregnancies, however, none of the girls delivered their babies at the Iverson Maternity Home. The 329 women who completed patient registers at my great-grandmother's home between 1943 and 1958 identified themselves as married, provided information about their husbands, and indicated that their children were "legitimate." Had any single woman, teen or adult, become pregnant out of wedlock in a place like Echo, her reputation and her family's social standing likely would have suffered "the heavy hand of moral ostracism," as one Twin Cities social welfare worker put it, the scandal spreading through word-of-mouth if not the local newspaper. So instead of turning to familiar doctors and midwives, many such small-town unfortunates took their troubles to the big city, where institutions such as Booth Memorial Hospital provided shelter and anonymity. In 1946–47, ninety-five Booth girls hailed from rural counties, compared to a combined total of ninety-two from Hennepin and Ramsey Counties. Booth and other far-off homes for unwed mothers helped preserve the appearance of sexual propriety even as they dealt with the consequences of its breach.[7]

Dating, not to mention sex and pregnancy, may not have been much on Mom's mind when she lived in Echo, but when she moved back to the Twin Cities with her family in 1953, she was a thirteen-year-old entering an age and an environment permeated by mixed messages about sex and anxiety about teen behavior. That year, Dr. Alfred Kinsey's research on women's sexual behavior stirred controversy across the country. Despite the insistence in many a church pulpit, school classroom, and family conversation that marriage was and should be the sole province of sexual activity, Kinsey found that American women were engaging in a wide variety of erotic behaviors. In August 1953, the Minneapolis papers published lengthy reports on Kinsey's findings, among them that nearly all of his respondents had experienced orgasm and 81 percent had engaged in petting while teenagers; almost half of married women had had premarital sex, and about a quarter had had extramarital sex. For some Minnesotans, acknowledging such behavior was as threatening as the behavior itself. A Minnesota Poll conducted in late August asked respondents not about the study's results, but whether they should have been made public. Of the 73 percent who had heard about the study, 37 percent of women, but only 26 percent of men, believed that publicizing its contents would prove harmful to society, especially the young.[8]

Even before the release of the Kinsey report, the dating habits of teens were being scrutinized by social scientists, cultural critics, and the mass media. Minneapolis newspapers were filled with stories about young people's dating habits and authorities' attempts to mitigate the attendant risks. In 1950, when Mom was just ten years old and still living in Echo, the Minneapolis papers had published articles such as "Teen-Agers Told of Love Pitfalls," "Teen-age: Time for Gayety, Not for 'Going Steady,'" and "Love Can Be an Illusion, Young Told." Two years later, when Mom was on the cusp of becoming a teen herself, the *Minneapolis Star and Tribune*'s Sunday magazine ran a two-part article on "The Truth About Teenagers" and, in between, a five-part series on "Teens in Trouble." These series conveyed adults' concern that teen sex would lead to crime and degeneracy, even while pointing out that the worried parents of the 1950s had made similar kinds of mayhem during the 1920s, in their own roaring youth.[9]

The flurry of stories continued unabated after Kinsey made headlines, throughout Mom's high school years and into her days at the University of Minnesota. In 1959, the "Truth From Youth" series reported on teens' responses to Minnesota Poll questions about going steady, necking, and sex education in public schools, with 47, 38, and 67 percent, respectively, approving of such activities. Clearly, there was widespread disquiet over a "sexual liberalism" that many believed would undermine social order and common decency.[10]

Girls and women bore the brunt of this scrutiny as well as the responsibility for maintaining the sociosexual order. The "Your Dating Days" articles from 1955 capture the gendered nature of what historian Elaine Tyler May calls "sexual brinkmanship"—sexual behavior stopping just short of intercourse. Excerpted from sociologist Paul Landis's book of the same title, the series argued that, despite recent trends toward gender equality in American dating practices, girls were less interested in sex—physically, emotionally, and socially—than boys. Both boys and girls would benefit if girls acted on their natural inclination toward restraint by controlling boys' natural inclination toward sex. "Boys worth dating respect a girl for drawing the line. They are more likely to love and respect her and to want to marry her if she keeps control of the situation." Girls' virtue, then, would pay off in the form of a marriage proposal.[11]

These articles thus convey some of the prevailing and conflicting assumptions about girls, boys, and sex in the mid-1950s. Dating often took the form of "going steady," which was viewed, sometimes with comfort, sometimes with concern, as the gateway to early marriage. Girls took active roles in romantic relationships, though their parameters differed from those assumed by boys. Boys and girls alike engaged in physical expressions of affection, but to different degrees and for different reasons. Petting was de rigueur, but intercourse was not. Relationships between the sexes were moving toward increased egalitarianism, but the double standard persisted. Dating was a hallmark of teenage life, and young people went to great pains to make themselves appealing to the opposite sex, but many boys and girls didn't date at all. When they did, however, the ultimate goal of dating and the site of full sexual engagement was marriage.

By her own account, Mom traveled among the 40 percent of high school girls who never or rarely dated, so matters of petting and going steady probably were moot for her, marriage and children prospects for a remote future. At a time when a teenage girl's greatest aspiration was supposed to be taking her place on the arm of the captain of the football team, Mom stood shoulder to shoulder with many of the boys. She had reached her full height of five foot ten inches in junior high, while her male peers still sported peach fuzz and feet that only hinted at growth spurts yet to come. In her senior class picture, she and two other tall girls stand on the top row of risers, surrounded by boys, their female peers clustered in the front row. The good looks that would attract so much attention at the university were apparent even then,

though, her dark hair and eyes and high cheekbones—even her height— foreshadowing the beauty contestant to come. But at Spring Lake Park High, her stature and modest excess of weight became social liabilities, ones she tried to minimize with flat shoes, poor posture, and a self-consciousness that would accompany her for the rest of her life.[12]

Mom, about 1959.

Mom matched her insecurity about her physical appearance with an energetic bustle of activity, however. She was a joiner and she was well liked, attributes that would also follow her throughout her life. She played drums in the band, sang in the choir and glee club, worked on the student newspaper and yearbook. She played badminton and basketball and volleyball, served as librarian for the Future Homemakers of America, and joined the Spanish and Rooters clubs. She and a boy classmate (along with thirteen other boy-girl pairs) appeared on the "Senior Superlatives" page of the yearbook, her image labeled "Personality Plus," his captioned "Prettiest Smile." Her friends inscribed her yearbook with fond memories and called her a "swell girl" and told her to have fun and be good. They offered her generic wishes of good luck and specific wishes for success in her "secretarial career."

By anyone's account, then, Mom was a good girl.

It's hot and the 5:20 bus from downtown Minneapolis to Blaine is crowded. She stands in the aisle, fanning herself with her hands, stomach churning at the smell of exhaust.

She hasn't been feeling well for a while. Yesterday after work, she'd lost the battle with nausea in the middle of Marquette Avenue.

It's just a bug, she tells herself.

Maybe the stress of final exams, she tells herself.

On the bus, her vision narrows, grows dark. She feels her knees giving way.

Then two businessmen in white shirts are helping her off the bus, the driver having pulled to the curb along Central Avenue. She sits on the grass and gulps the fresh air, mortified at the spectacle she has become, rush-hour motorists slowing to get a glimpse of the goings-on.

The driver and passengers, their sweaty fatigue lightened by the excitement, wait for her to recover. She takes a seat in the front of the bus and it gently pulls back into the traffic. Now it's worry that roils her stomach. ●

Coed Beauty Queen

Mom had enrolled at the university in the late summer of 1957, just before classes began, not out of passion for education but out of dismay at the realities of full-time work. She had taken a secretarial job after graduating from high school, with the goal of eventually working for the foreign service, but the day-in, day-out routine of work left her disillusioned and dispirited. College seemed a better option.

In many ways, it was, at least in terms of enjoyment. Her time in the journalism program at the university represented a personal renaissance, less a matter of intellectual growth and more a matter of social progress. She thrived in the big-city school where her classmates knew nothing of the self-conscious, demure high schooler she had been. She lost weight and stood tall, and the boys came running. Rob brought her flowers and noble intentions. Clayton took her to fraternity parties in his Corvette. Dickie flirted constantly, but still couldn't measure up at a mere five foot seven. Dark-haired Howie trailed after her everywhere she went. As good girls were supposed to do, Mom toed the line of respectability with all of her suitors, including

Howie. They saw each other for a few months, passion flaring but, as she later wrote, "always stopping just short of actual consummation for an agonizing dance of denial and desire." When the romance fizzled, Mom moved on to the next suitor, her virginity intact, her good looks still attracting attention. In May 1960, just before the nausea and fainting spells took hold, she rode in a parade through the Minneapolis campus for the university's Miss Engineering Day contest. Though the queen's crown would elude her, she took pride in being named to the royal court.[13]

In most of her writing about this time period, Mom portrays herself as a somewhat vacuous young woman bobbing along on life's currents. "The new me was visible as a slim, attractive young woman, ready to have fun, ready to play, but without a serious thought in my head about what I wanted from life," she wrote many years later. "School was only a vehicle to avoid the terrifying prospect of working fifty weeks a year for the rest of my life. It was a supplier of boys and parties and fooling around instead

Mom, at left, as the University of Minnesota's 1960 Miss Engineering Day winner was crowned.

of going to class." For all the emphasis she put on the good times her good looks afforded at the university, however, there was more to the story. She was, after all, a full-time, working college student pursuing a degree in a field dominated by men.[14]

Attending college in itself was not especially unusual for young women in 1957. Whatever pressure, expectation, or desire pushed women toward married motherhood in the 1950s, the pursuit of some sort of postsecondary education had become an increasingly common experience. As overall numbers of college students continued to rise after World War II and in the early years of the Cold War, so too did those for women specifically. During the 1959–60 school year, approximately one-third of women between eighteen and twenty-one years of age were attending colleges across the country; these coeds constituted more than a third of the total college student population. Local trends reflected these broad currents. About twenty-three girls were among Spring Lake Park High School's first-ever graduating class in 1957, and Mom was one of the ten of them who attended a four-year college or university for at least a year.[15]

Many women of Mom's race and social class viewed a college degree as a waystation en route to marriage and motherhood, one that would allow them to work outside the home around their children's schedules, thus helping the family's ascent to the middle class, or to better equip them to perform the functions of a stay-at-home wife and mother. The media perpetuated such ideas as well. "The expectation today is that all college girls will at one time or another be wives and mothers *and* work at something outside the home," Nevitt Sanford wrote in a 1957 article for the *Ladies' Home Journal* titled "Is College Education a Waste of Time for Women?" (He declared it was not.) *Minneapolis Star* columnist Cedric Adams suggested that coeds agreed, albeit for slightly different reasons. "College graduates themselves," he wrote, "deem a college education for girls as valuable in its own right, not just because it can lead to a job or business career, but because of the usefulness of their college experience in helping them in their present or future roles of housewife or mother." Some white coeds in the postwar period seemed to take this view as well. According to historian Elaine Tyler May, they were twice as likely to have enrolled in college than their mothers had been, but more likely to drop out before earning a degree in order to marry. Though the absolute number of Black women attending college was smaller than white women, they attended at higher rates, and 90 percent of them completed their degrees. For some white women, however, the gap between the

stimulation of their education and what they came to view as the stultifica-
tion of their domestic lives led to the "problem that has no name" that Betty
Friedan described in 1963.[16]

While I'm sure Mom entertained ideas of marriage and family somewhere down the line, she also wanted to write. So, instead of following in the
footsteps of the 33 percent of women who graduated from college in 1957
with a degree in education, Mom stepped in line behind the 0.8 percent of
women graduates who earned a degree in journalism. She even became a
member of Theta Sigma Phi, an honorary society for women in communications. Though she would not complete her degree with the rest of her
classmates or become a journalist, she would go on to enjoy a long career
that combined business acumen with her skills as a writer.[17]

Mom's grades suffered as she enjoyed her newfound popularity; she
earned a solid 3.0 average for courses within her major field, but a dis-
appointing 2.2 in general studies. By her junior year, the allure of the party
scene was beginning to fade, too.[18]

Just about this time, Earl came home from the navy. Mom's adoration
of her big brother hadn't waned, even during their teen years. He had married his high school sweetheart not long after graduation, but the marriage
faltered during his time in service, and his wife filed for divorce. When he
came home to find her engaged to his best friend, Mom felt the pain almost
as much as Earl did, and, for once, she stepped in and took care of him. She
put her newfound popularity to use and tried to console her brother with
good humor, good friends, and good fun. They partied with her friends from
school and they partied with his friends from work.

Enter Jack.

APRIL 1960

He's taller than she is. That's the first thing she notices.

Then, his brown hair and blue eyes. His lean and muscled body. A
self-confidence that falls disarmingly short of arrogance.

She feels a spark of lightning shudder through her body as he draws
closer in the noisy room.

I know your brother from the navy, he says over the music.

That is enough for her. If he is her brother's friend, that is all the recommendation she needs.

That night begins their romance. They take walks under the stars, go for drives in his convertible, dance close and slow at parties. She learns that he had married young, had a child, divorced, dropped out of school, joined the service.

This is no college-boy flirtation.

She falls hard, gives in to his soft words and knowing hands.

It is her first time. ●

Sex Talk

I don't know the details of Mom's sexual relationship with Jack, only that he was her first partner and she believed that sexual intimacy signified a serious commitment. Because she saw herself as a "good girl," she felt guilty about violating the values with which she had been raised. At home, however, the specifics of those values had been communicated only obliquely. She knew one thing: sex was a private matter. One time during her teen years, Mom had ended up in the middle of an awkward conversation between her parents and a social worker. My grandfather's drinking had become cause for concern by then, and he had been cycling in and out of treatment programs and doctors' offices. On this occasion, Mom had accompanied my grandparents to an intake session with a social worker. When the (male) social worker asked my grandparents about their sex life, my grandfather erupted while my grandmother and mother stifled giggles. "What the hell kind of question is that? . . . dad-gummit, my daughter's sittin' right there and you ask such a thing! How in the hell is your sex life?" Even if it was understandable that my grandparents would be reluctant to discuss their personal relationship in front of my mother, it seems they didn't touch the subject of sex at all with her, even as she grew into young womanhood. "The only admonition or instruction I'd ever received was a tense warning from my Mother that I should be careful," Mom later wrote. "I knew what that meant and I didn't know what that meant. I didn't know that the emotions that would overtake me would be more powerful than anything I'd ever felt before."[19]

The sparing conversations Mom and Grandma seem to have had about sex were not uncommon. Commentary in the Minneapolis papers at the time and retrospective accounts make that clear, despite the widely held belief that instruction in matters of sex should ideally occur at home, whether through direct conversation or loving example. The American Medical Association produced a series of booklets that parents could rely on to help facilitate such a discussion, but authorities such as Dr. Marion Hilliard, chief of obstetrics and gynecology at Women's College Hospital in Toronto, suggested that good parental role modeling could be just as effective. "A father can teach his son a good attitude toward sex in the courtliness and consideration he shows his wife," she wrote in 1957. "A mother can teach the grass-roots principle of happy adjustment in the respect and admiration she shows her husband. This is sex education in its finest, most intelligent form." She described the "tenderness and responsibility of having a baby" communicated lovingly by mothers made "radiant" by pregnancy. "Babies are the result of warm love that overflows into physical union. That is my idea of sex education."[20]

Twin Cities clergy had a less sanguine view of home-based sex education and believed that parents had "fallen down on their job," whether out of reluctance to broach the awkward topic or lack of proper knowledge. Some churches attempted to take up the slack, in part to stem the rising tide of divorce among their parishioners, but even they, according to Kinsey and others, were missing the mark. Kinsey told a reporter from the *Minneapolis Sunday Tribune* that "Not more than a few per cent, perhaps not more than 5 per cent" of children were learning anything useful about sex at home or at church. "The other 95 per cent," the reporter claimed, "pick up their facts from each other, from older children, or from the gutter."[21]

Should public schools step into the breach? From at least the 1940s on, the answer, increasingly, was yes. According to Susan Freeman, school-based sex education earned broad support from parents, educators, and students themselves throughout the 1940s and 1950s. As one letter writer told the *Minneapolis Morning Tribune* in 1949, "most parents have a great deal of faith in our public schools and it seems that most parents would welcome the school's relieving them of the seemingly awkward job of sex instructing." The schools could supplement the subtle education provided by parental role modeling with more factual instruction that would still, according to columnist Albert E. Wiggam, prepare boys and girls "for dating, home, love, marriage and children."[22]

Public health organizations such as the American Social Hygiene Association (ASHA) promoted sex education as a means of preparing young people to assume conventional gender roles within the nuclear family. Even Kinsey himself, an advocate of free-ranging sexual behavior, sought to reassure a wary public that his scientific research could be deployed to strengthen the institution of marriage. Public schools across the country offered family life and human relations courses that often included screenings of two 1947 films: *Human Growth* for junior high students and *Human Reproduction* for senior high students. Between 1948 and 1962, more than two million students, including those in Minneapolis public schools, learned about anatomy, reproduction, and childbirth—but not sexual intercourse per se—through *Human Growth*'s depictions of middle-class morality.[23]

Whatever the specific content of available films, not all young people had the opportunity to view them. There were no federal standards to guide educators in matters of sex instruction. Although Minnesota teachers could access a rather forward-thinking, frank curriculum guide prepared by the state department of health and the University of Minnesota in 1947, implementation of its recommendations was not required. In 1949, the state commissioner of education said that no district in Minnesota had instituted any "comprehensive" program of sex education.[24]

Several years later, neither parental nor public school instruction about sex had improved, at least according to Jane Browne, executive director of Planned Parenthood of Minneapolis. In 1954, the organization began offering an "Education for Marriage" program for engaged couples and, a year later, a series of classes aimed at junior and senior high students. "Young people get almost no information of this kind in school," Browne wrote in 1956, so Planned Parenthood took up the slack in cooperation with the YMCA, the YWCA, and a number of local churches. The courses were led by doctors, nurses, and family life educators, included screenings of *Human Growth* and *Human Reproduction,* and promised frank discussion of questions such as "Who is the more at fault when necking goes out of control—the boy or the girl?" Nearly four hundred young people participated in these courses in 1955 and 1956.[25]

It's doubtful that these specific efforts, based in Minneapolis, affected Mom directly, though they reflect the general local climate in which she came of age. But her family, church, and school were in Anoka County, where there was no Planned Parenthood. Perhaps she had viewed *Human Growth* or *Human Reproduction* in school, or participated in a youth group discussion about family living at her Lutheran church, but I can't be sure. What I do know is that, like so many other women of her generation and station, she later recalled more silence than conversation about sex, especially at home. As late as 1963, teenage girls waiting out their pregnancies at Booth St. Paul described the scattershot sources that constituted their sex education, from mothers who discussed only periods to school friends who shared rumors to boyfriends who provided hands-on learning. A seventeen-year-old commended Booth for its instructional program, noting, without irony, that "the health education here is really helpful about pregnancy." The women Ann Fessler interviewed years later for her book about unwed pregnancies in midcentury America recalled a similar lack of information. As one woman said, "My mother talk about sex? Oh, god. Please. 'You can't be kissing boys. You can't be letting anybody touch you. Sex is dirty. Sex is bad.' It was always bad things. Always taboo. It was never healthy, never, never a healthy talk. My mother was twenty-four with four kids. Probably that's why sex was bad."[26]

The lesson this woman learned wasn't the sanitized, romanticized version of marriage and reproduction that Marion Hilliard had envisioned, but it may have been closer to what Mom had learned at home. In her time in Echo, she had overheard the harsh and mysterious realities of childbirth. Then, during her transition from wallflower to beauty queen in the Twin Cities, Mom felt the tension in her parents' marriage. According to Mom, Grandma and Grandpa "scrapped and carried on" during these years. There were now six children in the Moore family; the youngest, a boy, had arrived in 1955. My grandfather was still tending bar at night, and in 1959 my grandmother took a job in the library at the *Star and Tribune*. The family needed her income, and my grandmother enjoyed working, finding it a respite from the demands of childcare and cooking and cleaning. That she was still primarily responsible for those domestic duties as well surely made her tired, if not also a bit resentful—especially as my grandfather's drinking became more problematic.

Still, the alliances that had formed during the Echo years held. Mom described her mother as "stern, critical, and unforgiving" and remained true to her father, even, perhaps especially, when she felt like a "pawn" in their arguments. "My sentiments were almost always with Dad," she wrote later, "and since my two brothers and one sister who were old enough to pay attention sided with Mom, my loyalties grew fiercer, more protective, and more predisposed to see Dad's side in every argument." Though she planted her stake squarely on her father's side of the divide, she also understood, at least later, that it was her mother who kept order in the family, both internally and in the eyes of the neighbors.[27]

Indeed, my grandmother went to great lengths to present a certain image of the family to outsiders, one that equated a tidy house with harmonious living, whatever the realities behind the gleaming countertops and clean-swept floors. Keeping order meant keeping up appearances, preserving privacy. She wasn't the only one to put a fine polish on the scarred truth, however, as historian Wini Breines has shown. In an era "fixated on family life," when happy families headed by a working husband and homemaking wife were supposed to be the site of both personal fulfillment and national virtue, "the appearance of a happy marriage was more important than happiness." So, Mom wrote, "Our house became a garden of secrets, a walled fortress where we could be ourselves when no one was looking, but, should company come calling, we had to hide our true natures, clean our already-clean house, and disguise our true thoughts and inclinations under smiling and agreeable company manners." The Moore family may not have been living in glorious harmony, but it endured in spite of its frailties, my grandmother remaining loyal to my grandfather as he battled his demons. "Dad was still an alcoholic," Mom recalled, "but at least we were all together, more or less."[28]

The gap between exterior image and interior reality that had shaped Mom's growing-up years and the Moore family dynamics defined a whole culture. Anxieties about what teenagers were up to when out of adults' sight; debates over how and where to teach kids about sex; the insistence that the nuclear family could fulfill the economic, social, and sexual needs of individual and nation—all of these pointed to an uneasy duality in white, middle-class American life. Despite pressures to maintain the appearance of a gender-specific sexual propriety, the reality was that girls and women were having sex, mothers and marriages weren't always happy, and the keeping up of appearances could be stifling.

For Mom, as for many others, it was a zero-sum game. She couldn't be a "good" and "bad" girl at the same time. She later described her time at the university in terms of personal emergence: her uncertain, ungainly teen years were a cocoon that had both obscured and harbored her real self so that it could appear fully integrated, internal spunk matched by external appeal. She would soon come to understand, however, that the butterfly wasn't any more "real" than the caterpillar. "Little did I know that my new 'visible' woman was also an illusion," she wrote, "a very popular type of illusion to be sure, but still not the real me."[29]

She's on the Central Avenue bus again.

Her symptoms—the dizziness, the nausea, the fatigue—haven't improved since the day she fainted on the bus. Then she missed a period.

This time, she gets off the bus of her own accord, crosses Central Avenue, and enters a low-slung brick building. This time, it's fear that makes her knees weak.

You're pregnant, Dr. Goode says as he stands in front of her in his white coat, a pack of Camels in the front pocket. About two months.

She had known this was a possibility but had willed herself into believing it would not be so. The illusion shatters in five words.

All she can say is, Oh.

Dr. Goode drones on, about eating better and taking vitamins and gaining weight, but the words come to her through a long, dark tunnel. Until, By the way, are you married?

Not yet, she replies. ●

In June 2015, I was part of a summer research program at the university where I was teaching. I had recruited a student to help me with my Booth project and arranged for us to visit the former maternity home, now the Booth Brown House. A staff person led us through parts of the original building, showed us photographs of its history, pointed out the physical remnants of its past. The addition of a new wing to the east end of the building in 1969 had destroyed the entrance at which two decorative stone lions had stood sentry for more than half a century.

A few days after our walk-through, I received an email from the staff person. A woman who had delivered a baby at Booth in the early 1960s had stopped in just after our visit and was interested in learning more about my research. That's how I met Pam—by email in 2015, then, finally, in an interview at her home in Michigan in 2017.[30]

Pam was born in 1943 in Iowa but spent her growing-up years in Minnesota, first in Two Harbors and then in Brainerd. She was a shy, insecure girl whose harsh father kept a tight rein on her activities. By her senior year of high school, however, she had begun to rebel against his restrictions, sneaking out of the house at night to meet a boy. "I would take my horse and ride five, six miles around the lake to meet my boyfriend on the other side. . . . [My bedroom] was on the second story and I'd sneak out on the porch and I'd slide down and then I'd try to sneak back in the house through the door and up the stairs back to my room."

One night, her father drove her to town so she could attend a school basketball game. After he left, however, Pam and her boyfriend drove out to the golf course and had sex in the car. "I really didn't want to do [it,]" she recalled, "but in order to go steady with this very popular boy, that was something I had to do. He said, 'Well, you can't be my girlfriend if you don't do this,' and I really wanted this popular boy to like me, so we did it in the back seat. It was very uncomfortable."

The next day, Pam felt ashamed and confused, but the boy bragged to his friends that he had "popped a cherry." Pam's girlfriend had to explain what that meant. Pam didn't know anything about sex or reproduction. She recalled no sex education in school and little conversation at home. Back in Two Harbors, when her mother had suggested they have a talk about girls and growing up, Pam declined, insisting that she knew all about it because a friend had explained everything to her. Never mind that the friend had said that babies came out of belly buttons, which then just tucked back in once the child had been cut away. Never mind that Pam had failed to make the connection when she saw cows giving birth on the farm. Never mind that she had been having her periods for a while and had only a vague understanding that something was "going on down there." "It was all very embarrassing to me," she said, "We didn't talk about those things."

So when Pam became pregnant after just two sexual encounters with her boyfriend, she was surprised and her parents were outraged. "My mother was worried about what people would think," she recalled. "My father said I was a bad influence for the other children." They offered her no consoling words, no support, no offers of help. Instead, they drove her to the hospital, where her father released himself of responsibility and made her a ward of the state. "One minute I was a part of a family and then the next minute I was in a hospital headed for I didn't know where."

Pam's boyfriend, the back-seat Romeo, did not help much, either, though he did not abandon her. His mother wanted Pam to get an abortion so that the "taint of scandal" wouldn't follow her son. Pam refused. She knew she couldn't keep the baby, but she also knew she couldn't have an abortion. So she decided to relinquish her baby for adoption, provide a gift to a couple struggling with infertility. "That was my choice. Much to my boyfriend's chagrin, and his mother's fury, I stood up to them and that was my act of bravery."

Once her parents had relinquished her, a pregnant teenager turned over to the impersonal guidance of the state, Pam moved from place to place: a harsh and judging foster family, then a kind and loving foster family, then Booth in the summer of 1961. "I remember walking up the steps," she said. "I remember how imposing this building was . . . you walked up between these lions and you entered these huge doors and you went in and you sat with this imposing woman, but [she was] very gentle and kind."

Pam remembered other things, too. The girls rubbing each other's backs and helping with breathing once labor started. The thirteen-year-old street-wise girl who knew more about life than eighteen-year-old Pam. The smell of hot, dry cotton sheets as she fed them into the mangle. The sound of the animals at the nearby Como Zoo. "Sometimes at night, if the wind was right and the night was quiet in the summer and the windows were open, you could hear the lion's roar." One beautiful, confined creature singing to another.

When Pam's time came, they took her to the delivery room on the second floor. She labored by herself and without benefit of pain medication. Her resolve to surrender her baby did not waver, even after her dark-haired girl arrived. "I had no resources. I didn't even know how to take care of myself," she recalled. Still, saying goodbye hurt and she did it by herself, no parents or family or friends there to comfort her. The social worker picked Pam up from Booth and delivered her to an apartment near the university. It was September and classes were about to begin, so Pam signed up and moved on, eventually reuniting with her baby's father.

Pam got pregnant again but this time refused to release her baby, despite her boyfriend's pleas. She kept her baby and lost her boyfriend. For eighteen months, Pam raised her son alone, but when her boyfriend came home on leave from the army, they married. The family of three grew to four with the arrival of their second son, but when Pam, a lonely and isolated army wife, took comfort in the arms of another man, her husband left and took their two boys with him. In 1968, she married again, a navy man with whom she would have four more children. The last four kids didn't know about the first three kids until child number two, by then a twenty-one-year-old man, showed up at Pam's door. Then everybody knew, Pam's full story finally released.

Pam's second marriage dissolved in 2000. She and her ex-husband are on good terms, and six of her children are now in her and each other's lives. One remains absent—her first, her dark-haired daughter, her Booth baby. At this point, Pam said, she's too tired to entertain the thought of a search; she cannot absorb any additional drama in her life. Should her daughter find her, she would welcome her into the fold, but she can't initiate the reunion. That part of her life, the time she spent at Booth, a lonely girl listening to a lion's roar carried by the summer breeze, seems like it belonged to a different person. "But it's still a part of me. It's still who I was and am but it's rolled into this being that I am now, who's comfortable with myself, who feels strong and is not afraid to stand up for what I believe." ■

In the spring of 1960, Mom knew she was on the cusp of a new life. Some thirty years later, she described the day she took the bus to see Dr. Goode:

> *Standing on the grass again, the spring*
> *Air now cloying, the sun sinking*
> *The lights coming on in the*
> *Houses and shops that lined the thorough—*
> *   Fare, she knew that her life had*
> *Changed, irrevocably, in the heat*
> *Of a passion she could barely*
> *Recognize in the daylight, with a man who had*
> *Shown her the ways of the flesh*
> *But who was already*
> *Slipping out of her life.*

The before, the after. The then, the now. Innocent schoolgirl, burdened adult. This day divided them all.

The pain is unbelievable.

It's a beautiful June morning, the kind whose fresh breeze and dancing sunlight promise good things. For the past several weeks, I've been reveling in the afterglow of having completed my PhD. Although I don't yet have any work lined up, I've decided to take the summer off, enjoy a break from the arduous teaching and writing schedule of the last few years.

But on this morning, with its cerulean skies, I crouch in a contorted child's pose on our living room floor, hammering the rug with my fists. I've had horrible menstrual cramps all my life, but this pain is of a different order altogether. I cannot straighten my abdomen enough to stand up or lie down. I cannot see straight. I cannot articulate anything but a string of furious curses. Sweat soaks my pajama shorts and T-shirt.

Steve stomps into the living room, first annoyed, then concerned when he sees me on the floor.

"What in the—what's wrong, Kim?"

I muster up just enough coherence to tell him we need to go to the hospital. He looks for his wallet and keys.

Another spasm of pain.

"Call an ambulance," I say.

The first diagnosis: ruptured ovarian cyst. The second diagnosis: stage four endometriosis. Major surgery results in the loss of one ovary and fallopian tube and severely compromised fertility.

There's an irony in all of this. For the first ten years of our marriage, I had told Steve I wasn't ready for kids. He had been ready since the moment we said, "I do." I, however, had never expressed a desire for children. I grew up watching my mother thrive in her profession and, when my father took ill, become our family's primary breadwinner. I shared her suspicion of those who claimed that childrearing was a woman's highest calling and was wary of babies and their helpless, constant neediness. Besides, I had things to do: finish my bachelor's degree, get a job, travel, quit my job, grad school.

Finally, after I finished coursework and was working on my dissertation, I agreed that the next step in my life's plan would be to start a family. We stopped trying not to get pregnant.

We had taken such care to prevent a surprise pregnancy for so long that I thought it might happen right away once we relaxed our vigilance, but no. A year and a half of not trying not to get pregnant and nothing.

Now this.

2

CALIFORNIA DREAMING

The Greyhound to San Francisco was scheduled to leave Minneapolis at 6:00 on a Friday afternoon. I had saved as much money as I could, dropped out of my classes, written a note to my parents, and given notice at my part-time job. I had done everything but think through what I'd do when I arrived in San Francisco . . .

I still had the notion that everything would be all right. I would go to San Francisco, get a job and an apartment, have my baby, and then, I didn't know what. I'd just have to see. I had the flimsy confidence of a young woman who'd never been tried, who'd always gotten by easily, and who'd been able to count on good genes, good luck, and a good family to see her through. [1]

MOM WAS THREE MONTHS INTO her surprise pregnancy when she decided to take her troubles to California. She bought a one-way ticket to San Francisco, where she intended to start a new life with her baby, in the process sparing her family the shame of neighbors' condemnation or, worse, self-righteous pity.

She'd bided her time after that fateful day in Dr. Goode's office, waiting for an opportune moment to make her escape. She kept up appearances by riding the city bus to and from work each day and eating sparingly enough to compensate for the weight gain of pregnancy. She learned to manage the pulsating waves of nausea and the realization that she faced this situation alone. Jack was working out of state and had not replied to her letter containing the news of her pregnancy. Then, on a Friday night in July, after her parents and four younger siblings departed for a weekend of camping, she made her move. She packed her bags, left a note on the kitchen table explaining that she had set off in search of adventure, and said a silent goodbye to everything she knew and loved, including Jack.

So it was that she found herself sitting in the anteroom of the Northland Greyhound bus station, long before it would become the renowned music venue First Avenue, waiting for the bus that would be her deliverance.

Always given to introspection and self-condemnation, she must have wondered how she had turned from a self-conscious good girl to a scandal-tainted bad girl and what she might have done to prevent such a fall from grace. Held fast to her sexual morals, for one thing, she must have thought. But what about other options? Couldn't she have taken steps to prevent conception once she found herself in the thrall of love and sexual intimacy? Was she really as alone as she felt that evening in the bus station? Why did

Passengers at the Greyhound bus depot in 1952, eight years before Mom's trip.
Minnesota Historical Society collections

she flee? How did her cross-country journey reflect the options available to white, unmarried pregnant women in 1960?

Answers to these questions stem from the same mid-twentieth-century ideology that had shaped sex education and emphasized sexual restraint for the unmarried. Policies and practices regarding access to birth control, abortion, and services for single pregnant women and mothers reinforced the white, middle-class, nuclear family ideal.

JUNE 1960

Jack is gone.

He's out of state on a construction job, but she tracks down an address and writes him a letter.

I'm not looking for a ring, she says. Neither of us wants that. But there will be expenses.

She drops the letter in a mailbox and waits.

Nothing.

He's just busy, she tells herself after a week passes without a response.

Maybe my letter got lost in the mail, she tells herself after a couple more days.

He's gone, she finally admits.

This man, the one who knew just what to say, just what to do, is saying and doing nothing.

This man, who has an ex-wife and a child, is washing his hands of his girlfriend and their child.

This man, who had seemed so mature and responsible, is proving himself to be anything but.[2] ●

The Other Boom

Mom may have felt terribly alone when she realized Jack would have nothing to do with her, but the milestones of her young life placed her squarely within her generation and its booming population trends, both celebrated and condemned. She graduated the same year the post–World War II baby boom peaked, the 4.3 million newborns arriving in 1957 hailed as a sign of American prosperity and virtue. The number of babies born to single women also reached an all-time high that year, at more than 200,000, though they were certainly not celebrated as part of this nationwide "reproductive mania." Her pregnancy in 1960 contributed to this unheralded explosion, the out-of-wedlock conception and birth rates for white women having doubled and tripled, respectively, since the 1940s. In 1960, 224,300 unmarried women—82,500 of them white—had babies, their numbers rising more sharply than the number of overall births in the waning years of the baby boom. The 2,589 children born to single women in Minnesota from June 1960 to June 1961 represented an 8.8 percent increase in the number of such births; the 87,505 children born to all Minnesota women during the same period signaled a mere 0.4 percent rise overall.[3]

Clearly, then, Mom was part of a rising demographic when she became pregnant out of wedlock in an era that reveled in marriage, family, and parenthood. But given the emphasis on marital childbearing, why were so many more women getting pregnant outside of marriage? Certainly, more women were having more premarital sex as cultural practices, if not attitudes, were changing, for whatever combination of reasons. But couldn't Mom have taken measures to prevent pregnancy once she became intimate with Jack? If it were a one-time occurrence, perhaps not. But if she and Jack were having sex more regularly during their brief courtship, couldn't one of them have taken precautions? It seems Jack, worldly wise as he was with an ex-wife and child already, should have had condoms on hand. But what about Mom? Why hadn't she used birth control?

An Ounce of Prevention

There's a short, two-part answer to that last question. First of all, in order to secure birth control, Mom would have had to admit to herself that she was the "kind" of young woman who had sex outside of marriage. She got pregnant early enough in her relationship with Jack that she may not have had time to reimagine herself as someone who knowingly violated the social and moral codes of the day, as someone who needed birth control.

The second part of the answer relies less on speculation about Mom's interior logic and more on the hard facts of history, for even if she had sought to obtain contraceptives of some sort, they were hard to come by, especially (but not only) for single women. The Pill was not yet available; FDA approval of it for pregnancy-prevention purposes came on June 23, 1960, as an already-pregnant Mom was planning her escape to San Francisco.

Condoms had been around since 1918 and were the most popular form of birth control in the United States in the 1950s, but their effectiveness depended on men's willingness to secure and use them. One of the women I interviewed, Mary, said her boyfriend "promised, promised, promised to use a condom" in persuading her to have sex. After she got pregnant, however, she learned that he had only pretended to wear the rubbers. "I had been too naive to turn on the lights and throw back the covers and see what was going on," she said. Mom may well have been as naive as Mary, but I cannot account for Jack's actions or motivations, whether he acted in good faith with a faulty condom or in self-interest without one.[4]

No Pill, no condom. What other options might Mom have had? For years, women had tried to prevent pregnancy by relying on inexpensive and ineffective over-the-counter products such as foams, douches, and suppositories—marketed as "feminine hygiene" products to circumvent laws prohibiting the distribution of birth control. In the 1950s, the most effective and most often prescribed form of female contraceptive was the diaphragm and jelly, but it required a doctor visit, instructional fitting, and willingness to abide a difficult and messy insertion and removal. Moreover, it cost more than the over-the-counter options. These factors combined to make it an unpopular choice for most women, according to historian Andrea Tone; instead, before the Pill era, women got most of their birth control information and devices from sources beyond their physician's office.[5]

Had Mom mustered the courage to broach the topic of birth control with Dr. Goode in 1959, however, he likely would have refused her request anyway. Even though law, custom, and many religious organizations had come to accept the notion of intentional control of conception by the mid-twentieth century, many states still had active "little Comstock" laws—statutes modeled on the federal Comstock Law of 1873 that criminalized the publication, possession, and distribution of information about contraceptives and abortion. Some prohibited the dissemination of birth control altogether, while others explicitly limited contraceptive use to husbands and wives. It had been hard enough to convince skeptics that birth control had a place in the marital bedroom, much less to assuage critics who feared that it would unleash rampant promiscuity among the unmarried. In the aftermath of the 1965 *Griswold v. Connecticut* decision guaranteeing married couples access to contraceptives, legal codes in twenty-six states still expressly denied them to unmarried people. Minnesota repealed its "little Comstock" law, which had made it a crime to provide birth control information and contraceptive devices, in May 1965, but it would take another seven years for the Supreme Court to grant single men and women (in *Eisenstadt v. Baird*) the same rights that their married counterparts enjoyed. Single women found creative ways around such limitations—feigned menstrual difficulties, fake wedding rings—sometimes with the knowledge and support of their doctors, but Dr. Goode's inquiry as to Mom's marital status suggests he may not have been willing to play along had she manufactured a story about a nonexistent engagement.[6]

Thus the same logic that framed sex education as a matter of preparing for proper family life cast birth control as a means of planning for proper family growth. Cultural authorities argued that both sex education and birth control could be deployed in support of the nuclear family ideal. By the late 1950s, many Jewish and Protestant leaders had come to support the use of contraceptives (and the Catholic Church the rhythm method) so that husbands and wives could fulfill the sexual responsibilities of marriage without producing children that would strain their relationship or risk their faith. "Husband and wife are called to exercise the power of procreation responsibly before God," declared the United Lutheran Church in America in 1956. "This implies planning their parenthood in accordance with their ability to provide for their children and carefully nurture them in fullness of Christian faith and life."[7]

Churches were not themselves distributing contraceptives, though, so whatever Mom's Lutheran church's stance on the matter, she wouldn't have turned to her pastor for help. But what about the University of Minnesota, where she was a student? In all likelihood, her search would have been just as fruitless. As late as 1970, ten years after the Pill was approved for contraceptive use, 72 percent of college health services across the nation offered no birth control to female students, married or single. Although doctors at the University of Minnesota student health services appear to have been prescribing contraceptives to married students for disease-prevention purposes since 1918, as of September 1965—more than five years after Mom got pregnant—they were still offering them only to "married girls, plus girls who are soon to be married and who furnish for the records a date of impending marriage, together with the name of the husband to be" or to single women who took the Pill to regulate troublesome periods. As of January 1970, the student-fee-funded service no longer explicitly prohibited doctors from prescribing the Pill to unmarried students, but its priority was to aid married women in regulating conception. For Mom in 1960, though, the university would have been another dead end.[8]

Planned Parenthood would not have been of much help to Mom, either, as its Twin Cities clinics also limited their birth control services to married women in the 1950s and early 1960s. Originally established in 1928 as the Motherhood Protection League, Planned Parenthood of Minnesota had by the mid-1950s adopted the national organization's stance linking birth control to marital health and happiness as well as to population control. Indeed, concerns about the "population bomb," especially in poor and nonwhite communities in the United States and abroad, had escalated after World War II and fueled the growing support for birth control in general and development of the Pill in particular. Contraceptives would allow "child spacing" to prevent a family from growing beyond a couple's means just as they could prevent the neediest populations from expanding beyond a nation's resources, a point made by Jane Browne, executive director of Planned Parenthood of Minneapolis (PPM), in a Twin Cities radio broadcast in June 1956. She made no mention of using contraceptives to curb births by single women, however, noting that the clinic was open to married women seeking birth control and engaged women seeking premarital education.[9]

Planned Parenthood's policy may have left single women like Mom in the lurch, but many married women were equally desperate to control their fertility. In 1958, one woman wrote that the Minneapolis clinic "is a life saver to people like me who have enough children & cannot afford private Doctors. . . . I wouldn't part with any of my 11 children [but] I have been talking planned parenthood to every one I get a chance to." In 1959, a worker at Planned Parenthood's booth at the Minnesota State Fair noted a "Woman with 10 children, pregnant, 2 of them retarded" who stopped by to ask for help. The worker gave the woman the phone number for the St. Paul clinic and turned to call a taxi for her, but by then the exhausted woman "had trudged off with 8 offspring trailing." Of course, Planned Parenthood generated hostility from its critics, too, as when a male visitor to the 1955 state fair booth advised PPM staff that they "should all commit suicide" if they were truly concerned about overpopulation, and a Catholic nurse spat that birth control was "against nature." Other men (and women) simply saw no need for PPM's services, including the man who claimed in 1958 that he "had a magic computor for the 'safe period' that was in constant demand by all of his friends."[10]

In an era when birth control for married couples still sometimes came under attack for being "intrinsically evil," Planned Parenthood opted to stay within the bounds of respectability by limiting its services to married women.

It wasn't until 1965, when the Minneapolis and St. Paul branches merged, that the organization vowed to "make birth planning services available . . . to all women in Minnesota regardless of socio-economic, marital, or geographic circumstance."[11]

The debates about and policies regarding birth control—who should have access to it and for what purpose—expose the racist contradictions of postwar pronatalism. The baby boom was celebrated as a sign of American health and prosperity when it was the "right" kind of babies born to the "right" kind of women. As historian Rickie Solinger has argued, the conversation and arguments around birth control thus became a matter of *rights* for white and middle-class women and *restraint* for poor women and women of color. Contraceptives would allow white women to exert control over their bodies in the name of private family planning and economic well-being, but they would allow the state to exert control over the bodies of Black and Brown women in the name of limiting population growth and public welfare expenditures. Many Black women (and men) eagerly sought access to birth control for the same reasons white women (and men) did—to determine for themselves if and when to have children. But in the 1960s, the appearance of government-funded birth control clinics in otherwise underserved communities with large nonwhite populations raised suspicions among people of color who had long been victimized by state efforts to control their reproduction, including through compulsory or coerced surgical sterilization.[12]

Though rates of eugenic sterilization of the "feeble-minded" had subsided by the early 1940s, African American, Native American, and other women of color continued to face permanent loss of their childbearing capacity at the hands of doctors who often viewed them with racist contempt. According to legal scholar Dorothy Roberts, a court case originating in 1973 discovered that 100,000 to 150,000 poor women had been sterilized annually in federally funded programs and that half of those women were Black. In Puerto Rico by 1968, more than one-third of women had been sterilized under the auspices of a "population control" plan begun in 1950. One-quarter of Native American women were sterilized in reservation programs in the 1970s, 3,000 cases of which occurred in four hospitals run by the Indian Health Service from 1973 to 1976. Many of these procedures were performed without adequate (or any) consent, under coercion or threat, with deceptive record keeping, and/or for financial gain or training purposes.[13]

Sterilization procedures—tubal ligations and hysterectomies—weren't always coercive; many white women and some nonwhite women chose this method of birth control for its permanency, reliability, or accessibility. In another example of race-based control of women's reproduction, however, while nonwhite women were experiencing high rates of coerced sterilization, many doctors were reluctant to grant white women's requests *for* such procedures. In the 1960s, the American College of Obstetricians and Gynecologists recommended that doctors perform tubal ligations only on women whose age times the number of children they had equaled 120 *and* who had letters of support from two physicians and a psychiatrist. Clearly, there was a two-tiered race- and class-based system governing women's ability to control their own childbearing.[14]

Mom would not have been subject to such discriminatory rhetoric or practice on the basis of her race or social class, but she was caught in the gap between the celebration and condemnation of white women's fertility on the basis of marital status. State, private, and university policies left women like her stranded if they were unwilling to fabricate engagements or menstrual difficulties or unable to find sympathetic doctors willing to violate law and community norms. Instead, they had to rely on their boyfriends' willingness to wear condoms or men's assurances—often borne of exaggerated sexual expertise—that they knew how to withdraw just in time or that it was impossible for a virgin to get pregnant during her first experience of intercourse or that they had a "magic computor" for identifying the risk-free safe period. If they were unwilling to turn over their fertility to their partners, they could peruse the feminine hygiene products at their local drugstore, the Zonite and Lysol douches, the Norform suppositories and Tannette powders, and hope that a fifty-nine-cent bottle of Lysol would prevent an unwanted pregnancy as effectively as it disinfected the kitchen sink. (It didn't.) Or, if they were unwilling to abstain from sex altogether, they could use nothing and hope for the best.

I don't know where Mom stood in this landscape. I don't know if she and/or Jack used condoms or douches or withdrawal or nothing at all. I don't know if they had intercourse one time, several times, or many times. She didn't spell out such details in the essays about her pregnancy, skittering around the subject with vague statements about intimacy and naivete and carelessness. I suspect that she and Jack had had sex on more than one occasion and that she'd have considered the idea of securing birth control, as a report in the *Saturday Evening Post* put it, "too great a transgression of standards." She had already felt "demoralized" by her "lost virginity." The effort involved for her to access contraceptives, whether from a druggist or a doctor, would have given the lie to the idea that she was merely succumbing to passion in the heat of the moment, a momentary stumble on the path of feminine virtue. In an era when women's identities were defined in binary terms based on sexual activity—good/bad, virgin/whore, virtuous/promiscuous—her self-image was at stake. "I simply didn't think about consequences," she later wrote, "believing that a 'good girl' like me wouldn't get caught."[15]

The Other Side of the Boom

It was difficult to be single and pregnant in an era that emphasized the nuclear family ideal. It was also difficult to be married and childless. As historian Elaine Tyler May has documented, cultural pressures to procreate and deep personal disappointment at their inability to do so turned the infertile into outsiders gazing longingly at the warm glow of familial bliss from just beyond the white picket fence. So it was that at the same time that medical, moral, and political leaders debated strategies for helping husbands and wives limit their fertility on the one hand, they also considered means of assisting white couples to enhance their fertility on the other.[16]

For medical researchers, fertility and sterility were two sides of the same reproductive coin, the study of one advancing understanding of the other. John Rock, for example, had made a career of treating sterility long before he helped develop the birth control pill. In 1944, he and colleague Miriam Menkin had announced the first successful in-vitro fertilization of human eggs, which laid the groundwork for the eventual birth of "test-tube baby" Louise Brown in 1978. He also promoted the study of male infertility, contributed to the increasing popularity and success of artificial insemination, and conducted some pioneering research with sperm cryopreservation. In 1954, three women in Iowa made history by giving birth to babies conceived with frozen sperm.[17]

As was the case with birth control, however, such "interference" with what was supposed to be the natural or divine process of human reproduction generated controversy. Some saw it as providing new hope for the infertile and for "improving the human race through selective breeding," while others found it morally troubling, spiritually offensive, and legally confounding. In 1949, Minnesota legislators debated the legal limitations and moral implications of artificial insemination. Catholic leaders lobbied for making the procedure illegal, even for husbands and wives, while the *Minneapolis Star* urged legislators to regulate a legalized practice. A report prepared for the American Lutheran Conference in 1952 approved of artificial insemination for married couples, but "frowned on" using another man's sperm. In June 1958, the *Minneapolis Star* reported that the New York archdiocese had defined artificial insemination as "adultery" for "[isolating a woman's] motherhood from her husband's love," akin to the National Catholic Conference's description of contraceptives as "unnatural and repugnant to Christian thinking."[18]

The trends and debates surrounding what is now known as assisted reproductive technology (ART) were clearly far afield of Mom's concerns in 1960. The stress, both personal and cultural, of being unable to conceive would shape my life forty-five years later. By that time, ART had become yet another site where race, class, and reproductive politics converged: low-income Black women were more likely to experience infertility than white women, yet high-income white women were twice as likely to turn to high-tech assistance to try to achieve pregnancy. But in 1960, Mom's dilemma revolved around how to prevent conception. The cultural tensions surrounding both birth control and artificial insemination show how secular, medical, and religious authority loomed in the background of private bedrooms and intimate relationships, attempting to define what constituted a "proper" and desirable family formation. Mom got caught outside of those bounds, her pregnancy revealing her transgression. If she had to confront her fall from grace, however, she hoped she could hide it from her loved ones. And so she boarded a bus headed west.[19]

A Pound of Cure

Mom made the decision to set out for California in a context that offered her limited options for handling her surprise pregnancy, none of them easy. As a 1961 article on unwed mothers in *True Love* magazine noted, "There are just three possibilities for the unwed mother-to-be: getting rid of the child by means of an abortion, having the child and legitimizing him by marriage, or having the child out of wedlock." Though *True Love* may not be an authoritative voice on the experiences of single pregnant women, the broad options it laid out were generally on target.[20]

Mom would have faced daunting legal, logistical, and moral hurdles if she had considered having an abortion in the pre–*Roe v. Wade* era. Minnesota law had prohibited the practice, except when necessary to save the mother's life, since territorial days, and in 1960 she could have gone to prison for one to four years if she had been convicted of terminating her pregnancy. Such strictures forced many women and providers to circumvent the law, either by operating deceptively within it or entirely outside of it. Women of means, both financial and social, could sometimes secure safe and sanitary abortions, but Mom had no such resources at her disposal. Feigning mental illness or threatening suicide in hopes of securing a "therapeutic" abortion sometimes carried the attendant risk of being permanently sterilized at the same time. Women who couldn't or didn't dare turn to professional help in terminating their pregnancies sometimes tried to induce miscarriage themselves, with folk remedies, drugs, or more dangerous means. Most women who died from illegal or self-induced abortions were women of color, while most women who obtained therapeutic abortions were white.[21]

Although Rickie Solinger argues that the primary threat to the health and well-being of women seeking to terminate their pregnancies in the pre-*Roe* era was the law and that "decent, competent practitioners performed the lion's share of abortions in the criminal era," the specter of the "back alley butcher" permeated the culture. Confessional magazines and mainstream newspapers alike disseminated horror stories about incompetent abortionists and the damage they inflicted. During the time that Mom was studying journalism at the university and dating Jack, the Minneapolis papers ran stories about a "machinist and gunsmith" who had been arrested for the second time for performing an illegal abortion and was found carrying a bag with "rubber gloves, medications, surgical instruments and a doctor's head mirror"; a married woman who was sentenced to probation for seeking an abortion from a dentist, who was also criminally charged; and a Duluth woman who, charged with manslaughter for an abortion gone wrong, killed herself before facing trial.[22]

There are no firm figures on the number of abortions performed in the United States during this era, but estimates range from hundreds of thousands to more than a million each year. Mom never mentioned having considered abortion in any of her writings or discussions of the matter, though in later years she took up a pro-choice position. As a churchgoing, law-abiding woman of twenty in 1960, however, she probably didn't view it as a viable option, even if it was among her fleeting thoughts in those desperate, fearful early days of her pregnancy.[23]

I wonder, too, if Mom might have felt so frantic as to have wished herself dead. It's horrible to consider, but she wouldn't have been the only woman to have entertained such dark thoughts in an era when single pregnancy carried such stiff social and emotional penalties. Some single pregnant women's contemporaneous firsthand accounts and retrospective memoirs and interviews include references to thoughts of suicide. "I was so desperate I thought I would kill myself," a nineteen-year-old Booth girl told a researcher from the University of Minnesota in 1963. One of the women I interviewed said that, upon learning of her pregnancy, she tried to muster up the nerve to "walk in front of a bus and end my life." A study of maternal deaths in Minnesota from 1950 to 1965 reported no incidents of suicide but twelve deaths from illegal abortions among unmarried pregnant girls and women.[24]

Mom obviously did not have an abortion or commit suicide, nor did she seriously contemplate the idea of marriage, though she'd have been in good company if she had. In 1960, 69 percent of twenty- to twenty-four-year-old women in the United States were married and, from 1960 to 1964, a full 60 percent of women who became pregnant while single married before that child was born, thus converting an illegitimate pregnancy into a legitimate birth. In fact, Ann Fessler points out that marrying after the discovery of pregnancy was the most common solution to the problem for white women, 67 percent of them walking down the aisle in 1960 compared with only 40 percent of pregnant Black women.[25]

Having ruled out abortion and marriage, Mom chose option number three: having her baby out of wedlock. In California.

JULY 1960

She sits near the front of the bus, trying to ignore the leering, chain-smoking man in the seat behind her.

Nausea strikes in South Dakota, turning her pale skin sallow. She falls asleep, then wakes up to darkness as the bus rolls to a stop at a wayside diner somewhere near the Nebraska border. She straightens her hair in the mirror of the dank bathroom, rolling her tongue along fuzz-covered teeth. She has little appetite, but buys some saltines and a 7UP to help ease her stomach.

Back on the bus, she dozes on and off, in her waking moments watching small-town America pass outside the window. In daylight, she is hopeful; at night, despondent. Another truck stop, another suggestive smile from a strange man, another wave of sickness. By Nevada, her head is pounding. The closer she gets to California, the more expansive the sky and the land become, the smaller she feels. Instead of relief at the shrinking distance between herself and San Francisco, she feels only the yawning gap between herself and Minneapolis.

The bus arrives on Sunday evening, emerging from the Oakland hills to cross the Bay Bridge to San Francisco. There are no colorful Victorian row houses in sight, no picturesque cable cars or gleaming Golden Gate Bridge or romantic Telegraph Hill. Instead, her first taste of the city is a cavernous bus station.

She uncoils herself from her seat and descends from the bus. She catches her reflection in the streaked windows of the station, clothes wrinkled, hair mussed, makeup vanished. She tries to shake off her fatigue and swallow the rising tide of nausea as she retrieves her suitcases, catching a whiff of salty sea breeze in between the exhalations of buses. Her lonesome gray reality begins to settle in, but the sun is setting and she needs to find a place to stay.

The YWCA on Powell Street has a room available and is only a short taxi ride from the bus station. The room is on the second floor, small but clean, with a shared bathroom down the hall. It is there, ensconced in a toilet stall, that the tears finally begin to fall. They come slowly at first, then in a torrent, splashing on the black and white tile floor. She heaves silent sobs and cries herself dry. Then, slowly, she steps out of the stall, washes her face at the sink, and returns to her room, where she sleeps for twenty-four hours straight.[26] ●

Mom's cross-country trek made her part of a nationwide movement of single pregnant women. She joined the many other white, middle-class good girls who hid their illegitimate pregnancies with girdles and visits to far-off relatives or dime-store wedding rings and made-up military husbands. Some young women in trouble left home for jobs that lasted fewer than nine months, while others watched the seasons change from behind the curtains of their homes. These migrants formed a web that spread across the country, their travels covering sometimes thousands of miles, other times only as many footsteps as it took to walk from one end of a house to the other. Mom's pregnant sojourn traversed both spans, beginning with her flight to California.

After rising from her slumber, Mom found an employment agency in the phone book and filled out an application, deciding for the moment not to acknowledge her pregnancy. Federal protection against sexist employment practices wouldn't come until 1964; it would take another fourteen years for Congress to prohibit employment discrimination on the basis of pregnancy. If married teachers and nurses could be fired for becoming pregnant, what were the chances that an unwed mother-to-be with no references would find a job with an income that could support two? Mom figured she'd fight that battle once she had a paycheck in hand and could no longer hide her condition. She searched the classifieds for an apartment and looked at several of them, each small and drab and depressing.[27]

There's no indication that Mom contacted any social service agency that provided assistance to single pregnant women while she was in San Francisco. She may have been unaware that such services existed or too overwhelmed by the myriad challenges ahead of her to seek them out. Still, unwed mothers had long been identified as a population in need of guidance from social workers employed by public and private welfare organizations, for their own well-being as well as that of their children and the taxpaying communities of which they were a part. In 1959, the National Association on Services to Unmarried Parents (NASUP), a national umbrella organization for agencies serving unmarried parents, listed among its members several organizations in the San Francisco Bay Area. But what if Mom had decided to relocate not to San Francisco but to Minneapolis or St. Paul instead? Of course, she would have run the risk of exposing herself to friends, family, and acquaintances, but she'd have been operating on more familiar terrain. What resources might have been available to her and other expectant single women in the Twin Cities?[28]

Minnesota's mandate to care for single expectant women dated from 1917, when the legislature passed thirty-five laws designed to centralize planning for defective, delinquent, and dependent children that would shape the state's response to illegitimacy, adoption, and maternity home care for much of the twentieth century. The Children's Code, as it was known, made the state responsible for providing the "illegitimate" child "the nearest possible approximation to the care, support, and education that he would be entitled to if born of lawful marriage." This included providing "aid and protection" for "the unmarried woman approaching motherhood." By the time Mom was pregnant, county welfare boards had been administering such aid, including Aid to Dependent Children (ADC), for two decades. Had she stayed in the metro area, she could have tapped into those resources with the help of a county welfare agency or a sectarian agency such as the Lutheran Welfare

Society. A social worker trained in the individualized casework method could have helped Mom confront the "inner conflict" that had supposedly led to her pregnancy and access financial assistance, housing, medical care, and hospital delivery services. But first, Mom had to decide where to live, a decision that would trigger a complicated set of negotiations over which entity would assume financial responsibility for her care.[29]

Public assistance depended to a large degree on the county in which one lived and the particular system by which that county administered its welfare funds. Unmarried pregnant women were a mobile population, often moving from one county to another in order to avoid "censorship, condemnation, and non-acceptance," according to the Hennepin County Attorney's office. A 1959 Ramsey County report noted that more than 40 percent of unmarried mothers served in the county in 1957 were nonresidents. Given the circumstances prompting their move, most women had not established the two-year residency requirement for claiming public funds. Had Mom moved to Hennepin or Ramsey County in 1960, she would have been encouraged to contact Anoka County for help. If she refused to do so, the county welfare board or private agency with which she had been working may have considered absorbing some of her expenses, but they did so on a very limited basis.[30]

Mom also would have had to find a place to live, even if it was just across town. If she couldn't afford to pay rent on her own, she could have considered one of several housing options available to single pregnant women: a maternity home, a foster home, or a wage home. Foster homes, in which a pregnant girl lived with a family that received compensation for providing room and board, were typically used by younger girls, as was the case with Pam. Residence at maternity homes often came in the later stages of pregnancy. In the meantime, Mom could have considered a wage home, where she would live with another family and perform agreed-upon work—usually housekeeping and/or childcare—for pay. Mom may also have made arrangements on her own if she'd responded to one of the ads for "expectant unmarried mother, live in, small salary" that appeared in the classified section of the local papers.[31]

Finally, Mom would have had to make arrangements for the delivery of her baby and, ideally, medical care along the way, both of which would have incurred considerable cost. If she'd had to rely on public assistance, she could have sought care at Minneapolis General or University Hospital in Minneapolis or Ancker Hospital in St. Paul. Booth Memorial Hospital was alone among the three maternity homes in the metro area that also provided on-site delivery services. If she'd used any of these hospitals with public funds, the issue of residency would have surfaced once again.

In many ways, then, Mom would have faced the same challenges in Minnesota as she had in San Francisco, the situation made only slightly easier by familiarity and the fact that she'd have been crossing only county, not state, lines. Had she remained committed to the idea of going it alone, without asking for help from her family, she'd have spent the months of her pregnancy trying to manage her most immediate needs—food, housing, income, medical care—while also planning how she would support herself and her child in the future. She could have kept the office job she'd had, at least until her pregnancy became obvious, thereafter at her employer's will. Perhaps this would have provided sufficient income to rent a small apartment. If—when—her funds ran low, however, she'd have faced the prospect of becoming a welfare recipient, an object of scrutiny and supervision and pity, a "case" to be worked and bandied about. Had Mom been securely economically self-sufficient, she could have avoided many of these entanglements for, as one letter to the *Minneapolis Star* said, "With funds, you don't end up in need of public aid." But she was a twenty-year-old college student who had never lived on her own before. It may not have been impossible for her to have her baby on her own, but it would have been difficult and isolating, whether in the Twin Cities or in San Francisco. [32]

JULY 1960

Back at the Powell Street Y after another day of fruitless searching—no job, no apartment, no prospects—she decides to go home. The decision comes quickly and with certainty. She'd known that California would never be home to her and her baby as soon as she'd gotten off the bus, the way Dorothy had longed for grayscale Kansas the moment she landed in Technicolor Oz.

She packs her bags, hauls them down two flights of stairs, and catches a cab back to the bus station. This time when she buys a one-way ticket, she feels nothing but relief.

When the Greyhound crosses the Bay Bridge back into the Oakland hills, she realizes she never laid eyes on the Golden Gate Bridge.

She doesn't care. Though her California experiment has failed, she is going home a wiser woman, armed with Dramamine and a wary countenance.

This time, neither dingy truck stops nor strange men detract from her sense of calm.

This time, she's going home. ●

GAYLE

For Gayle, home was elusive. She led a transitory life as a child, moving from here to there with her family, never landing in one place long enough to feel anchored. And even if she'd lived one place her entire young life, home would have been a complicated refuge.

I found Gayle—or, rather, she found me—through an article I'd published in *Minnesota History* in the summer of 2017 about Booth girls' decisions to surrender their babies for adoption. She responded to the "in search of former Booth girls" call with which the piece ended and said she'd be willing to talk to me either in Atlanta, where she now lived, or in Minnesota, where she could travel. I told her I'd come to her. A few months later, I was on a plane heading to Georgia.

Gayle greeted me with a hug when I arrived at her house in a quiet, wooded neighborhood near Emory University. Petite, energetic, and with an academic's quick-snap mind, Gayle said she'd been getting increasingly nervous about the interview as it approached, even dreaming about the past, but she had prepared a list of topics she wanted to be sure to discuss. The brutal truth that haunted Gayle for years wasn't her pregnancy per se, she said. It wasn't the time she spent squirreled away at Booth. It wasn't even the surrender of her son. Gayle's heart wounds, the ones that began to heal only years later thanks to good therapy and Buddhist teachings, stemmed from a lacerating silence and the shame it implied.[33]

Gayle came of age under the intellectual guidance of her father and the judging eye of her mother. Her "nomad" father moved his wife and four children from town to town around Minnesota as he pursued work and education—bachelor's, then master's, then doctorate; to Brookings, South Dakota, when he took a faculty job at South Dakota State University; then to Ankara, Turkey, when the Agency for International Development decided to use his talents there. From him, Gayle acquired a healthy skepticism, an agnostic atheism, and a high regard for philosophers and scientists and politicians. From her mother, Gayle learned to look at their family from the outside in, to keep up appearances, to put her best face forward. "She cared about what the neighbors thought," Gayle said of her mother, the sixth child of immigrant parents who had struggled to adapt to life in the United States. Gayle chafed at her mother's insistence that she attend church, fold a handkerchief just so, leave no trace of her presence in the living room lest the neighbors stop in for a visit.

The shame set in even before Gayle got pregnant, when, at age fifteen, she slept with a twenty-six-year-old US airman in Ankara. Gayle's parents had found themselves "in a whole new world" in Turkey, with new professional obligations, which meant she and her younger siblings were often left to their own devices. Gayle took advantage. She was young and free and living a "very fast life"—drinking, smoking, having sex—"doing way too much for someone my age." Though her father had expressed a certain open comfort with matters of sex, Gayle had internalized her mother's moral strictures. So when she fed her own sexual appetite, her mother's lessons won out. "There were parts of me that were really the good girl, and there were parts of me that were the bad girl," she said. But after the airman, Gayle was all bad girl, any vestiges of the good girl having slipped away in the arms of an older man. And, she says, "I started not liking myself."

When she and her family returned to Brookings, in time for her junior year of high school, she felt awkward and out of place. She started dating a college freshman with a fancy car and got pregnant soon thereafter. When one morning at breakfast Gayle's roiling stomach wouldn't let her eat the oatmeal her mother had prepared, her mother knew. "I think she wasn't surprised," Gayle said, "Mainly, she would talk about it in terms of how disappointed Dad would be, to make me feel even guiltier." Later, Gayle speculated that perhaps she'd wanted to "get even with my parents or something" for sending mixed messages about sexual behavior, for giving her too much freedom too soon, for taking an odd pride in their daughter's popularity without considering the daughter herself.

Angry, hurt, and ashamed though they were, Gayle's parents considered other options before Booth. There was a road trip to Colorado with her father in search of an abortion that didn't happen because the doctor was under the watchful eye of the authorities. They came home and turned to plan B: marriage. Her parents, his parents, Gayle herself—everyone wanted the college boy to marry Gayle, but he remained steadfast in his refusal. Her mother even thought fleetingly about keeping and raising Gayle's baby. Finally, Gayle's parents wrote to Ann Landers, and Ann Landers wrote back about Booth. This time, the three of them took a road trip from Brookings to St. Paul.

Confinement at Booth was no punishment for Gayle. She loved being out from under her mother's critical eye, fast-tracking through her high school studies, disappearing into the books in Booth's library, *Rebecca* and *Wuthering Heights* and *Jane Eyre*. She reveled in the company of the other Booth girls. "The upstairs room was all these bunk beds and it was just girls, just talking and being, and telling their stories and whatever. And I thought, *This is heaven to me. There's no judgment, no parents, no pressure.*" Still pregnant, she left Booth for a wage home in St. Paul, where she cared for a couple's two children in exchange for room, board, and pay, and she loved that, too. The family operated a jewelry store and welcomed Gayle into their home with kindness, inducing such relaxation in Gayle that she stopped gnawing her fingernails for the first time in years.

Not that there wasn't also subterfuge and loneliness. There was still the family image to protect from the disgracing daughter. Her parents helped her concoct a story to cover her disappearance: she was in Sweden, working as an au pair for a friend her father had made through his international connections. This friend would send Gayle blank postcards from Sweden, which she'd fill with imaginary adventures and return to him so he could mail them to her friends and family in the United States, the Swedish postmark evidence of the good family name. Sometimes she'd get so lonely she'd telephone a favorite relative just to hear her voice, then hang up before saying anything.

It was the jeweler who brought Gayle to the hospital when her time came, who waited in the hall listening to her curse as she delivered her bottom-first baby boy. Her parents came, too, her mother bringing an outfit for her new grandson. Despite his adorable blond hair and his obvious likeness to her, Gayle remained resolute in her plan to surrender. "I did not want to keep that child," she said. "I had other plans . . . it seems like a lot of the girls [at Booth] were conflicted, and I don't remember being conflicted." It was Gayle's mother whose resolve wavered. "She always thought that she should have kept him [but] that wasn't an issue for me." She took comfort in the idea that giving her boy to an educated, married couple would give them a family, him a secure home life, and herself a second chance at a life of her own.

Gayle took advantage of that second chance, driven by a compulsive need to "prove I was a good girl again." She earned one degree, then another, and a third, ending with a doctorate in intercultural communication. Her work, her studies, her curiosity took her all over the world: West Virginia and Vermont, Uganda and Mexico, Lebanon and Kuwait, Turkey again. She married, had another son, enjoyed a successful career as an academic.

But then there was the pain. The anger. The "wet, gray blanket" of judgment that threatened to smother whatever happiness Gayle had found. Therapy and meditation helped her express a latent rage at her condemning mother, give voice to the silent shame that had surrounded her first pregnancy. Gayle had suffered a nearly paralyzing fear when she was pregnant with baby number two. She'd lost her first boy to adoption, and some years later, her beloved younger brother died at age nineteen. When, counting the heartbeats of the baby inside of her, she realized she'd likely have another boy, "I just fell apart," she said. "I didn't want a boy because I'd [already] lost two boys."

She didn't lose the third boy. She and her husband raised him and loved him and watched him become a husband and a father. Then her second son became a brother to her first son. In the mid-1990s, Gayle started searching for her lost boy. With the help of Children's Home Society and after the sting of her son's initial disinterest in knowing her, Gayle finally reunited with her first child. Son number one came with a wife and a son of his own. There were letters and meetings and visits back and forth and family get-togethers. It was "wonderful," a "relationship from heaven." Then he "started closing up," and Gayle wondered if she had become an imposition. "I can be really high energy," she said, "and I thought, *I'm just too much for him, I guess.*" Then, a rebound before another dip. And so it went, highs and lows, peaks and valleys.

How does it all fit together, these pieces of her life—the good girl/bad girl, the unwed mother/successful academic, the rage-filled daughter/loving grandmother? For Gayle, the answer is in the question: they are all contributing pieces, no single one of them defining her more than the others. Even the shame has taken its place as a mere tile in the mosaic of her life. "It's not like all the time I'm living with the shame . . . because you go on, whether you just move on and repress it or whatever, you still move on. I've had a really great life, and so I can't say my life was messed up because of that." She sees Booth and surrendering her son for adoption as part of the greater context in which they occurred, one that placed undue emphasis on marriage and unfair responsibility on women but also preserved opportunities for her and gave her the chance to live the life she's led.

Her final plea to others is to let go of the judgment. "The message I have to people is love. Really. Open your heart to the mothers, to the children, to the fathers." ■

The curved front of the bus station is a welcome sight. Though the waiting room is the same sad place she had left just a few days before, it feels like home. The checkered floor, the leftover humidity of a hot Minnesota summer day, the faces of strangers . . . everything feels familiar and comfortable.

She decides to splurge. Instead of lugging her suitcases onto another bus, she uses some of the money she had saved for San Francisco for cab fare to Blaine.

She stands at the foot of the long driveway as the taxi pulls away. It's late and she's tired, but she needs a moment to take it all in: the house dark and silent save for the flickering light and muffled laughter from the television in the front room, the little kids' toys littering the front yard, the crickets chirping their summer song. A fan whirs in an open window upstairs, trying to draw the cooler night air into the bedroom under the eaves. Home.

She picks up her bags and walks down the driveway to the side entry, the one that opens into the kitchen. A lifetime has passed since she last crossed its threshold.

She takes a deep breath and opens the door. ●

I am pregnant. Against all odds and without too much effort, I am pregnant. I didn't know how much I wanted to have a child until I was carrying one.

We don't tell anyone at first, hewing to the common practice of keeping a pregnancy close to the chest for the first few weeks, just in case.

In private, though, Steve and I revel in the promise that a white stick with two pink lines portends, our happy little secret. The home remodeling project we have begun takes on new overtones. In the frame of our new basement and kitchen and bedroom I see the outline of our life to come, playrooms and high chairs and rocking chairs. I study the stages of fetal development and envision stroller walks and bedtime stories and booties and bonnets. I am realist enough to forecast the struggles as well, the sleepless nights and noxious odors and baby wails and thankless giving and giving and giving of oneself to another. These latter concerns have dominated my view of parenthood for more than a decade, but now they are eclipsed by maternal feelings that have, surprisingly, bubbled to the surface. Pregnancy casts a warm glow on everything around me, softening sharp edges and bathing everything in sepia as it mellows my flaming temperament.

I have a part-time teaching gig at a local community college and, to escape the noise and dust of our remodeling project, I spend nearly half of every week at Mom's house in Crystal. Eric is there, too, as he transitions back to Minnesota from Brooklyn. Though they don't know our secret, I carry it with me. Just wait, I say silently, relishingly. Just wait till you find out that our family is growing.

We have a doctor's appointment scheduled for Monday, December 1. I will be almost eight weeks pregnant by then. We plan to tell the grandmas the news before the appointment and everyone else after. On Sunday afternoon, we bring Steve's mom, who has been visiting from Duluth, to the Greyhound station in St. Paul. As we sit in the car in the weedy parking lot outside the tiny station, we tell Evie we are expecting. Though she has heard such news before—fourteen times, from her four other children—she is happy. She asks how I am feeling and says she didn't get too sick with her pregnancies, either.

After Evie waves goodbye from the bus, we drive across town to Mom's. She is elated, but tries to tamp down her enthusiasm a bit, knowing how we all tease her for being a "gusher." Mom, like most others, has stopped asking about our plans for children. Never particularly baby-oriented herself, she had respected our—mostly my—focus on other things: school, work, travel. But now she is thrilled at the prospect of being a grandmother. She already is—to Kim's son Christopher, but they are in Detroit, and we are here, and she and I have spent my lifetime together. Steve and I leave Mom on a happy note, promising to call her with an update after the next day's ultrasound.

No heartbeat.

When we get home from the obstetrician's office, I go directly to bed, seeking the comfort that only the consciousness-less of sleep can provide. As I fade away, I hear Steve making phone calls in the other room, to his mother and mine, to his siblings and mine. Our secret revealed in its failure.

It's a long week between learning of the death of our pregnancy and the removal of its remains by dilation and curettage.

Nurses, doctors, friends, fellow miscarriage survivors offer reassurance. Ten to twenty percent of pregnancies end in miscarriage, says one doctor. Miscarriage is nature's way of taking care of a fetus that was not developing properly, says another. I had a miscarriage, too, says a friend, a mother of three. Don't worry, honey, says a nurse. You'll get pregnant again.

But somehow, I know.

I just lost my one and only pregnancy.

3
UNDER THE EAVES

When I got back to Minneapolis, I had no job, no school, and no money. I had to go back home to my parents, and I did. But I didn't tell them the truth about my situation right away. I knew I couldn't wait much longer, though, because I was starting to show. My plan was to stay at home until my time came, then go to a place in St. Paul called the Booth Memorial Home for Unwed Mothers, have my baby, and give it up for adoption. I had written to Booth and to the Lutheran Social Service, and I was trying to gather up my courage to tell mom and dad.

When that bitter day finally arrived, I discovered that mother already knew after intercepting a letter from Booth Memorial. She hadn't told dad, though, so that was up to me. . . . I don't think mother was terribly surprised at what happened to me, because she never seemed to have much confidence in me. But she didn't want anyone else to find out . . . not the relatives, not the neighbors, not even my little sisters and brothers.

And so I was tucked away in the upstairs bedroom, the one that had been my brother Earl's until he moved out, the one upstairs under the eaves, the only room on the second floor. [1]

SO BEGAN THE LONGEST PHASE of my mother's pregnancy, the one when she was hidden in plain sight, when shame and uncertainty and anger and boredom collided in a modest house on Tyler Street. For the next five months, my mother's world shrank from the expansive possibilities of California to the stifling space between the knotty-pine walls of that room under the eaves. She moved through the rest of the house in an awkward silence about what was happening to her, under strict orders not to discuss the situation with her littlest brother and sister, who were too young to fully understand the situation, or her teenage brother and sister, who might learn the wrong lesson from her example. Those terms, whether arrived at through negotiation, agreement, or command, extended to her relationship with the outside world as well. They defined her existence through the dog days of summer, when neighborhood children staved off the heat by running through sprinklers and sucking on popsicles. They regulated her activities through the crispening fall, as days made bright by red and golden leaves gave way to the ever-earlier evening shadows. They prevented her from feeling the bite of winter and appreciating the hushed silence of sparkling cold nights. For the next five months, my mother was not to set foot outside the house.

This scenario casts my grandparents' house, and my grandparents themselves, in a harsh light—house turned prison, room turned cell, parents turned guards. But this image does not mesh at all with my memories of Grandma and Grandpa and their house on Tyler Street. I loved making the trek across town to visit them, my mood rising in happy anticipation as the small house came into sight. When the whole family gathered for the holidays, we would fill every nook and cranny, gathering around a long, pieced-together table in the basement, the only room large enough to accommodate my grandparents' six children and children-in-law and thirteen grandchildren. After dinner and the all-hands-on-deck cleanup, we kids would fan out around the house while the adults visited. This often led us up a narrow set of stairs off the kitchen to that room under the eaves. By that time, it served mostly as a storage room, but it seemed like an adventure-land to me. Trinkets and old magazines and worn-out toys lined the shelves along the walls. The room smelled of cold winters and hot summers and yellowed newspapers, its winding path through the piles holding out the promise of hidden treasures. I didn't know that a painful piece of my mother's past also lay buried in those mounds.

I knew my grandfather, Earl Moore Sr., as a gentle, creative man from whom my mother and brother and I had inherited our dimples. He wore his hair slicked back from his face, traces of its youthful black still evident in the dominant gray. He was tall and quick to smile, with a bit of a flush to his face. Mom liked to tell me how he would ride his bicycle from the house in Blaine to his job at the Target store in Crystal and then to our house—a trip of fifteen miles—to bring me baby dolls when I was small, a gesture of love for me and her both. Later, he worked at the Ambassador Resort Motor Hotel in St. Louis Park, caring for the plants and flowers that made the pool area a tropical paradise. I spent many happy occasions—birthday parties and family gatherings and midwinter escapes—at that hotel, swimming till my eyes burned from the chlorine, proud that I had a personal connection to such a wonderland.

But it was Grandma who took center stage. She was unfailingly kind and indulgent with all of us grandkids. She hosted sleepovers for me and my brother, took us clothes shopping at the beginning of each new school year, and treated us to ice cream at the counter in the back of Merwin Drug. She called me Kimberly—the only one ever to use my full name—and did so without making it seem formal or awkward. She worked hard at home and at her job at the *Minneapolis Star and Tribune.* She did all this with gentle good humor, a laugh always at the ready. But underneath her calm exterior lay a strong will and authoritative presence, while Grandpa seemed to occupy unstable territory within the family, a quiet man who retreated into his basement workshop and his crafts and his plants. Though as a child I was not privy to the details, I overheard whispers of excessive drinking and problems keeping a job. One day, as Mom and Grandma drank coffee at the house in Blaine, I ran into the kitchen for a glass of water and headlong into the first and only time I ever heard my otherwise even-tempered grandmother curse, in a hushed but urgent conversation about my grandfather. Mom shooed me away before I learned anything more, but the impression lingered.

Mostly, though, concerns from the grown-up world barely permeated my relationship with Grandma and Grandpa. I loved them for what they were to me, not what they were or had been to my mother. They were the adults in my life who bestowed the gifts of time and affection without expecting anything but the same in return. They were the heads of the family that, to me, meant aunts and uncles and cousins playing and laughing and eating and sharing, and their house on Tyler Street was the site of many of these happy gatherings.

How, then, could these two beloveds have shunted their daughter aside, banishing her to a half existence in that room under the eaves? Why did my mother agree to hide herself away, first at home, then at Booth? What filled her days during those long months of confinement, when she stayed behind as everyone else in the house came and went, the obligations of work and school reflecting a luxurious freedom that she lacked? And how was it that she had learned about Booth in the first place?

Let's start with that last question first.

Finding Booth

In November 1960, in the middle of my mother's period of home confinement, television news anchor Dave Moore appeared on screens across the Twin Cities to introduce a new programming initiative, WCCO Television Reports. Moore was three years into what would become a three-decade career as the trusted voice of the evening news in the metro area. The public service series was to focus on some of the most pressing social issues of the day, and the first installment tackled "a true story and also, unhappily, a continuing one," as Moore explained. "It's a story that may shock some viewers,

The clapboard at the beginning of Dave Moore's WCCO Television Reports program on "Unwed Mothers," which is available at https://tinyurl.com/WCCOReports. *Peabody Awards Collection, University of Georgia*

but the fact that it is true demands that it be told. It's a story of confusion and heartache. It's a story of unwed mothers."

The music swelled as the camera panned back from Moore and cut to the opening credits. Moore thanked the program sponsor for shedding light "on areas of life that don't generally come within our view." The image then shifted to a fuzzy view of a "darkened hallway in St. Paul," hints of light emanating from a door opened just a crack. To the sounds of stifled grunting, Moore reported that "the actions of an age-old drama had begun": a young woman was delivering a baby. Yet the arrival of the "reddish, crying mass of boy" would not be met with the joy typical of such occasions, he noted. As the camera focused on the infant squalling in the doctor's arms, Moore remarked that the new child's "very existence had caused pain, other than the mother's labor. He had brought with him embarrassment and confusion. His entry into this world was not a happy one and it was duly recorded on the birth records. Our little newcomer was illegitimate."[2]

And this "little newcomer" had been born at the Salvation Army's Booth Memorial Hospital in St. Paul.

My mother had already made arrangements to deliver her baby at Booth by the time the WCCO program aired, so she obviously had learned about it elsewhere. By 1960, the stately building on Como Avenue had been serving as a home and hospital for unwed mothers-to-be for forty-seven years, one of three such maternity homes in the Twin Cities area at the time. It could be that she had heard about it through the grapevine, in whispered conversations about other unlucky girls. But the historical record suggests other possibilities as well.

Stories about unwed mothers saturated the local and national media. Indeed, the unwed mother had, by the late 1950s, become a recognizable character in US popular culture, the terrible denouement to all those warning stories about "teens in trouble." She was a perfect dramatic figure, one who elicited curiosity, pity, and revulsion in equal measure. Like the stars of reality television in the twenty-first century, the unwed mother of the mid-twentieth century embodied a lifestyle familiar enough to be relatable to viewers, deviant enough to spark their prurient interest and moral criticism. In Minneapolis in early 1959, a year before my mother would have taken such personal interest in the topic, she might have read in the *Minneapolis Morning Tribune* about how the unwed mother symbolized the failings of the modern family; learned from Dear Abby that even girls in trouble could find a "door open to happy future" at a home for unwed mothers; watched *In*

Lonely Expectation, a television drama set inside a fictional maternity home, on WCCO's channel 4; attended a public talk about unwed mothers at Central Free Church in downtown Minneapolis; then caught *Unwed Mother* and *Joy Ride* at the Heights Theater, a double feature about "today's most dangerous teen problem" and "kids who live for kicks," respectively. She may have, but probably didn't, preoccupied as she was with her newfound popularity at the university.[3]

Still, it would have been difficult for her to avoid entirely the public conversation about the unwed mother and the maternity home, characters writ large in post–World War II culture. Perhaps media stories that mentioned Booth specifically lodged somewhere in her brain, ready for retrieval when she found herself in need of help. The Salvation Army operated a network of Booth Memorial Hospitals across the country, not just in St. Paul, and national magazines such as the *Saturday Evening Post*, *Ladies' Home Journal*, and *True Love* mentioned them in stories about unwed mothers, sandwiched between advertisements for belly-flatteners and Maidenform bras. "Are you really lovely to love?" the makers of Fresh Cream Deodorant asked in *True Confessions* magazine, while in the adjoining column, a real-life unwed mother recounted the terrifying realization that she was "in trouble." Luckily for her, a benevolent minister pointed her in the direction of the local Salvation Army Booth Memorial Home. As she had done for Gayle and her family, Ann Landers advised a worried mother, whose daughter was growing plump despite the fact that she was hardly eating anything, to contact the Salvation Army. The *Minneapolis Morning Tribune*'s own advice columnist, Mr. Fixit, provided information about homes operating in the metro area, including Booth. And long before Dave Moore brought viewers on a virtual tour of Booth, local newspapers had praised Booth's services in stories such as "Booth Hospital Offers Help—Haven for Unwed Girls" (1950) and "Girls in Trouble—Booth Hospital Offers Security" (1959).[4]

For Mom, however, the most likely scenario is that an intermediary directed her to Booth. Perhaps Dr. Goode had told her about the Salvation Army's services during that visit to his office on Central Avenue, or maybe she had confided in the minister at her Lutheran church. Although I can't know exactly how my mother learned about the Salvation Army home, statistics show that most girls learned about places like Booth from counselors, doctors, pastors, and county social workers. These professionals were often the first point of contact for single pregnant women, and the Salvation Army and Minnesota Department of Welfare disseminated information about available resources to their offices. The Salvation Army promised young women that they could find at Booth "a life rekindled, a faith renewed, a new beginning."[5]

In any case, Mom had already decided on Booth for her confinement by the time she came into contact with Anoka County officials. Her illicit pregnancy triggered her involvement with the labyrinthine state and county bureaucracy. According to Patricia Peart, Mom's Anoka County caseworker, "Sharon came to our office with her plans well formulated. She is a very intelligent girl and we helped her with her plans for Booth."[6]

JULY 1960

It's time.

She has to tell him.

She creeps down the stairs, heart in her throat.

He's in his workshop, standing at the mirror in his T-shirt, combing his dark hair, getting ready for his evening shift at the club. Her handsome father.

She is his favorite and he is hers. She is immune to the wrath he sometimes unleashes on her brothers; she hungrily absorbs his doting affections; she champions his cause in family disputes.

Dad? she says, hoping her status as favored child will shield her from his temper when she tells him the news.

It doesn't.

His face goes red, his eyes flame. He yells so furiously his slicked-back hair falls onto his forehead. He rages with accusations and invectives. And then:

How could you?

And then: a slammed door, a car engine.

And then: silence.

For three days, there is silence.

Finally, a summons, an apology.

A plan. ●

Through whatever pipeline of information she found, Mom had chosen Booth, and before she turned herself over to its care, she hid in the room under the eaves. But why hide at all? Why would my grandparents have insisted she stay out of sight for so long? And why would she have agreed to these terms, then turn herself over to Booth?

The short answer: shame.

My mother and grandparents lived in a culture that barraged its members with messages about proper sexual behavior, especially for girls and women. Churches, schools, and families; social policy, state law, academic research; movies, magazines, and newspapers—the entire social structure seemed to be telling young women how to behave and yelling at them and their parents when they failed to follow the rules. Although premarital sex had become increasingly common among young people in the postwar period, cultural mores had yet to catch up. White wedding dresses concealed many potentially damning realities. The pretense of sexual purity evaporated when a single woman became pregnant, however, and she faced a gauntlet of disapproval. High schools and colleges were not legally required to provide their services to pregnant students until Congress passed Title IX in 1972. If she had decided to continue her classes at the University of Minnesota, Mom likely would have faced raised eyebrows and snickers, as she would have among her neighbors on Tyler Street or congregants at her family's church. In February 1959, a seventeen-year-old girl who had had to quit school upon becoming pregnant wrote Dear Abby about the guilt-by-association mentality that stripped her of any potential support from her friends. "My girl friends say they still like me but their parents won't let them associate with me because it might ruin their reputations." Many of the women Ann Fessler featured in *The Girls Who Went Away* also recalled painful scenes of "social shunning." One woman's story could have been Mom's: "I had been this girl who didn't smoke, didn't drink, didn't do anything wrong. I took care of my kid brothers and sisters, and everybody's parents wanted their daughters to be with me. Now, when I walked down the street, all the parents made their daughters cross the street."[7]

Neighbors and friends who ostracized single pregnant women for being sexually transgressive "bad girls" may not have given much thought to the causes of such aberrant behavior, but others certainly did. Social welfare experts sometimes mentioned the shortcomings of sex education or the limited availability of birth control, but often they focused on factors internal to the erring girl herself. By the 1950s, those studying unmarried mothers no longer viewed them as innocent victims of predatory men or bad circumstances, feeble-minded deviants incapable of moral behavior, or girls of low class and breeding. Instead, in what was heralded as a more humane approach to illegitimately pregnant women, experts considered them—or at least the white women among them—to be psychologically ill. Drawing on psychoanalytic theory, psychiatrists, social workers, and maternity home staff argued that white women who conceived outside of marriage had been driven by subconscious, neurotic desires. Prominent social work theorist Leontine Young suggested in 1954 that the (white) unmarried mother deliberately sought out sexual encounters with men about whom she cared little in order to achieve pregnancy. "The logical and seemingly inevitable result of her psychological development is an out-of-wedlock child," she wrote, "and, like a sleepwalker, she acts out what she must do without awareness or understanding of what it means or of the fact that she plans and initiates the action." Social welfare professionals in the Twin Cities agreed that "the bearing of an illegitimate child is symptomatic of an inner conflict," as a 1956 Hennepin County report put it.[8]

African American women, on the other hand, were often portrayed as welfare sponges acting on innate, intractable impulses and, according to historian Rickie Solinger, "their *absence of psyche.*" These attacks were especially common as the civil rights movement made inroads in its fight against white supremacy, and racist officials sought to reassert political and economic power. Leontine Young argued against this view of Black illegitimacy, however, suggesting instead that some "Negro" unmarried mothers were motivated by the same neuroses as white unmarried mothers. Most often, these Black women lived in the industrialized North and came from families and communities that had adopted shame-based white standards of propriety. In contrast, Young wrote, Black girls and women in the rural South came to their out-of-wedlock pregnancies "naturally and normally," not because they were acting on biological defects, but because the matriarchal culture in which they lived, one shaped by the legacy of slavery, made single motherhood commonplace. Young's relatively nuanced view of Black unmarried mothers stood in stark contrast to, as she put it, the "stupid and clearly fallacious" stereotype that the "Negro is constitutionally immoral," a myth advanced by those seeking to "prove the Negro racially inferior." Yet the vehemence with which she denounced that view is evidence of its currency among social welfare professionals and politicians who viewed Black single mothers and children as a threat to the moral, economic, and racial hierarchy of the nation.[9]

For white women like Mom, though, illegitimate pregnancy was thought to emerge from deep-seated inner conflict. So, too, apparently, was the *inability* to bear *legitimate* children, at least in the eyes of some health professionals. Psychological explanations for atypical childbearing—whether in excess or in absence—provide another example of how the narrow vision of "proper" social and sexual functioning cast those beyond its margins as deviants. Although many doctors argued that physiology played the most significant role in inhibiting conception, others turned to Freudian psychology to understand the 50 percent of infertile couples for whom no physical cause had been diagnosed during the post–World War II period. Medical professionals had become more attuned to the physiological basis of and treatment for male sterility—a long-overdue corrective to an almost exclusive focus on the "'incompetent' female body"—but when it came to theories about the psychological underpinnings of fertility problems, women were the target. Experts conceded that work-related stress *may* have had some bearing on a man's fertility, physically and/or psychologically, but viewed him as otherwise psychologically sound and prepared to accept his masculine role as father and breadwinner. Merely having a job, however, could be taken as evidence that a woman had not adjusted to her feminine role and was subconsciously avoiding motherhood. Overeducated, career-minded, "aggressive and masculine women who are competitive, strong, ambitious, and dominating" had given themselves over to their neuroses, rejected their natural drive toward "motherliness," and become "frigid." One authority renowned for his study of the psychology of infertility warned that helping such maladjusted women bear and raise children would contribute to the "endless processions of neurotics."[10]

Authorities cited the generational impact of female neuroses when discussing girls who became pregnant outside of marriage as well, laying blame for their maladjustment squarely at the feet of their parents. Young women engaged in illicit sex and subconsciously sought to become pregnant because, somehow, their parents had failed them. "The predominant factor in this difficult problem is an unwholesome child-parent relationship," social worker and former maternity home director Sara Edlin wrote in 1954. Leontine Young described many unwed mothers-to-be as "mother-ridden": girls who had grown up in the care of a self-absorbed, domineering mother "who has never accepted her own femininity and whose life adjustment is a constant struggle with that fact." Though fewer in number than the mother-ridden, the "father-ridden" sought solace in unmarried pregnancy as a means of rebelling against a "rejecting and tyrannical" father who "demands unquestioning obedience and conformity to his wishes." In contrast to Young, Edlin found that most of the pregnant girls she encountered had troublesome relationships with "strong but neglectful" fathers.[11]

I'm certain that neither Young's nor Edlin's book would have been on my mother's or grandparents' bookshelves, but these ideas about neurotic pregnancy-seekers and faulty parents trickled into mainstream society via the popular media. Mom and my grandparents may have seen movies such as *A Summer Place* (1959) or *Too Soon to Love* (1960), which depicted overbearing fathers and sexually repressed or domineering mothers as contributing to their daughters' sexual improprieties. They may have read cautionary tales such as "Today It Could Be *Your* Daughter" (1958) and "My Daughter Is in Trouble" (1962) in coffee-table copies of *Ladies' Home Journal* or *Look* magazine. Perhaps they would have chanced upon Kenneth Eric's article in a 1961 issue of *True Love* in a doctor's waiting room. "What sort of woman is the unwed mother?" Eric asked. "Is she a criminal, is she simply stupid, or is she an innocent victim?" Mostly, he answered, she "is an unhappy person who comes from an unhappy home." Donna's was "shabby and fatherless"; Jean's "a muddle of alcoholism and promiscuity." Sally's mother commanded her household, leaving the girl desperate "for attention from a father always too busy to notice her." These young women got pregnant to replace the love they couldn't get at home.[12]

Would my mother or grandparents have read *Ladies' Home Journal* or *Look*? Maybe. *True Love*? Maybe not. But it is almost certain they would have read the local newspapers. My grandmother worked in the library at the *Minneapolis Star and Tribune*, after all. The Minneapolis and St. Paul papers published stories that echoed these themes about white unwed mothers' motivations and home environments with the same backhanded gestures of sympathy and understanding. The *Minneapolis Morning Tribune* reminded readers in 1956 that unwed mothers were not "statistics or sinners," instead noting that they "may have been trying to 'solve' something by having a child." In 1959, the same paper blamed daughters' pregnancies on "dominating mothers who cluck over them like angry hens," while the *St. Paul Dispatch* claimed that "the defect in family relationships is basic," more influential in the increasing incidence of single pregnancy even than youthful rebellion, sexual desire, and a lack of sex education and birth control. Three years later, the *St. Paul Pioneer Press* identified the problem and its apparent root: "Unwed Mothers Increase; Permissive Parents Blamed."[13]

All of these accounts suggested the same thing: a daughter's morality was the responsibility of—and a reflection on—the parents. Accordingly, mothers and fathers of single pregnant girls were judged as harshly as the girls themselves. They were seen as failing, not only in their parental responsibilities but also at upholding the standards of their entire sex. Best, then, for my grandparents to hide my mother's deviant behavior from prying eyes for as long as possible, to maintain the illusion that all was well in the Moore household.

Putative Fathers

Yet, for as much shaming and blaming as these sources spread around the unfortunate pregnant woman and her family, the intent, by experts and journalists alike, was often sympathetic. Dave Moore of WCCO-TV reminded viewers that unwed mothers were not so unlike themselves; they had friends and family; they were someone's daughter. "All parties," he insisted, "the parents, the young mother, the young father—need understanding."[14]

The young father. Where did he fit in this landscape and how might Mom have called Jack to account? The state of Minnesota had an economic interest in identifying fathers so that they, and not taxpayers, could assume financial responsibility for the "care, maintenance and education" of "illegitimate" children and medical care for the woman during pregnancy and delivery. Barring a man's outright admission and in an era when the best scientific testing could only exclude a man from fatherhood rather than provide positive proof of it, the process of establishing paternity was more legal than biological. Had Mom or Anoka County chosen to pursue the matter, the municipal court could have required Mom (and Dr. Goode) to declare under oath "the time when and the place where [the child] was begotten," after which it would issue a warrant to bring Jack before the court to answer Mom's allegations. If the court had adjudged Jack to be the father of Mom's child, it would have imposed a legal financial obligation upon him with the prospect of jail time hanging over his head if he refused to pony up. Such proceedings were acrimonious all around, expectant mothers in some instances refusing to name their male partners and in others standing accused of either intentionally identifying an innocent man or having been so promiscuous that it would be impossible to pinpoint one man as the father.[15]

So it was that "putative" or "alleged" fathers often escaped notice while girls and women faced denunciation from peers, neighbors, and family members for the inescapable fact of their pregnancy. Some young men behaved honorably, acknowledging their responsibility by proposing marriage, providing financial and moral support, or offering to raise the child with (or even without) their girlfriends. Others, like Jack, left their partners to fend for themselves and single-handedly deflect the slings and arrows of public and private reproach. In a culture that demanded women bring sexual activity to a screeching halt before petting turned to penetration, pregnancy branded single pregnant women as moral failures. "When [a couple] has relations, the man's ego is flattered, yet the woman is looked down upon," a nineteen-year-old resident of Booth told University of Minnesota social work professor Gisela Konopka in 1963. "My boyfriend's mother has sort of condemned me because I am unwed," a seventeen-year-old reported. "I do not think the double standard is fair."[16]

Social theorists and journalists perpetuated this double standard in their relative examination of fathers and mothers. Leontine Young had taken up the subject of the unmarried father in 1954, describing him as "in almost every case a counterpart of the neurotic personality of the unmarried mother." Still, she pointed out that he had only recently become the subject of study, shielded from examination by his limited biological role and scared off from accepting responsibility by punitive laws and presumptive stereotypes. In 1956, public welfare officials in Hennepin County admitted they knew little about the fathers of out-of-wedlock children; ten years later, they had made only minor headway in their understanding.[17]

Media stories about single pregnancy focused even more intently on the mother. Moore's brief nod to the role played by the young father was typical of such accounts in the early 1960s. Journalists acknowledged that men had had a hand in creating the situation and should be held to account for it in some way—financially at the very least—but only as a sidebar to the feature story about neurotic young women about to bring a child into the world. In Kenneth Eric's twelve-page report on unwed mothers for *True Love* magazine, for example, the "putative fathers" merited only a few paragraphs in the section discussing marriage as a possible option for the expectant mother. The *Minneapolis Morning Tribune*'s 1959 series on the failing American family included one article devoted entirely to unwed mothers as an "index of the problem." The article presented critical and sympathetic views of expectant girls, discussed the incidence of premarital pregnancy among "Negroes" and Puerto Ricans, and cited judges, social scientists, and children's bureau officials. There was nary a mention of fathers, however, putative or otherwise. This skewed representation of the issue was not an isolated incident: a search of the online archive of the Minneapolis newspapers from 1954 to 1974 using the term "unwed mother" yields 6,119 results. The number of stories containing the phrase "unwed father" for the same time period? Fifty.[18]

This almost exclusive focus on unwed mothers would begin to shift by decade's end, when welfare officials and journalists alike started referring to "unmarried parents" and social service agencies, including Booth, extended services to unmarried pregnant couples as well as single fathers. But in 1960, when Mom lived in secrecy in that room under the eaves, single pregnant girls and women found themselves in the crosshairs of public and expert attention, as did their parents. However benevolent the intentions of academics, welfare officials, and reporters, the images they crafted and circulated were unflattering to say the least. In this collective cultural narrative, Mom and Grandma and Grandpa would have seen themselves portrayed as defective, neurotic, and dysfunctional. Little wonder, then, that my grandparents felt compelled to hide my mother's pregnancy. They must have felt that they were protecting the whole family from scrutiny and judgment, trying to maintain their sometimes-tenuous grasp on middle-class respectability. Little wonder, then, that my mother conceded to the plan, agreeing to hide herself away, first at home, then at Booth. In the world in which they lived, they undoubtedly saw these strategies as the best of a bad set of options.

Confined at Home, Consigned to Memory

And so my mother spent the second half of 1960 in hiding. In everything she wrote about her first pregnancy, she devoted just a few lines to those long months:

> It seems to me that I spent most of my time in that room, looking out the window, watching for the bus that brought the little kids home from school or the one that dropped my weary mother off after her working day at the Star and Tribune. I heard dad get up in the afternoon to get ready for his bartending job, wishing I could go down and talk to him

and kid and laugh with him the way we used to. But those days were past, and I paced the floor of that upstairs room repenting about my sins from July until the end of December.[19]

I suppose there wasn't much to say about this period of lonely monotony, one day bleeding into the next. Still, I wonder: What did my grandparents tell friends and other family members about Mom's whereabouts? What did Mom's four younger siblings make of these circumstances? Marcia and Dave, ages ten and five, respectively, may have been too young to understand what was happening, but Diane was seventeen, Sam fifteen; of course they knew. Did they talk about it, to each other, to Mom? What about Mom's friends? Was she able to stay in touch with any of them by telephone? Even if my grandparents had forbidden such contact, might she have attempted it anyway, or was she too defeated to challenge any such proscriptions? Did she still somehow make her way across town to Dr. Goode's office for prenatal checkups? Did she never step outside to feel the sun on her face?

I know she did the latter at least once.

NOVEMBER 1960

The table is set, dinner made, cake studded with candles awaiting a match.

She's coming! she yells when she sees her mother walking up the driveway after a long day at work.

She herds her brothers and sisters into the kitchen, gets them settled at the table.

Surprise! they yell when the door opens. Happy birthday!

Her mother's weary eyes begin to lighten, then go cold when she sees the gift on the kitchen counter.

Where did this come from? her mother asks, staring at the ribboned package.

I got it from Dayton's, she says. For you. For your birthday.

Downtown? How did you get there? Her mother is glaring at her now.

I took the bus, she says. I wore that big coat, Mom. No one could tell.

Her mother holds her gaze a moment longer, then turns and walks past the laden table, past the birthday cake, past the package, into her bedroom in the back of the house.[20] ●

After the failed attempt to please her mother with a surprise birthday gift, Mom spent her remaining days at home alone in her sanctuary-cum-prison under the eaves.

This, at least, was the story Mom's essay "Greyhound" had led me to believe. For years, I had an image of Mom pacing and ruminating in that thousand-square-foot prison for months on end as her belly grew. Then, in late 2018, while looking through a box of her personal papers that had been sitting in our basement since her death nearly ten years earlier, I found something: a résumé she had prepared in late 1964 or early 1965. On it, she listed three separate secretarial jobs she had held since graduating from Spring Lake Park High School, from 1957 through the first half of 1960. Then, she noted a fourth . . . from August to December of 1960, the last five months of her pregnancy, the exact period during which she was supposed to have been confined to the house under strict orders not to show herself publicly. She claimed that she had worked for a man named Jerry Voyle at Shoppers Charge Service in Minneapolis. Then there's a five-month gap in her record, until she began working for Gold Bond Stamp Company in May 1961.

These starkly different accounts of this five-month period raise the question: did Mom fabricate a job on her résumé or fabricate a story in her essay? It seems a stretch for her to have done either of these things. A search of the Minneapolis papers confirms the existence of a Shoppers Charge office headed by Jerry Voyles (not Voyle) in Minneapolis in 1960. It would have been a bold falsehood indeed to have randomly chosen a specific company and specific person to falsely pad her work history. Could she have worked for him from her home in Blaine? Maybe, but the job duties she described—she "helped set up the office" for the new Minneapolis branch of the company— seem site specific. Had she embellished her essay, then, exaggerated her actual circumstances in the fall of 1960 to communicate her interior circumstances? That also seems unlikely, out of sync with the tone and truthful intent of the rest of the piece. Had she forgotten that she had left home every day for a job in downtown Minneapolis during the very time she says she was home in the afternoons to hear her father get ready for work? This would be a major, almost unimaginable, failing of memory. Besides, Mom had repeated the story of her isolation in another essay, "Birth Rite"—in which she wrote that "my shamed parents hid me in the upstairs bedroom until my time came"— and in verbal accounts to both me and my sister Kim. As Kim recalled of her conversations with Mom, "She definitely said she did NOT leave the house."[21]

Ultimately, I believe Mom was confined to the house for the last several months of her pregnancy, shielding herself and her family from public scrutiny. Though there is no way to verify with absolute certainty this account over the one presented in her work history, there is ample evidence of how harshly single pregnant women and their families were judged in 1960. I can't muster up comparable explanations for why she would have manufactured the confinement story almost forty years later. Times had changed; single pregnant women were no longer the scorned women they once had been, especially those whose pregnancies had occurred decades ago.

Mostly, though, I believe Mom's later account because it is in keeping with the person I knew her to be. Plagued by self-doubt and self-consciousness all of her life, not given to self-aggrandizement or self-pity, she'd have been more likely to "adjust" the facts of her work history to preserve her good standing in others' eyes in 1965 than she would have been to exaggerate her suffering years later to elicit undeserved sympathy from her writing professor and classmates. Whatever the literal facts of the matter, however, the larger truth is that Mom felt trapped, condemned by the judgment of her community, her parents, and her own conscience to a circumscribed life as penance for her transgression.

In November, two months before the baby was due, WCCO television broadcast its documentary about unwed mothers at Booth St. Paul. There is no way to know if my mother or her parents watched the program. If they did, I imagine they absorbed it with mixed emotions—curiosity, regret, relief. Mom may have taken comfort in Dave Moore's call for sympathetic understanding of single pregnant women as she got her first glimpse of the inner workings of Booth: the social worker counseling the residents, the doctors and nurses tending to their medical needs, the girls masking their status with fake wedding rings during excursions to nearby Como Park. Though her relationship with my grandparents was strained, she may have felt better about it after hearing about the "angry father who left his daughter a half block from the hospital" or the mother who told her pregnant daughter "I'd rather have you dead than bring this shame upon me." Grandma and Grandpa may have felt relief in hearing that the unwed mother's parents often "have to suffer more than the girl" and that their sometimes-harsh treatment of their daughters stemmed not from "lack of love" but "lack of understanding, or confusion as to how to help these young girls." They would have taken comfort in Moore's assurance that the professionals at Booth were well equipped to handle such difficult situations.

It would likely have been the final scene in the program that stilled their hearts, however. Moore had already pointed out that seven of ten mothers at Booth surrendered their babies for adoption, and the closing scene focused on one such separation. Set to the strains of "The Old Rugged Cross," the camera followed a young mother as she hands her baby over to a social worker, who carries the baby down a long hallway and to a life as someone else's child. As the social worker exits the building, the mother dashes away up a spiral staircase. Then she, too, leaves Booth to start a new life. "She's a young girl who has had her first child," Moore noted, "but the child is no longer hers."

As strained as these months in seclusion at home must have been, greater pain lay ahead.

MARY

Mary's story begins and ends with pain.

I met Mary in February 2016, when I gave a talk about my research at St. Catherine University's Abigail Q. McCarthy Center for Women's brown-bag lunch series. I explained the origins of my research, how it began with my mother and my sister and my failure of curiosity. During the Q and A, a woman in the audience said that she, too, had delivered a baby at Booth and surrendered it for adoption. She reassured me that accepting my adopted-away sister into my life and my relationship with Mom had probably been gift enough for Mom. Though I would not fully understand this until much later, I was moved by the gesture this woman made. I asked if she would consider telling me her story.

Thirteen months later, Mary and I sat down in a study room at a library in Edina. I began the interview with the same brief questions with which I opened every interview, then asked her to tell me about her family and growing-up years.

That's all it took. Mary's story unspooled in an eloquent, pained howl.

Between the ages of five and sixteen, Mary lived in northern Minnesota in the "grim surroundings" of her stepfather's hostility and her mother's mental illness. Her mother's husband "resented every spoonful of his potatoes" she and her older sister put in their mouths, played favorites with his two biological daughters, and kept his wife and girls isolated on a farm where slop buckets stood in for flush toilets while he enjoyed the amenities of modern life during his workweek in the Twin Cities. When Mary was nine, her mother swallowed a handful of sleeping pills. The county nurse told her stepfather it was too late for a stomach pump, that she would either live or die. Mary clenched her teeth on a dishtowel "to keep from screaming, not so much about her dying" but about the prospect of being turned over completely to her stepfather's harsh care. Her mother survived—her suicide attempt, her illness, her controlling husband—and several years later gathered the courage to end the marriage that had itself begun with a surprise pregnancy. When Mary graduated from high school in 1963, she and her mother and three sisters moved to the Twin Cities. She worked for a time as a seamstress at Munsingwear, then took a job at Nevens Dry Cleaners.[22]

In 1965, after more than two years of dating and two years of refusing, Mary gave in to her hometown boyfriend's pleading promises to advance their relationship. When she learned she was pregnant, she also learned how limited her options were. She considered suicide, then tried to self-abort. Then she made a plan. She couldn't tell her family her shameful news, but she told her boyfriend. He wanted to get married, just as his two older brothers had when they impregnated their girlfriends. The trouble was that he wanted a wife, not a child, and Mary knew better. "I knew what it was like to have someone detest your very presence, and I couldn't do that to this child," she explained.

So Mary refused the offer of marriage and got another job to bolster her savings while she bided her time at home. When it was time to leave, when she could no longer conceal her pregnancy, she concocted a story. She told her mother and sisters that she would be on traveling assignment for work. She would phone and write when she could. The job might last four to six months, she said. She waved goodbye to her family when they dropped her off at the airport for her phantom job, then called a cab to take her to the room she had rented on the West Bank in Minneapolis, near the University of Minnesota.

Mary spent four months in that room with a "tiny kitchen and a tiny bedroom and a tinier bathroom," her only contact with the outside world the weekly delivery of groceries by her baby's father. She took one, two, sometimes three baths a day to soothe her nerves and fill the hours. Then, Mary recalls, "under the cover of darkness, every Friday night, I would walk down to the pay telephone booth, which was about a block and a half away from my room, and call [home] and pretend I was in Boston or Chicago or New

York or wherever I was and talk to them and assure them that I was fine. I'd go back to my room and hang out there until the next week."

When it came time to deliver her baby, the baby's father delivered Mary to Booth. She endured an excruciating labor—the baby was breech but Mary refused a cesarean section because it would leave a telling scar. As the hours wore on, the doctor turned her case over to the next one, callously remarking that neither her nor her baby's prospects were good and that she was not to receive a blood transfusion. To Mary, this seemed a punishment issued by a condemning doctor, whether for her moral transgression or her unwillingness to undergo a cesarean procedure. When her baby arrived in a flood of pain and blood, the nurse who had stayed by Mary's side, who had held her hand and comforted her in the face of the doctors' seeming indifference, took care to follow Mary's wishes: she whisked the child away so that Mary wouldn't have the chance to touch him or smell him, to lose her resolve. In letting him go, in sparing him a childhood as pained as hers had been, Mary believed she had saved her child from a "fate worse than death."

Mary spent a few bleary days in Booth's hospital ward until finally the baby's father came to bring her back to her room in Minneapolis. She had bought herself a dress, a tan shift made of a coarse fabric, that she wore while she recovered. Then it was time to go back home. She slipped into the clothes she had arrived in, took a cab back to the airport, feigned excitement when her mother and sisters picked her up, and slipped back into her life.

There were jobs that turned into a successful design career and relationships that turned into a challenging marriage. But there were no children. She and her husband could not conceive, and there was no discussion, with anyone, of her Booth baby. Then, one day in the early 1990s, in the safety of her trusted therapist's office, the words flowed out of Mary in a torrent. "I should probably tell you, I had a baby when I was twenty," she began, and out it all came: the shame, the desperation, the fear. It would be another two years before Mary found the courage to share her story with the women's group she had joined, two more years before she could tell her husband, and several more months after that that she broached the subject with her mother and sisters.

It took years to break the decades of silence, to chisel an opening in the wall she had built. When her husband, burdened by familial shame of his own, heard Mary's news, he suggested they both commit suicide rather than face the embarrassment her revelation would cause. When her mother learned about Mary's baby, she said she wished Mary had taken her secret to her grave. Mary refused to bow to such harsh reactions, however. She told her husband that he could leave her if he wished, but she was no longer going to punish herself for her past; she maintained a cool relationship with her mother.

And then Mary met her son, her amazing, wonderful, too-good-to-be-true son. It started with a letter she deposited in his file at Children's Home Society, which turned into a written correspondence, which turned into a phone call, which turned into a face-to-face meeting at the Hotel Sofitel in Bloomington, which has turned into a long and loving relationship with him and his wife and her children. Mary's husband came to love her son almost as much as she does, but her mother refused to acknowledge him. Her husband and mother both have since died, as have her son's adoptive father and brother. But Mary and her son and his adoptive mother live on, a three-way mother-son relationship born out of heartache.

But heartache is not distributed equally. Mary contacted her son's father once she began telling her story, offering him the chance to tell his family that he had fathered a child when he was young. The whole experience had been "life-changing [and] damaging" for her, she told him, and she wanted to spare his parents any potential discomfort. "I'm sorry that it's been such an issue for you," he told her, "but I really never thought about it again."

He never thought about it again. "That is the biological privilege [men] are granted," says Mary, and it is this unfairness that haunts her. "There are rewards from the struggle," Mary admits, her son being the brightest of them all. But she has an "ongoing argument about the inequality of the consequences." Her long-ago boyfriend put the experience behind him, as Booth girls were supposed to do, but boys didn't have to endure the physical pain of birth and separation, the public shaming that condemned girls but winked at boys, the lifelong ramifications of enforced silence. To this day, Mary's stomach turns if she sees a piece of clothing, however beautiful, crafted from the same fabric as that tan shift she wore around her room after releasing her son. The whole experience has taught Mary about strength she didn't even know she had, but it has taken a toll. "I will never think that it is an equal opportunity—this sexual arrangement that we've been given. It isn't equal, no."

So why do an interview? I asked. Why dredge up all the pain? Because, Mary explained, "It'll go into that basket of healing and accepting and understanding and shining a light on it one more time so you get a way to carry it that doesn't destroy you."

But even now, despite the joy that her son brings to Mary's life, the cost outweighs the benefits. "There isn't enough goodness; there isn't enough time to heal the pain and agony and misery that I lived with," she says. "If you ask, 'Which is the bigger basket, the pain or the happiness?' Oh, it's the pain by far. It's the pain." ▪

Just as 1960 drew to a close, the period my mother had spent hidden away in the bedroom under the eaves came to an end. Her due date was drawing near, and Dr. Goode told her it was time to go to Booth. She packed a suitcase, took one last look at her secret hideaway, and left behind the life she had known. Her mother drove her from Blaine to a red brick building on Como Avenue in St. Paul, leaving her in an empty dorm room on the second floor.

On December 31, 1960, my mother became a Booth girl.

I drop Steve off at the airport in Miami, then drive back to the Extended Stay in Coral Gables that will be my home for the next six weeks. I am here to attend a National Endowment for the Humanities Summer Seminar for college faculty who teach about the US–Vietnam War. I am also here to escape the failure of our final attempt to get pregnant.

Medications to stimulate and suspend ovulation. Laparoscopies to remove endometriosis adhesions and, eventually, my remaining fallopian tube. Semen analyses and sonohysterograms, ultrasounds and blood tests. Visits to gynecologists and reproductive endocrinologists and acupuncturists and chiropractors and mind-body therapists. Injections at the clinic, injections at home, delivered subcutaneously and intramuscularly, in the belly and in the butt. Z-Pak, Estraderm, Repronex, Gonal-f, hCG, Ganirelix Acetate, tetracycline, Medrol, progesterone in oil, Valium. Intrauterine insemination and in vitro fertilization and intracytoplasmic sperm injection—the invasive medicalization of intimacy. Steve and I have submitted ourselves to all of it.

This submission comes at a steep cost. Our insurance covers some of the diagnostic testing, less of the treatment, none of the labyrinthine IVF procedures. We pay thousands of dollars for clinic visits and lab tests and medications and high-tech procedures. I am working part-time as an adjunct, making a subsistence-level income. Steve's salary is good, but not sufficient to cover these exorbitant costs. We dip into savings and investments, grateful that we have them to tap, aware of the discriminatory nature of the potential solutions for the indiscriminate problem of infertility.

But there are other costs, too. Infertility treatments and the cycles of hope and despair are all-consuming. I find it hard to separate our struggles from our friends' easy fecundity: one friend, then another and another gets pregnant with no trouble. We endure the social isolation of being involuntarily childless in a pro-family atmosphere. I have started boxing as a new form of exercise and find satisfaction in beating out my frustration on the heavy bag.

We try to maintain our sense of humor, even when an office assistant at the ob-gyn clinic informs us in her carnival-barker voice that we are in the wrong location for our latest procedure.

"I'm sorry, sir!" she shouts toward Steve.

The waiting room goes silent. Chatty parents-to-be suspend their conversations. Babies stop crying. Even SpongeBob and Squidward seem to halt their hijinks from the television in the toddler area.

"We don't do that here! You'll have to give your . . . *sample* at our Maplewood location!"

Abashed, we turn to make our way back to the elevator, through the gauntlet of patients now intently studying their reading material or cooing at newborns. A *Sesame Street* ditty comes to mind and I sing "Two of these things are not like the others" under my breath as I give an imaginary royal wave to the assembly.

For me, the hardship also stems from my inability to achieve a goal I have set for myself. I can't think of anything else I have so completely failed, any other objective that has resided so clearly and distantly beyond the reach of my efforts. I don't see it as a failure of my womanhood or a denial of my femininity; I see it as a failure of my personhood, my self, my effort and desire and deservingness.

Fail, fail, fail.

So when we get the news, on April 19, that the IVF didn't work, I am despondent.

In Miami, I am blessedly preoccupied. I immerse myself in literature and conversation about the US war in Vietnam, the focus of my dissertation and much of my teaching. I do my reading at the beach, box at a local gym, eat Cuban sandwiches, go to movies by myself, gaze in wonder at the towering thunderheads that produce downpours in the subtropical heat. For the first time in a long time, I do not feel defined by my (in)fertility.

Mom visits for a few days, treats me to a stay at the Eden Roc, a luxury resort. We lunch on the patio, lounge by the pool, take a dip in the Atlantic. She has provided me an oasis within my oasis. We do not discuss anything having to do with pregnancy, fertility, or babies. I am sad to see her go.

Soon afterward, back in my room at the Extended Stay, I learn that Vietnam has opened to international adoption again.

4
BOOTH GIRL

Mother took me [to Booth] on a cold, sunny January [sic] afternoon. All the paperwork had been completed, and, after a brief introduction to the social worker and nurse, my mother left me in the empty second-floor dorm room with my suitcase.

The place seemed completely deserted. I sat and looked at the shiny floors, the neatly made narrow beds, and the immaculate orderliness of the place. It was very quiet, and I was truly afraid of what was about to happen.

It wasn't long before I discovered that everyone was down in the basement, where the kitchen, dining, smoking, and lounging rooms were. Before supper was served, I had been assigned my tasks, introduced to the other girls, and invited to the smoking room to have a cigarette.[1]

FROM HER ARRIVAL on New Year's Eve until January 25, Mom's life unfolded within the walls of Booth Memorial Hospital, her attention focused on the imminent arrival of her baby. She had traded one cloistered environment for another, but now she was surrounded by others who faced the same daunting situation that lay ahead of her. Young women from across the state flocked to Booth to hide their distended bellies and escape the condemnation of neighbors. They came from small prairie towns like Jackson and Dodge Center and from midsized cities such as Rochester and St. Cloud. Some crossed state borders to seek shelter at Booth, while others merely crossed the river from Minneapolis to St. Paul. A handful of these girls were listed, in the parlance of the day, as "Indian" or "Negro," but most of them, like Mom, were white. Although the Salvation Army welcomed girls of all faiths to Booth, they tended to be Protestant. Other pregnant Lutheran girls may have turned to the Lutheran Girls' Home in Northeast Minneapolis, while Catholic women were more likely to take up residence at the Catholic Infant Home on Carroll Avenue in St. Paul. Of these three homes, only Booth provided hospital delivery services on-site; the others directed their wards to affiliated community hospitals.[2]

But what was it like to be a Booth girl? Mom's essay provides some insight on the matter as a testament of one woman's experience. But "Booth girl" was a cultural identity forged in the fires of history, one shared by thousands of single pregnant girls and women across the country. One woman's account of her individual experience, however deeply it may resonate with others, cannot provide a full understanding of the context in which those events had unfolded. So, once again, I turned to the archives and to oral history to learn about Booth girls in general so I could know my mother in particular. How did residents spend their time at Booth? What was their relationship to Salvation Army staff and other authority figures? How did the Salvation Army generally, and Booth St. Paul specifically, approach its work with these young women? Aside from the decision about what they would do with their babies—the subject of chapter five—how did Booth help its residents prepare for what would be one of the defining moments of their lives? And for the girls themselves—what was it like to be inside?

Answers to these questions emerge in the interplay between broad social trends and intimate personal history, in the tension between competing professional ideologies and practices, in the relationship between Booth girls and Booth staff and among Booth girls themselves. For as they crossed Booth's threshold, these young women became both less and more than the people they had been at home, reduced by culture and circumstance to the status of their transgression. They arrived in fear and in anger, in defiance and denial, in shame and sorrow and relief and anticipation. They were greeted by Salvationists who saw in them the potential for spiritual rejuvenation, by social workers who saw the capacity for social regeneration, by psychiatrists who saw the hope of psychological remediation, and by doctors and nurses who saw the promise of human birth and rebirth.

They were assigned beds and chores and caseworkers. They assumed abridged identities—Sharon M. and Mary S. and Sandy T.—and they came to know each other quickly and deeply, as is common among young people at once cast aside and cast together. They whispered and argued and laughed and cried, they smoked and played cards and gossiped. They watched as one, then another, went off to be delivered, each awaiting her own call to mother-hood, however proscribed or circumscribed. During their time at Booth, these mothers-to-be shared a common experience and developed a camara-derie born of the "shared ordeal," even as each brought her own history and departed to her own future.[3]

Salvationists and Social Workers at Booth St. Paul

When Mom showed up on the steps of Booth Memorial Hospital in Decem-ber 1960, she joined a cohort of mostly young, mostly white women who took shelter in a nationwide network of maternity homes for unwed moth-ers. These homes saw their occupancy rates peak in the late 1950s and early 1960s. Each year from 1945 to 1965, 25,000 women left behind families, friends, schools, and jobs to spend the last few weeks of their pregnancies at homes run by the Salvation Army, Florence Crittenton Association, Catho-lic Charities, or other social service organizations. More expectant mothers sought shelter than the homes could accommodate, however, and many—up to one-third—were turned away for lack of space. In 1961, 8,227 single pregnant girls and women stayed at a Salvation Army maternity home for an average of fifty-two days, while more than 13,000 obtained services on an outpatient basis. Of those served in residence at a Salvation Army maternity home that year, 85.6 percent were white.[4]

In order to understand what Mom experienced at Booth, I had to under-stand how Booth functioned and its location within a network of agencies that had a stake in its operation, from its host organization to associated reg-ulatory, public, and funding agencies. It turns out that Booth Memorial Hos-pital in St. Paul (Booth St. Paul) is as much a "character" in this story as are the women who walked its hallways. Like them, it was the subject of cultural debate and ideological tugs-of-war. Such dynamics shaped Booth's programs, policies, and personnel, which in turn influenced its residents' experiences.

To understand Booth St. Paul is to understand its origins and evolution as part of the Salvation Army, a London-based evangelical organization established in the nineteenth century and famed for its open-air street preaching and work with the urban poor. Uniformed Army officers and rank-and-file "soldiers" mingled with the downtrodden, providing them with food and shelter and offering by lived example a pathway to redemption. The Army's Women's Social Services Department took special interest in "fallen" women—prostitutes, drug addicts, runaways, unwed mothers. The Army believed these women needed protection from the male predators who had led them astray, training in proper womanly skills and comportment, and spiritual regeneration for their souls, all best accomplished under the loving guidance and sisterly influence of female Salvationists in the wholesome environment of the rescue home.[5]

The Salvation Army first opened a rescue home in St. Paul in a small rented building at University Avenue and Jackson Street in 1898. Eleven years later, bursting at the seams with young women in need of assistance, the home moved to another temporary location, then celebrated the grand opening of its permanent location at 1471 Como Avenue in October 1913. State architect Clarence Johnston designed the new facility with funding provided by Jewish brothers and prominent businessmen William and Joseph Elsinger, who, the story goes, had been moved by the rescue home's warm embrace of a pregnant Jewish girl. The new building could accommodate seventy-five women and babies and boasted "every modern convenience for an up-to-date Rescue Home and Maternity Hospital": an operating room, isolation rooms, multiple bathrooms and bedrooms, two porches, a nursery and playroom, steam-plant heating, and gas and electricity. Yet it was the "love, sympathy and wise counsel" provided by Salvation Army women that was the heart of the program, the inspiration that would help erring girls "start life anew."[6]

If one battle had been won with the move to Como Avenue, however, another was just beginning, and it was occurring in rescue homes across the country. The evangelical women who had founded the homes in the late nineteenth century struggled to maintain control of them in the first decades of the twentieth as social workers, attempting to establish professional credibility through their work with the US Children's Bureau, brought their scientific expertise to bear on the problem of illegitimacy. The crux of the problem: religious women attempted to redeem unmarried mothers (who by 1920 would become the sole focus of rescue home work) through spiritual regeneration induced by the good example of committed Christian sisters, regimented routines, and the practice of motherhood. Social workers, on the

Salvation Army Rescue Home and Maternity Hospital under construction, 1913. *Minnesota Historical Society collections*

The completed building, 1920. *Minnesota Historical Society collections*

other hand, aimed to treat them through objective, individualized casework services provided by trained professionals whose primary interest was the well-being of children and the restoration of proper family function.[7]

Not long after the Salvation Army Rescue Home and Maternity Hospital, as it was then known, moved to Como Avenue, the social work approach to helping unmarried mothers earned the imprimatur of law. Minnesota's 1917 Children's Code legislation granted the state the authority to oversee services to "illegitimate" children and their mothers, and in 1919, the state boards of health and control assumed regulatory and licensing oversight for "any maternity hospital [or infants' home] that is for the public good," including those designed specifically for unwed mothers. The board of control established operating standards regarding staffing, record keeping, medical care, and vocational training for maternity hospitals across the state, including the Salvation Army facility in St. Paul, and sent inspectors to ensure those standards were being met. It investigated complaints against the hospital and monitored occupancy rates, births and deaths, dietary regimens, and finances.[8]

The tension created by this encroachment of public authorities into what was supposed to be a Christian sanctuary came to a head in 1934 when a state social worker wrote a scathing report describing the Salvation Army home's treatment of unmarried mothers as outdated and overly restrictive and recommended that social workers be allowed to set it aright. Adjutant Lillie Kittelson, the superintendent of the home, marshaled the support of the Salvation Army's territorial commissioner, who responded by insisting that there would be no sharing of authority. Eventually, aided by the intervention of the St. Paul Community Chest, which provided a substantial portion of the home's budget and so wielded another form of external control, the state children's bureau and the Salvation Army agreed to form an advisory board in which social workers and Army representatives would enjoy equal status. By 1940, to the great satisfaction of Minnesota child welfare authorities, the maternity home, now called Booth Memorial Hospital, had hired a full-time social worker to provide modern counseling services to the young women in residence, a trend that was taking hold in Salvation Army maternity homes across the country, so much so that Army officers themselves sometimes earned social work degrees and certifications.[9]

After World War II, Booth St. Paul carried out its work according to national Salvation Army philosophy regarding unmarried mothers, which mirrored the widespread psychological understanding of premarital pregnancy. According to a 1952 Salvation Army handbook, single pregnant girls and women suffered from "deep emotional maladjustment" stemming from broken homes, disadvantaged circumstances, lack of sex education, and a dearth of parental affection, all of which led to the "desire . . . to escape reality." It was the job of trained Army caseworkers to help them face it. Salvationists' focus on individualized counseling and "differential diagnosis" led to greater freedom and a closer approximation to life outside the home for those temporarily residing within it.

Gone were the days when residents' attire, appearance, activities, and mail were closely regulated by maternity home staff. Instead, the Army recognized the girls' need for independence, privacy, and personal liberty. Mail flowed freely and girls could leave the home unescorted to go shopping or get their hair done. Army maternity homes offered optional chapel services and personal pastoral counseling; educational classes for secondary students; books, television, and radio; social activities and holiday parties. They provided individual casework counseling and pre- and postnatal care, labor and delivery services, and pediatric care for babies. The Army charged for its services but maintained its policy of not turning anyone away for an inability to pay, and it did not refuse admittance based on race, color, or creed. Still, the Army maintained that "the strength of the entire endeavor is still its original strength: unlimited faith in a great God and unbounding [sic] faith in the rights of the individual to a better chance in modern society." Single pregnant women would be uplifted through the good example set by Salvationists even while they were counseled by skilled social workers, thus preparing them to assume roles as happy wives and mothers in "wholesome family situations" upon their release.[10]

Many of these ideas were still in operation in 1961 when Mom was at Booth St. Paul. By this time, the Army was drawing even more heavily on the language and tools of psychotherapy in describing its unmarried mothers program. Despite its recognition that a combination of factors, both external and internal, contributed to premarital pregnancy, the Army's goal was to effect permanent "personality change" in the expectant mother through a combination of religious guidance, casework services, and psychiatric counseling. "Increasingly, the Maternity Home and Hospital has become a multi-service health and welfare center," a 1961 report by the national Salvation Army pointed out, and among its modern offerings was "psychiatric consultation." In using the language of psychiatry to describe its desired result in those with whom it worked—personality change—the Army's report reflected the "medicalization of a social problem," to use historian

A religious service at Booth Memorial Hospital in the early 1960s. Salvation Army Brigadier Gunborg Fugelsang (standing) presides. *University of Minnesota Libraries, Social Welfare History Archives*

Cara Kinzelman's phrase, that occurred when social workers embraced the psychiatric approach to understanding unwed motherhood.[11]

The final major player from outside of Booth and the Salvation Army that had a stake in its operations was the University of Minnesota. Academics focused on illegitimacy, child welfare, and social work made studies of the home and hospital, but the most direct connection was through the university's medical school and hospital. From its earliest years, the rescue home relied on the medical expertise of university doctors, such as Dr. Jeanette McLaren, who served as the physician in charge of the facility from before it opened on Como Avenue until 1921. Dr. Jennings Litzenberg, head of the obstetrics and gynecology department at the university, replaced McLaren as chief obstetrician. It was during his tenure that the university took "more or less complete control of Booth Memorial Hospital." University doctors provided on-site labor and delivery services for Booth residents with low-risk pregnancies and sent complicated cases to the university for more extensive care in a fully equipped hospital. In return, the university used Booth as a teaching site for its medical students, who held prenatal clinics and provided routine care for its expectant mothers. Booth also paid the university $1,000 annually to cover the cost of "extra expenses" incurred for its service to the maternity program. Dr. John McKelvey replaced Litzenberg at the university and at Booth in 1938, and in 1963, during a long and controversial campaign to expand its facilities, supported the effort to license Booth as an affiliate of University Hospitals.[12]

Mom wouldn't have realized when she arrived at Booth how many institutional hands were stirring the pot in which she had landed. The Salvation Army and US Children's Bureau, the state of Minnesota and Ramsey County, the St. Paul Community Chest and University of Minnesota—each had a stake in Booth's operations, and each had a particular view of how to solve the problem of illegitimacy and help unmarried mothers and their children. The combination of passionate belief, political maneuvering, and professional rivalry—and no small amount of paternalism—made for a complicated web of authority, with young women like Mom at the center of it all.

She met these larger historical and institutional forces in the shape of the specific individuals she encountered: Patricia Peart, her Anoka County caseworker; Captain Pearl Norberg, Booth St. Paul's superintendent; Evelyn Headen, Booth's social worker; Pauline White and her staff of nurses; Dr. John McKelvey and the residents under his supervision. If these people and the agencies they represented shaped Mom's experiences at Booth, however, so, too, did her peers.

JANUARY 4, 1961

She is summoned to another meeting with another caseworker for another conversation about her situation.

The caseworker wants to know where she was born, where she grew up, where she went to school and to church and to work. The caseworker makes notes about her mother and father and brothers and sisters.

Were you born a legitimate child? the caseworker asks.

Then the caseworker asks about the alleged father of her baby, if she's certain it's Jack, if she wants to pursue a paternity claim.

It's him, she says. It could be no one else.

All right, then, the caseworker says.

The caseworker wants to know about Jack's family and education and employment and religion. How tall is he? What color is his hair? His eyes? Has he a history of mental illness?

Her answers are brief, factual.

Then: How would you describe his personality? the caseworker asks.

People like him, she says. He's a leader, a real individual, his own person. The words come more quickly, with more heat.

He seemed so mature, like a man, not a boy. He likes to think he's a real ladies' man. Maybe he is. He was married and divorced and already has a child, you know.

She pauses, catches herself before she loses hold of herself.

Does he know about this baby? the caseworker wants to know.

I wrote him, she says.

Anyway, she says. We're through. I'm through with him.

Okay, then, the caseworker says, putting her pencil down. I'll be in touch after the baby comes. ●

Inside Booth: Staff

On January 4, 1961, Anoka County child welfare caseworker Patricia Peart made a number of observations on the intake form for Sharon Moore, my mother. They included:

> 12. Sharon is 5'10½" tall and weighs 150 lbs. She has medium bone struc-
> ture. She has a fair complexion, has brown eyes and brown hair. Sharon has
> attractive features and looks much like a model.
>
> 13. Sharon likes music and has taken piano lessons. She enjoys all types
> of sports.
>
> 14. Sharon's personality is easy going. She is very likeable and can engage
> in an intelligent conversation. She has very pleasing mannerisms and no bad
> habits.[13]

Mom had been at Booth for five days and had already encountered a host of other professionals whose jobs were to care for the increasing numbers of single pregnant women and their children.

Nineteen sixty-one was shaping up to be one of Booth's busiest years. Over the next twelve months, the forty-six licensed beds in the facility's home section would fill to 102.1 percent of capacity and its nine hospital beds to 85.7 percent—the second-highest and highest occupancy rates in Booth's history, respectively. Though there are no precise records of the racial breakdown of Booth's residents in 1961, we can safely assume that they were overwhelmingly white, in keeping with trends at Salvation Army (and other) maternity homes across the country. And, of course, if the beds were full, so were the bassinets. Mothers delivered 414 babies at Booth through November 1961, compared with 198 newborns for all of 1955. Booth was so busy that, in December 1961, the Salvation Army approached the Greater St. Paul Community Chest and Council with plans to expand the facility, an undertaking that would evolve throughout the decade.[14]

By this time, Salvationists and social workers collaborated in relative harmony at Booth St. Paul, united in their mission to help both mother and child establish a secure future, as they defined it. Booth was still a Salvation Army institution, led by uniformed officers of the Women's Social Services Department who viewed their work as a spiritual calling. But these officers also believed in the importance of individualized psychological counseling for the young women in their charge. Captain Pearl Norberg, Booth's superintendent from August 1958 to June 1961, had grown up in a family passionately committed to Salvation Army religious doctrine; both of her parents were career officers. Norberg had received her commission in 1943, worked at Booth hospitals in Chicago and St. Louis, and earned a master's degree in hospital administration by the time she arrived in St. Paul in 1958. In June 1961, she assumed the position of assistant women's social secretary for the Central Territory of the Salvation Army, and from 1969 to 1979, she served as the territory's full secretary. Somewhere along the way, Norberg also became a certified social worker and was active in professional social work, hospital, and maternal and child health associations.[15]

Though she was a proponent of the casework method, as superintendent, Norberg was responsible for overseeing Booth St. Paul's entire program. Counseling the residents was left to Evelyn Headen, a member of Booth's "civilian" staff (i.e., those who did not necessarily subscribe to Salvationist gospel and were not part of its rank structure). Though Mom made only passing mention of having met her, Headen was the social worker at Booth for many years. She had earned an English degree from Jamestown College in North Dakota in 1927 and began her career in public welfare by investigating the legitimacy of families receiving public assistance during the Depression. She took a job at Booth sometime in the 1950s and had become supervisor of casework, with at least one staff member working for her, by 1961. In the mid-1960s, she did some coursework at the University of Minnesota, where she studied with renowned social work professor Gisela Konopka. In fact, when Konopka and her assistant, Vernie-Mae Czaky, made a study of teenage girls at Booth and other local maternity homes in 1963—interviews that provide uniquely compelling insight into the experiences and perspectives of Booth girls—Headen served as their in-house consultant and liaison. Records of these meetings show Headen as a passionate, self-possessed woman, confident in her abilities, who was, as her daughter-in-law suggested, unlikely to "suffer fools gladly." She retired from Booth in 1972.[16]

Headen wasn't the only non-Salvationist to work at Booth St. Paul. Its civilian staff also included teachers, housekeepers, cooks, laundry supervisors, and nurses. Mom wouldn't have had cause to work with the secondary school teachers supplied by the St. Paul school district, but certainly she had exchanges with the staff who kept the home running, supervised Booth girls

Evelyn Headen, supervisor of casework, counsels a woman at Booth Memorial Hospital in the early 1960s. *University of Minnesota Libraries, Social Welfare History Archives*

in their assigned duties, and tended to their health. She didn't mention anyone by name, referring only to "the nurse" whom she met the day she arrived and who would later guide her through labor. Records indicate that, at the end of 1960, Booth employed two full-time registered nurses (RNs), including head nurse Pauline White, five part-time RNs, one full-time licensed practical nurse (LPN), and three full-time aides.[17]

I found no trace of information about Pauline White or the other, unnamed nurses, but I would take heart if they were anything like June Wheeler, a labor and delivery nurse at Booth from 1966 to 1971. June was ninety-four years old when I met her in the fall of 2017, good-natured of temperament, sharp of mind, and compassionate of heart. She had earned a nursing degree from the University of Minnesota and worked as a public health nurse for the Red Cross, teaching "baby care" and sex education classes in local high schools, before taking the job at Booth. She worked the 3:00 to 11:00 evening shift so had only infrequent contact with the Salvationists. Mostly, she stationed herself in the nurses' room on the second floor, waiting to be called to duty. Sometimes the girls would stop by her office to chat; one young woman looked to ease what she presumed to be June's loneliness by "fooling around with the 'wheelie' chairs, entertaining me and keeping me company when I didn't have anybody in labor."[18]

June enjoyed these interactions with Booth girls. She had spent a lot of time with young people when she was teaching high schoolers about sex and anatomy, trying to prevent the exact thing that had led them to Booth. But she understood how they got there, too. "You're in love and that [sex] is a normal ending." She realized the difficulties the girls faced. She saw the double standard that allowed boys to escape the situation with reputations intact while the girls hid themselves away, though she didn't recall the girls complaining too much. "Sometimes they would talk to me and tell me what had happened or how they had ended up there," June said, but oftentimes, such communication was unnecessary. "They knew how I felt so they didn't have to talk to me about it." This kind of casual, friendly interaction with an empathetic nurse may have been as important to the girls as any medical care June provided.

These three women seem to have been competent, confident, and kind professionals. Whatever their job and whoever their employer, most of Booth St. Paul's officers, staff, and affiliated colleagues shared something else: with the exception of maintenance workers and visiting doctors and medical students from the University of Minnesota, they were all women. This doesn't mean, however, that the atmosphere was one of feminist solidarity or easy sisterhood, either between staff and residents or among residents themselves. Though Mom and the seven women I interviewed lodged no hard complaints about their treatment at the hands of Salvation Army officers or staff, one woman who contacted me after learning about my research described her experience at Booth in the mid-1960s as "degrading" and the staff as cruel and insensitive. She did not respond to my invitation to an interview, so I have no further details to offer, but her brief account stands in rather stark contrast to those offered by my interviewees and a handful of other former Booth girls with whom I have corresponded. Still, Ann Fessler, Rickie Solinger, and others have revealed some similarly troubling dynamics at other maternity homes across the country, if not at Booth St. Paul specifically. Whether individual Salvationists, medical personnel, and social workers held such punishing attitudes or not, they were part of a larger system whose policies, practices, and philosophies made single pregnant women feel ashamed, punished, and powerless, especially when it came to the decision about what they would do with their babies.[19]

As much as authorities attempted to assist, guide, or steer the young women in their care, though, Booth girls created a world of their own, one that was sometimes impervious to the intrusion of authority figures and sometimes heart-wrenchingly subject to its power.

Inside Booth: Community and Culture

They rose at 7:00 in the morning, after a night spent dreaming of innocence lost or love abandoned or future awaiting. They climbed out of their beds, one next to the other in the second- or third-floor dormitories, eyes bleary with sleep. After changing from a billowy nighttime frock to a billowy daytime frock, they took up their brooms and dustpans or sorted clothes for washing or helped prepare the oatmeal and coffee. They convened for breakfast at 8:30, their chatter slowly rising with the day. They discussed matters of fleeting concern and of lasting significance, plans for the afternoon and plans for their babies, dreams from the previous night and dreams of their forthcoming lives. They shared silly jokes and petty grievances and idle gossip about each other, anger and pain and bitterness about the boyfriends who had abandoned them or the families that had forsaken them or the experts who had evaluated them.[20]

After breakfast, devotions. Though much had been made of Booth's willingness to accept any girl in need, regardless of her religious convictions, they all felt the Salvationist desire to pull them into the flock of the redeemed. The Salvationists no longer reported how many girls they had converted, but they required the girls to attend daily devotions and twice-weekly services. The mothers-in-waiting sat through the prayers and the readings and the preaching and the singing, some adding their voices to the hymns with sincere conviction, some daydreaming of life outside the walls. When their spirits had been sufficiently uplifted, their bodies resumed the task of making Booth run. Their labor supplemented the fees they or their parents or their boyfriends or the community chest paid against the $140 (about $1,300 in 2020) they owed for room and board and medical care and delivery services. But they would also be able to take these skills with them when they became legitimate wives and mothers, when they had put all of this behind them. "Work therapy" was just one means of preventing the girls from "revert[ing] back" to the "mismanaged unorganized life of the past" that they supposedly had lived.[21]

Once they had completed that particular brand of therapy for the day, they could move on to other forms of rehabilitative and recreational activities. Actual therapy with psychiatrists and counseling with social workers. Sewing, handicrafts, music, volleyball in the yard, television and cards in the lounge. Health care classes with Red Cross workers, prenatal check-ins with medical students, high school coursework with teachers from the St. Paul Board of Education. Halloween parties and Miss America contests, wiener roasts and birthday celebrations. Visits with mothers and fathers or boyfriends or girlfriends on Wednesday and Friday evenings, free time to leave the grounds from 2:30 to 4:30 every afternoon and all day Sunday after morning services. Gayle read in the library. Sandy #1 played the piano. Karen did her homework. Pam and her boyfriend visited the lions at the Como Zoo.[22]

But mostly, Booth girls survived the social isolation and expert intervention and veiled judgment and frightening uncertainty about what was to come by enduring it all in each other's company. This, above all, was what the once and former Booth girls remembered: how important it was to be surrounded by other girls "in trouble." Memories worn thin by passing decades took a little more shape when aimed laterally, at their fellow boarders. If they had been the "bad girls" at home, singled out and cast out from their schools and families and communities for their transgression, it was this very transgression that bound them together at Booth. Girls from small towns and big cities, of high achievement and low expectation, who ran with the wild kids or the popular crowd or no one at all, who otherwise may have had nothing to do with each other, found themselves sequestered together, united by their unsanctioned pregnancies. Sometimes this unity was balm to aching hearts. "It was like a little sorority," said Pam. "We shared our stories. I didn't feel so lost and alone."

Sometimes, though, because even Booth girls were prone to the meanness and exclusions of social posturing, this unity faltered. There were arguments and jealousies, clashes of personality and priority, the singling out among the singled out. There was a mentally impaired girl, Pam recalled, whom the other girls teased and goaded to tell stories she only half understood about how she had gotten pregnant. "They would snicker and laugh at her behind her back, but they'd say, 'Tell us more.'" They were young women, teenagers mostly, behaving the way teenage girls sometimes do, the bonds between them making them neither more nor less angelic or devilish than they were on the outside. They created a world of their own, separate and distinct from the one Salvationists and social workers and psychiatrists and parents and teachers had made for them.[23]

Sometimes, an outsider would get a glimpse of the Booth girls' interior world. Vernie-Mae Czaky tasted it when she ventured into the smoker in 1963 to get to know the girls before she and Gisela Konopka started their interviews:

> There was a silence as I first walked in. The girl introduced me. I said I enjoyed a cigarette and if they didn't mind, I would like to join them. One girl said, "I like people who smoke to admit they smoke." There seemed to be some implication in this statement, but I said nothing. The others begin [sic] to talk about the fact that the Brigadier did not like them to smoke, that she told them they would have yellow babies, etc. One of the girls remarked, "I suppose if we eat lettuce we will have green babies; and if we eat grapes we will have purples ones."

They had circled up, drawn themselves together, established a line of defense through which they only reluctantly admitted this stranger, sizing her up as they made clear their refusal to bow unquestioningly to authority.[24]

For most Booth girls, the friendships lasted only for the length of their stay in residence, just one more element of an unfortunate experience that they were to put behind them when they left. But while they were at Booth, they were in it together.

The parting began when they went, each one of them alone, to have their babies.

She has finally fallen asleep, begins to settle into the dark dreamworld.

Then, urgent voices in the hall. The familiar bustle of activity that means one of the girls is going to have her baby. A cry, a moan, the soothing voice of the nurse.

Breathe, honey, the nurse says. Breathe, nice and easy, that's it. The doctor's on his way.

Then, a string of curses, loud but controlled.

Dammit, dammit, dammit, dammit.

It's Gerri.

The doctor arrives, takes control of the situation. The nurse translates his dry directives into kindness. Don't push yet, honey, she says. You're doing great, honey.

Gerri moans, curses, grunts. She does not scream.

A baby's cry. It's a boy, the nurse says.

Silence. ●

Inside Booth: Labor and Delivery

Like many single pregnant women who delivered their babies in mid-twentieth-century maternity homes or affiliated hospitals, the women I met reported being wholly unprepared for labor and delivery, as naive about childbirth as they had been about sex. This may have reflected the times in general, an era when male doctors assumed a paternalistic authority that did not invite question from their female patients, laboring women still sometimes descended into twilight sleep, and Lamaze classes were just beginning to advance the radical notion that women ought to be educated about and conscious during childbirth. Karen remembered only that "there were charts and discussions and this and that" and surmised that Booth must have offered some sort of educational class even if she could not call it to mind. There was the weekly check-in at the in-house clinic, twenty or thirty girls lining the corridor on the second floor while they waited for their turn with the doctor from the University of Minnesota, hoping, in Pam's words, that it would be the "tall and dark-haired and very handsome one" whose rotation brought him to Booth in the late summer of 1961.[25]

Naive though they were, Booth girls created a female society that provided its own form of solace before they separated from the pack and turned themselves over to the staff nurse and, eventually, the university doctor. Pam remembered "sitting on the couch, all cuddling together, three or four of us in a row on a couch, rubbing each other's backs. And when someone went into labor we'd help them with their breathing. We didn't know about Lamaze but we'd help them, rub their tummy."

Mom prepared for childbirth by scrubbing the floor. "Now I understood why Booth was so spotless," she would write later. "A stream of desperate young women shined and polished and scrubbed and dusted it constantly, trying to work off their unwanted pregnancies." Then it was her turn.[26]

> My labor came in the middle of the night, just as I knew it would. I crawled out of my bed about midnight to go down the wickedly clean hallway floor. As soon as I stood up, my water broke: I knew I was about to be delivered. And I was ready, no matter how hard or painful or scary, I wanted to be done with it.
>
> Slowly, I made my way to the small yellow delivery room, where the on-duty nurse confirmed that I was in labor. She put me in bed and went to call Dr. Goode. There was a big clock high on the wall, but the hands were moving so slowly, jerking each minute away with excruciating deliberation. The nurse still hadn't located Dr. Goode, and she told me to breathe, breathe, breathe, not push. 3:00 A.M. came and went. Then 4:00, and still no Dr. Goode.[27]

Though male doctors from the university attended deliveries at Booth, it was Booth's nurses whom the women I met remembered. I hope the nurse who helped Mom was like the "wonderful woman" who stayed by Mary's side and held her hand during a long, bloody breech birth, her tenderness a contrast to the "condemning tone" of the doctor. Or June Wheeler, who got to know the girls because she was there at Booth with them every day while the doctor just "delivered and left," who viewed her patients as "young girls [who] needed somebody to love them and accept them for what they were." Mom longed for her grandmother, who loved her unconditionally and had delivered so many babies in the front room of her house in Echo. "But," she wrote later, "I knew I wasn't entitled to such comfort, me with no husband and no excuse. So I did as the nurse said and kept breathing hard to prevent my baby from coming." I hope that nurse had been even half as kind as June.[28]

GAY

Gay was lucky enough to have a "wonderful" nurse guide her through labor and delivery in 1959.

When I had breakfast with Gay in March 2013, four years after Mom died, it was the first time I'd met anyone else who had had a baby at Booth. I brought a historian's curiosity and a daughter's longing to the table, and Gay brought a family photo album and an impressive memory. By the time we parted company, Gay had agreed to do an oral history interview. I promised I would be in touch to make arrangements once the project was underway.

Four years later, I visited Gay at her home with a recorder and microphone to listen to her Booth story.[29]

The youngest of three girls born into a Norwegian family in small-town Mound, Minnesota, Gay grew up under the harsh and watchful eye of a "strict" father and a "sweetie" mother. When she wanted to learn to tap dance, just like her older sister, her father "made it loud and clear that chubby girls didn't dance." When she went out riding around in a car with her boyfriend and their friends one warm summer evening, defying her father's directive to stay home and behave, he called the police. She had violated his rules and broken the social code of behavior for girls. In the 1950s, said Gay, girls "were just supposed to behave. They weren't supposed to smoke, and they weren't supposed to have sex. [They were supposed to] mind their parents, and I didn't always do that." She spent her freshman year of high school trying to mend her "incorrigible" ways at the Home of the Good Shepherd, an experience she described as "very positive."

When she was released on probation for her sophomore year, the same old restrictions were in place: no dating, no carousing, no late nights, no fun. In later years, Gay came to understand the root of her father's concerns. He had seen his widowed mother struggle to make ends meet while raising him and his four younger siblings. She took in a boarder, became romantically involved with him, got pregnant, got married. After they had three children together, he abandoned her, and she raised eight children by herself. Gay's father quit high school, took a job to support the family, and learned a harsh lesson about the consequences of sex and the difficulties of solo parenting. As a teenager, however, Gay felt only the stridency of her father's attempts to prevent similar hardship for her. Added to the list of nos: no sex education in school, no discussion of or access to birth control, no conversations with her parents about a young woman's social and sexual growth. A veil of silence.

And yet there was evidence that silence about sex did not mean the absence of sex: whispers, girls gone on long visits to far-off relatives, early marriages. One of Gay's older sisters married before graduating high school, her teenage years drawing to a close with the responsibilities of motherhood. Whatever cautionary tale the situation was supposed to have been, Gay saw instead the prospect of liberation. When she started dating a boy the summer after tenth grade—on the sly, sneaking out of the house every night—she viewed the possibility of getting pregnant as the possibility of escaping her father. "It got [my sister] out of the house, and so that was going to get me out of the house, too." Besides, she and her boyfriend were in love, committed to a future together. He had already bought wedding rings.

When the sickness came, she knew. And her boyfriend knew. He was proud, so his friends knew. Then Gay's probation officer knew, and her mother, and her father. Pregnancy was a violation of Gay's probation, so she spent the first days of her public pregnancy in juvenile detention. She sat alongside thieves and runaways, nursing her sickness, her only offense that she was going to have a baby: "I was put in solitary for twenty-four hours with just a bed and a sink and a toilet and a steel door with a little window. And so after twenty-four hours I got out with the other kids and [we started talking:] What are you here for? Well, I stole a car. What are you here for? Well, I broke into a house. What are you here for? I ran away. What are you here for? I'm going to have a baby."

Then, this sixteen-year-old girl had to recount the details of her sex life to two male detectives tasked with gathering evidence against her. The judge who heard her case gave her two options: report to Sauk Centre Home School for Girls or to Booth Memorial Hospital. The former was for bad girls, so Gay chose the latter.

For nearly seven months, Gay worked and studied and gossiped and laughed in the company of other unmarried pregnant girls and women. Her first work assignment was in the kitchen, but when the school year started, the teachers came. Gay tried to do her work, but she had other things on her mind. "I didn't learn a thing that whole year," she said, "nor did I care." She attended counseling sessions with Mrs. Headen and church services with Captain Norberg. She maintained some contact with the outside world, too. Her mother brought fried chicken when she came to visit; her boyfriend sent her money and snuck her out to parties; her father paid the bill for her room and board and medical care. When she went home for Thanksgiving, though, he ate in his room, unwilling to share a table with his disgracing daughter.

Mostly, though, Gay focused on the girls around her, at least one of whom became a lifelong friend. She avoided the smoker when possible, as her pregnancy turned her former habit against her, but she and the other girls made the best of their circumstances. The state fair was in full swing when Gay arrived, and she and her new friends walked down Como Avenue to the fair during their afternoon free time. As the leaves turned from summer green to autumn gold, the staff put on a Halloween party, and the girls had fun guessing the circumference of their expanding midsections, measuring them with a long piece of string—a baby shower game for girls whose pregnancies prompted shame instead of celebration.

The "girls" were a varied bunch. There was the older woman with white hair. There was the girl who seemed mentally ill, the girl who was deaf and had sworn off hearing boys henceforward. There were the two twelve-year-olds, one from a farm who did not understand how she had become pregnant, one an African American who stood out among the sea of white faces. "Those poor kids," Gay said of these two youngsters. "I was young, but I wasn't twelve."

Sixteen-year-old Gay had a plan: get through her time at Booth, deliver her baby, marry her boyfriend, become a family of three. The voices of authority had other plans for her: let a secure, childless couple raise the baby, move on with her life unencumbered by the weight of motherhood, forget this ever happened, go and sin no more. Teenage Gay, juvenile delinquent Gay, unmarried Gay, father-ridden Gay surrendered. "It worked," she said. "They got my baby." For eight days after she gave birth in March 1959, she spent as much time as she could with her baby girl. She named her, she fed her, she had her baptized. On March 19, Gay said goodbye to her tiny daughter. "The day my baby left I carried her from the second floor down to that same door [through which I had first entered Booth] and handed her to the social worker, and I told her, I will find you someday. And I thought, *How can I slip my name on a piece of paper into her skin?*"

Released from Booth, empty and aching, Gay went directly to her oldest sister's house to help raise her brand-new nephew, born that very day. Her father, at the house to celebrate the arrival of his newest grandchild—a real one, a legitimate one, a double-parented one—greeted Gay with a hug and a kiss, as if nothing had happened. Her mother, though, understood the depth of Gay's loss. She gave Gay a Mother's Day card that year, a tiny tear in the blanket of silence.

Gay remained under the jurisdiction of the juvenile court until she turned eighteen. She left her sister and brother-in-law's house, moved in with a foster family, attended a new high school, graduated in 1960. Got pregnant again, married, had another daughter, then divorced, became a single mother. She got pregnant out of wedlock once more, relinquished once more, formed a blended family with her second daughter and her new husband and his son. This relationship endured, and the family grew with the birth of another child and the adoption of two more. "We've had his, hers, theirs, and ours," Gay said. Six children, all told. Children came and went, came back again, left forever, stayed a lifetime. A long search, full of subterfuge and hired detectives, led to Gay's reunion with her "Booth baby," by then a young woman nearly six years older than Gay had been when she gave birth. Gay and this first daughter stayed connected, Gay becoming grandmother to her adopted-away daughter's two children. Gay reunited with her second adopted-away daughter, too, but the relationship waned. One of her adopted children left the family at seventeen and died young.

In the early 1980s, Gay connected with other women who had "walked the same walk" when she found Concerned United Birthparents (CUB), a support group mostly for mothers who lost children to adoption, but also for adoptive parents and adoptees. CUB prompted her search for that first lost daughter and gave her a way of looking at the world and her place in it, as both a birthmother and an adoptive mother. She turned her teenage trauma into a lifelong calling by helping hundreds of other women connect with their lost children through her work as a searcher.

As for Booth? "It was hard," she said, "but if you had to be somewhere, I guess it was a good place to be."

When I read the transcript of my interview with Gay, I am reminded of how incomplete it felt; there was so much left to talk about. But I had already been in her kitchen for several hours, and she was weary. I told Gay that perhaps we could do a follow-up interview later.

I stayed in touch with Gay over the next months as we processed the transcript or when questions arose as I continued work on the project. My funding was exhausted, other projects came and went, life rolled along.

Then, in 2019, Gay died of cancer. ▨

> *January 16, 1961*
> *At last, a young doctor rushed in, pulling on his white coat. I didn't care that he was a stranger, and, when he told me to push, it was a relief beyond telling.*
> *At 5:00 A.M., my baby girl was born.*

It had all come to this.

The teenage insecurities and the coed blossoming. The shortage of sex education and birth control. Angry parents and an irresponsible boyfriend. The shame that led to a short-lived venture in San Francisco and a long residence under the eaves. And, finally, Booth, with its young mothers-in-waiting and polished floors and social workers and Salvationists all trying to do right by mother and child in a time when the only "right" mothers and children were those bound together by a man, a husband who made the mother a wife.

All of it led to this moment in the early morning hours of January 16, 1961, when my sister made her long-awaited appearance in a yellow room in a red brick building on Como Avenue.

It has all come to this.

The years of disinterest and disappointment, of doctors and needles and procedures and failures. The months of adoption training and background checks, the intrusive questions and uncomfortable decisions. The home study started and stalled by a social worker who thought that Steve and I valued our independence too much, then turned us over to another social worker *so she could take maternity leave.* Paperwork, paperwork, and more paperwork. Waiting, waiting, and more waiting. It has all led to this moment when we meet another woman's little lost boy, the one who will become our son.

On December 4, 2006, we leave our shoes outside the door of the babies' room at the Ben Tre Child Protection Center in the Mekong Delta region of Vietnam. Steve and I go in last, padding in in our bare feet, trailing after the others who are meeting their children for the first time, too.

Tu is standing in his crib, the one with peeling yellow paint, the one in front of the window overlooking the soccer field outside.

He is wearing white cotton pajamas. He has a bracelet on his right wrist. His tiny hands grasp the edge of the crib. He is fifteen months old.

He does not cry, but he does not smile.

Nga, from the in-country adoption agency, tries to get him to reach to me. He's shy, she says. Of course, I say. I am, too.

I reach in, hesitantly, and pull him out of the crib. He comes to me, hesitantly, looking everywhere but at me.

The room is noisy, filled with babies chattering and nannies soothing and new parents exclaiming.

We three are silent, Tu and I in an uneasy embrace, Steve capturing it all on video.

We call him the Commander, one of the nannies tells Nga in Vietnamese, who tells us in English. He likes to stand guard over the room.

By the time we leave two hours later, Tu is laughing and playing and roaring around the room in a baby scooter.

This was only a visit.

On December 6, they tell us we can take Tu back to the hotel with us, though we are still waiting for the Giving and Receiving ceremony that will finalize our adoption in Vietnam.

The other families are ecstatic at the prospect of leaving the care center with their soon-to-be-adopted children. Steve and I exchange half excited, half terrified looks. The nanny weeps as we carry Tu away.

Tu is happy until we put him down to sleep. When he fusses, I let him crawl up on my belly and we fall asleep, lying cheek to cheek on the bed as we listen to the boats *putt-putt-putting* up and down the Ben Tre River outside.

At last, on December 13, it is our turn. All the other families have had their G&Rs and flown to Hanoi for final processing. Ours was delayed once, twice, three times.

But today, in a small, hot office at the Department of Justice of Ben Tre province, the Socialist Republic of Vietnam has made Tu our son. I wonder if his mother somehow senses this seismic shift, if her body feels the widening separation from her child.

Tu falls into an exhausted sleep as soon as we get in the cab. He doesn't wake up during the harrowing journey back to Ho Chi Minh City, over crowded, rough streets. He doesn't wake up on the flight to Hanoi. He doesn't wake up in the cab to our hotel or while we change him into his pajamas. He sleeps and sleeps and sleeps.

December 22 is Mom's birthday. I send her an email with good wishes.

We're still in Hanoi. The other families have left. We are (mostly) alone, our new little family of three, waiting out yet another delay in our paperwork.

Tu has been restless at night, tossing and turning in the bed between us, and temperamental during the day, alternating between inconsolable crying and charming good humor.

We visit museums and parks and restaurants. We walk the crowded streets of the Old Quarter and enjoy ice cream by the lake. Many people smile at us, nod, and cluck happily at Tu. Some glare. One person asks if we're bringing home a souvenir.

I can't wait to get home.

Finally, on December 26, it is our turn.

We board a plane in Hanoi.

We're coming home.

Tu is leaving his.

It has all come to this.

5
SURRENDER

She was so small and perfect, and I laughed and cried at her tiny red face and lusty squall. But, I didn't want to look too long, or I knew I'd weaken, so I allowed them to take her away. I couldn't escape naming her, though, and I chose 'Lynette' after a friend of mine from high school, a girl I'd greatly admired.

Mother came to visit, but not dad. Mom saw Lynette in the nursery and told me sadly how lovely she was, how small and fair, how much she looked like me. It was then that I realized that my ordeal had been hard on my mother, in ways I didn't really understand. Now it seems obvious that as the mother of six children, she had known better than I how hard it was going to be to go through with an adoption.[1]

MOM MIGHT HAVE HAD an inkling of the pain that awaited her when Gerri, she of the "quick wit and swaggering walk," crumbled. Sharp-tongued during labor and self-assured afterward, Gerri had lost her composure a few days after delivery. "She burst into the lounge on the third day, crying hysterically," Mom wrote. "She had just given up her precious little boy, the one with the tightly curled blond hair just like hers." When her turn came and her baby arrived, Mom allowed herself only a few maternal indulgences: a glance, a cry, a name. Then she too had to let go.[2]

My grandmother had come to meet her first grandchild and said her own sad goodbye. Then she returned to Blaine, where she had four other children still living at home. The youngest two, Aunt Marcia and Uncle Dave, were too young to have stored memories of this period. My two oldest uncles, Earl and Sam, surely would have had some recall, but they both died before my sister's return had released the story of Mom's first pregnancy from the vault of family secrets. It was only my aunt Diane, three years Mom's junior, who had been old enough to understand what was happening and lived long enough to speak of it later. She had known Mom was pregnant, remembered her being confined to the house and then going to Booth. But the next and last thing she heard about it was the day my grandmother returned from visiting Mom and her new baby in St. Paul. "Sharon had a beautiful little girl and she's fine," my grandmother had reported. "And that's all that was said, ever," Diane told me.[3]

That's all that was said because baby Lynette disappeared from view. Having her adopted allowed—or forced—Mom and Grandma and Grandpa and the whole family to pretend nothing had happened.

But if my mother had feared, and my grandmother had known, how difficult it would be to let this beautiful little girl go, why had they done it? Why did Mom choose to relinquish her baby for adoption? If the social work credo of the day was to provide unwed mothers with individualized counseling so that they could arrive at a considered, freely chosen plan regarding their and their babies' future, how do we account for the fact that, according to one scholar, 90 percent of single women who delivered babies in maternity homes ended up surrendering their babies for adoption by the late 1950s; that in homes run by the Salvation Army, including Booth St. Paul, seven of ten new mothers let their babies go? On what basis did these mothers make their decision and how did they feel about it? And what of those who bucked the trend and opted to keep and raise their babies?[4]

It hadn't always been thus, this rending apart of mother and child. In the earliest days of their existence, in fact, rescue homes went to great lengths to keep them together. But the same forces that altered the cultural understanding of unwed motherhood in the early twentieth century tilted the response to it toward separating child from mother by midcentury. They brought together the "illegitimate" and the infertile, each with their own kind of pain, and transformed the longing, love, and loss of parenthood into transactional elements governed by market forces.[5]

From Custody to Surrender: Illegitimacy, Infertility, and Adoption in the First Half of the Twentieth Century

In an essay written some thirty-five years after the fact, Mom seems to offer a simple explanation for her decision to have her baby adopted.

> *Nine months of pregnancy doesn't hurt, but nine months of unwed-mother-pregnancy can hurt very badly. By succumbing to the weakness that had landed me in such a predicament, I had fulfilled my own prophecy of being an inferior, and certainly an unlovable, person. So, I made up my mind early in my gestation that I would give my baby up for adoption rather than have it start life as an "illegitimate" little person doomed to failure because of me. Truth is, I didn't want to take on the responsibility either, which made me feel even more worthless than I already did.*[6]

She was not ready to raise a child or willing to impose the stigma of illegitimacy on a son or daughter. As such, it appears Mom had arrived at her plan of her own accord with the best interests of her child at heart, a view reiterated by Patricia Peart, her Anoka County caseworker. "Sharon is expecting an illegitimate child and wishes to place it for adoption," Peart wrote at her initial meeting with Mom on January 4, 1961. A few weeks later, after Mom had left Booth and her baby was in foster care awaiting placement, Peart made a similar observation: "Sharon came to our office with her plans well formulated. She is a very intelligent girl and we helped her with her plans for Booth and placement of the child. Sharon now wishes to return to University of Minnesota where she is a junior in Journalism."[7]

In Mom's and Peart's accounts, we see evidence of what midcentury social workers and child welfare experts touted as the "best solution" to the problem of illegitimacy. Adoption would shield a child from the social and economic privations of growing up in a fatherless household, allow a young woman to put her troubled past behind her, and help a deserving childless couple to achieve their dream of becoming a family. Single pregnant girls and women would willingly, though not without difficulty, arrive at this solution after careful consideration of all available options as discussed with a neutral, supportive social worker.[8]

Or so the story went.

ACCREDITED SCHOOL PROGRAM PROVIDED
BY THE ST. PAUL DEPARTMENT OF EDUCATION

RELAXING

OPPORTUNITY FOR
SELF EXPRESSION

UNDERSTANDING
PREGNANCY & BIRTH

CHECK UP TIME

A GOOD
BEGINNING

SPIRITUAL RENEWAL

I am very grateful for having a friend such as Booth Memorial Hospital. The work you people do is so tremendous that I cannot find words to express it...... May it continue throughout the ages. You have lifted me from the depth of despair into a new awareness of my abilities and into a life of peace with and within myself. Thank you unendingly.

May God bless you for your love and concern for me and others who share this problem.

Many Thanks
Linda

\# THIS IS A TESTIMONIAL TO THE BOOTH MEMORIAL HOSPITAL

A brochure from the late 1950s
or early 1960s proclaims the success
of Booth's program. *Salvation Army
Central Territory Museum*

But there was an inherent tension between social workers' view of adoption as the "best solution" for a collective social problem and their commitment to individualized casework counseling that would allow each young woman to decide for herself whether to keep or relinquish her child. In the end, most social workers favored the "best solution." As a result, there was an overwhelming trend toward relinquishment by maternity home residents. It was no coincidence that seven out of ten Booth girls released their babies for adoption in 1960, despite the Salvation Army's insistence that "the unmarried mother has the right to plan for the future of herself and her child. . . . She is given every possible assistance in considering alternate plans and in exploring resources to help her evaluate what is best for her and her child." Booth girls' decision to let their babies go reflected the pressure brought to bear by a system of beliefs, interests, and practices that steered them toward adoption.[9]

Perhaps the best evidence of the systemic bias toward adoption of "ille-gitimate" children in the mid-twentieth century is the bias *against* it in the early twentieth century—and its evolution thereafter. In the early years of the rescue homes, single mothers were encouraged to keep their babies in hopes that the maternal bond and practice of caregiving would cement their transformation into proper, if permanently marked, women. In 1912, only one of the 117 babies who left the Salvation Army Rescue Home in St. Paul did so by way of adoption—less than one percent. Nine years later, the home's superintendent, Brigadier Annie Cowden, reminded the *Minneapolis Morning Tribune* that "The Salvation Army never separates mother and child," and in 1932, an Army representative told prospective donors that Booth girls "must keep their babies with them." In 1944, Army officials lauded Booth St. Paul's high custody retention rate—85 percent—as evidence of "success-ful rehabilitation" of the unmarried mothers in its care. By 1950, however,

Nurses and babies at Booth in 1920. In those years, Booth provided childcare while working mothers took jobs and began to earn a living. *Minnesota Historical Society collections*

that rate had fallen to "about half," and in 1960, Dave Moore of WCCO-TV reported that 70 percent of mothers at Booth surrendered their infants.[10]

These increasing rates of surrender can be attributed, in part, to the post–World War II view of single mothers-to-be as suffering from psychological neurosis rather than inherent and immutable immorality, feebleminded-ness, or sex delinquency. A damaged psyche could be remedied through counseling, not mothering. Instead of viewing the child as a means by which a besmirched woman might restore her good name, as had the evangelical women of the early rescue homes, social workers saw an untreated mother as a potential liability to her child's proper future functioning. Though presumed to be free of what an earlier generation had seen as inherited defect, a child born to an unmarried woman faced better prospects in a stable home headed by two parents while its mother attempted to steer her own life back on course.[11]

Of course, this practice also offered a solution to the problem of the postwar adoption market, the pro-family atmosphere leading to soaring demand for adoptable white infants by infertile couples. A demand-supply imbalance had begun to take shape even while maternity homes such as Booth insisted on keeping mother and child together. In July 1921, just a few months after she had discussed the Salvation Army practice of preserving the mother-child bond, Brigadier Cowden spoke about the tension between mothers' desires and prospective adopters' demands. "Of course, the mothers want their babies," she told the *Daily Star*. "They are glad to keep them and glad to work for them. . . . We cannot begin to fill the calls we have for babies for adoption."[12]

Cowden's remarks signaled the transformation of adoption from a means of providing families for "needy" children (in the process preventing them from becoming a drain on public coffers) to a method of providing children for childless couples. Although social workers were initially rather slow to embrace the idea of severing the bond between mother and child, they felt it their duty to ensure that adoption occur under the watchful eye of trained professionals rather than through profit-driven black marketeers or liaisons from birth or adoptive parents' personal networks. In 1917, Minnesota law had required the state board of control to investigate and approve all adoptive placements. By the 1950s, national child welfare organizations and prominent social work theorists were advocating for the adoption of "illegitimate" children. Adoption is "an opportunity [that offers] the best life chance for both mother and child in the great majority of cases," Leontine Young (who

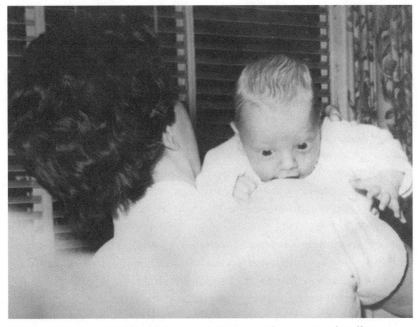

A baby at Booth, early 1960s. *University of Minnesota Libraries, Social Welfare History Archives*

had promoted the theory of the "mother-ridden" unwed mother) argued in 1954, and in 1958, the Child Welfare League of America recommended that social workers across the nation oversee the adoption process.[13]

Even in the 1950s, though, many rank-and-file social workers felt uneasy about separating a child from its mother. In response, the profession's leaders emphasized caseworkers' responsibility to help expectant mothers make "realistic" plans instead of dwelling in "fantasies" about how the baby would fulfill their disordered, oedipal longings. Leontine Young reassured caseworkers who worried about "snatching a baby from a mother" that they and the surrendering mother alike could take comfort in having made a difficult decision "in accordance with the way the world is." "When a worker can see that, had an unmarried mother wanted a baby for normal reasons, she would have fallen in love, married, and had a child under normal circumstances, the worker's problem begins to resolve itself." Similarly, in 1962, the Salvation Army noted that "considerable knowledge, skill and experience are necessary to help the unmarried mother reach her decision based on a realistic appraisal of the factors involved for all concerned" and that "where the rights of the child appear to be in jeopardy, efforts are made to insure the well-being of the child," presumably through adoption.[14]

Many birthmothers of this era harbor bitter feelings toward social workers who they said forced, coerced, or pressured them to part with their babies by using deceptive practices for punitive, prejudiced, and/or profit-driven reasons. Their accounts and scholars' research have demonstrated that such manipulations did occur. But the reassurances Young so firmly delivered suggest that many of them did not take the issue, or the recommendations of their professional leaders, lightly. Such was the case with Margaret Olson Seitz, a Ramsey County caseworker who worked with Booth girls from outside the metro area from 1960 to 1962 and whom I interviewed in October 2017.[15]

Margaret's job was to gather information about Booth girls that could be used in writing an adoption referral while also helping them make a decision about their and their babies' futures. "I wasn't telling them what to do," she explained. "I was . . . helping them through the process of deciding what they needed to do for themselves." All of her clients, she said, expressed some kind of desire to keep their babies, but there were realities to face, and it was Margaret's job to present them. "If your decision is to keep the baby, then what is your plan?" she asked them. "How will you support yourself and the baby? Where will you live? What will you do? Who can you count on to be by your side going through this?"

Were these women pressured to release their babies for adoption? I put the question to Margaret in the middle of our interview. "I would say there probably was an unspoken pressure to place babies for adoption," she admitted. Still, she maintained that the keep-or-relinquish decision was the mothers', not hers, though she couldn't recall a single woman from her caseload who kept and raised her own baby in the two years she worked with Booth girls. As our interview drew to a close, Margaret returned to the question. "I was so wrapped up in what exactly I was doing that I wasn't looking around at some of the other pieces," she said, "and it's easy for me to say that we didn't pressure the girls to give up their babies because we weren't the girls. They may have felt that we were. I hope not—I never set out with that intention, but the whole message that society was giving them may have made them feel that we were all on that side."

Margaret has a point. Though social workers spearheaded the drive for the "best solution," parents, doctors, lawyers, judges, educators, psychologists, legislators, and child welfare officials also believed that adoption was best, for child *and* mother. "I don't remember that we ever talked about, with the girls, a decision that was right for the baby that wasn't right for them," Margaret said. And of course, it would allow the many infertile couples longing for a child to live the American dream, too.[16]

These couples faced a gauntlet of their own, however. By the mid-twentieth century, infertility had become a necessary but not sufficient prerequisite for a white married couple to build a family through adoption, one way of managing the excess demand for adoptable children. Social workers conducted "home studies" to identify the most deserving couples, evaluating prospective adopters' social, physical, moral, economic, and psychoanalytic preparedness to raise a child. If they were found to be suffering from unresolved neuroses or a failure to adapt to proper socio-sexual roles, they too could be deemed unfit to raise a child. Unsurprisingly, these pressures and presumptions weighed more heavily on women than men. In an eerie echo of the explanation for premarital pregnancy, social welfare experts claimed that a woman's medically inexplicable infertility may have resulted from a childhood deprived of parental love, a subconscious hostility toward her husband, a refusal to accept her femininity, or an "unconscious rejection of motherhood."[17]

Clearly, then, social workers wielded considerable control over birth and adoptive mothers, both of whom faced scrutiny and stigma for their failure to conform to accepted standards of female behavior and paths to motherhood. In the middle of the twentieth century, illegitimacy and infertility became the twin pillars of adoption. Still, adoption "resolved" these dilemmas in a grossly differential way. The transfer of a child from birth to adoptive mother meant that the latter gained from the losses suffered by the former, all in the name of protecting the child's best interests.

Beyond the "Best Solution"

But the "best solution" didn't apply to everyone—or, rather, not every unmarried mother chose it for her child. If seven out of ten Booth girls relinquished their children in 1960, after all, three of ten kept them. They did so against great odds.

As social workers were quick to point out, there were some hard, cold facts confronting a young single mother who chose to raise her baby: the stigma of illegitimacy; the prospect of taking legal action to secure financial support from an unwilling father; parents unwilling or unable to support their daughters and grandchildren; full- or part-time, often low-paying, work that would incur childcare expenses and that may not be sufficient to cover the costs of housing, food, clothing, and medical care; and/or the prospect of relying on Aid to Dependent Children and confronting the insufficiency of and stigma associated with public assistance. The problem wasn't just this dearth of resources, however; it was also that caseworkers' predisposition toward adoption often precluded a discussion of whatever assistance was available and colored their service to their clients. In April 1956, for example, Roberta Rindfleisch of the Minnesota Department of Public Welfare acknowledged that "fuller and better service is given to the girls who give the child up for adoption than those who do not," and in 1967, the Minnesota Council on Illegitimacy noted that "the girl who chooses to keep her child does not often get the same continued warm acceptance as the girl who places her child for adoption." Even if caseworkers made a genuine effort to explore all options with their clients, however, University of Minnesota social work professor Gisela Konopka pointed out that "the provisions made for helping unmarried mothers raise their children with dignity are practically nil."[18]

Gisela Konopka, director of the University of Minnesota's Center for Youth Development, professor of social work, and an internationally known expert in group work, 1965. *University of Minnesota Archives, University of Minnesota–Twin Cities*

In arguing that unmarried mothers deserved the right and resources to parent their children, Konopka also railed against the widespread portrayal of them as selfish, immature, and emotionally troubled. In 1959, the director of child welfare services for Ramsey County, Beatrice Bernhagen, had declared that "the girl who is emotionally adjusted and intellectually capable of thinking things through will give up her baby." On the other hand, girls who kept their babies would end up raising them in "other than a normal family setting," resorting to public relief and using the child as a "punishment" against their parents. Drawing on the same psychoanalytic logic that portrayed single pregnant women as neurotic, employees of a New York adoption agency argued in 1960 that unmarried mothers sometimes used their babies as "love objects" to replace one or both of their own lost parents. "This inability to let go of the baby by surrendering it is related to the fear, substantiated in some cases, of being swallowed again by the depths of the depressions she had attempted to conquer by getting pregnant." A 1962 study that drew on a "personality factor test" described mothers who surrendered their babies as "confident," "poised," "mature," "intelligent," and "aggressive" in contrast to the "insecure, anxious," "tense," "unstable," "dull," and "submissive" girls who chose to keep their babies.[19]

These damning views of women who refused to relinquish their babies made their way into the popular media as well. In April 1961, just a few months after Mom had said goodbye to her baby, advice columnist Ann Landers chimed in on the issue by dismissing any unwed mother who claimed that she loved her baby too much to let it go. "Such 'love' is questionable," she claimed. "It is a sick kind of love turned inside out—an unwholesome blend of self-pity, mixed with self-destruction and a touch of martyrdom. . . . The unwed mother who has genuine love for her child wants him to have a decent life in a conventional, socially acceptable home environment. She is willing to give him up so that he can have such a life."[20]

Despite the general consensus on the "best solution," however, women who released their babies for adoption were not entirely immune from allegations of selfishness. In August 1965, a *Minneapolis Star* article titled "They Give Away 'Own Flesh and Blood'; Annual Event for Some," portrayed relinquishing mothers as callous, "dry-eyed," sexually promiscuous young women whom a Hennepin County court referee described as "unwilling 'to put forth the effort for [their] own flesh and blood,'" instead seeking "'selfish gratification' of desires." The day after the article appeared, local child welfare professionals, including representatives from Booth St. Paul, condemned the article's "destructive moralizing" and insisted that mothers made relinquishment decisions with care and guidance and that adoption was "usually . . . the best plan for the child."[21]

The article also generated a flurry of letters that appeared in the *Star*'s opinion pages over the next three weeks. Social workers, court workers, adoptive parents, and unwed mothers all wrote to condemn the punishing attitudes the article had revealed. These compassionate letter writers acknowledged the "anguish" with which mothers had undertaken the decision to release their children and uniformly praised them for doing so. Compassion for unmarried mothers thus seemed directly tied to their decision to let their babies go, thus reinforcing the cultural primacy of adoption for "illegitimate" children.[22]

That is, if they were white.

Race and the "Best Solution"

For all of its commanding power to shape the experiences of white unmarried pregnant women—including those who rejected it—the "best solution" was an ill fit for nonwhite women. While some "benevolent reformers," as historian Rickie Solinger calls more liberal-minded social welfare professionals, believed that African American and Native American women became pregnant out of wedlock for the same reason as white women and could therefore benefit from casework counseling, other officials viewed Black and Indigenous illegitimacy as evidence of inherited biological, cultural, or material dysfunction that merited neglect at best, punishment at worst, and in any case was not amenable to therapeutic intervention.[23]

Even those who believed that women of color deserved equal access to services for unmarried mothers, including adoption for their children, acknowledged that nonwhite children often languished in the state foster care system due to a shortage of adoptive homes. In 1965, the *Minneapolis Tribune* reported that, although "Negro" and "Indian" children were "more apt to be offered for adoption," they waited three to four times as long as white children to be paired with adoptive parents (nineteen months and fourteen months for Black and Indigenous children, five months for white children). "Billy," a six-year-old Black child, had been in foster care since his unmarried mother surrendered him at birth. "If he weren't a Negro, he would have been placed when he was an infant," a state adoption worker told the reporter. Seventy percent of white children who had been added to the state adoption registry in fiscal year 1965 had been adopted, compared to only 15 percent of Black and 47 percent of Indigenous children.[24]

According to the paper, increasing rates of illegitimate births, especially among Black and Native women, and a reduction in the incidence of infertility had led to the glut of nonwhite children in the adoption market. Because financial constraints limited the number of prospective Black and Native adopters, local adoption agencies were relaxing their requirements in order to recruit prospective white adopters. By 1965, would-be parents no longer had to be infertile, or married, or subjected to home visits by social workers, or endorsed by character references, or childless, or wealthy.[25]

Thus the supply-demand balance of the adoption market seemed to be inverted when it came to nonwhite children: too many children waiting for too few homes. Such a simple formulation obscures the more complicated reality, however. African American and Native American single mothers did not simply "offer" their children for adoption, and those children did not languish in the system due to lack of interest among potential adopters from their own communities. Instead, racism, class bias, and the economic concerns and assimilationist goals of government policy contributed to both the problem (an excess "supply" of Black and Indigenous children waiting for adoptive homes) and its potential solution (adoption of those children by white couples).

As Rickie Solinger has argued, Black unmarried mothers kept and raised their babies more often than they surrendered them for adoption, largely because they "accepted responsibility for [their babies] as a matter of course" and made decisions based on "an elaborated, shared, and distinct value system" that prized motherhood over marriage. Like their white counterparts, they often required financial assistance in the form of Aid to Dependent Children (ADC). Although the majority of Black single mothers did not receive ADC—and nearly twice as many white as Black unmarried mothers did—many politicians and taxpayers condemned the program for supporting supposedly immoral Black women who, they claimed, had one out-of-wedlock baby after another in order to claim welfare benefits. Solinger and others have shown how cutting ADC benefits punished these women, reduced state spending, and supported other racist policies designed to turn back advances made by the civil rights movement in areas such as housing and education, especially in the South.[26]

In response, the federal government enacted the Flemming Rule in 1961, which prohibited states from denying benefits to children on the basis of "suitable home" laws—laws that defined eligibility on the basis of the "moral" behavior of mothers. Instead, states were to use aid to improve the conditions of the home or to support children removed from the home and placed in foster care. The result, according to historian Laura Briggs, was the transformation of "ADC and foster care across the country from a system that ignored Black children to one that acted vigorously to take them."[27]

Once in the child welfare system, however, "illegitimate" Black children faced a paucity of adoptive families to take them in, as noted above. A study of unmarried mothers in Ramsey County in 1957 pointed out that the problem stemmed, in part, from "the failure to recruit such homes." Concerns such as these led to the creation of Parents-to-Adopt-Minority-Youngsters (PAMY), a two-year program launched in 1961 by the Minnesota Department of Public Welfare and supported by adoption agencies, county welfare departments, and the Minneapolis and St. Paul Urban Leagues. According to a 1963 report, PAMY's original goal was to find Black homes for Black children, but its plans to conduct a comprehensive recruiting campaign within the local Black community soon fell by the wayside as it decided to "reach a single community with a single approach" focused on finding parents for children in need. By the end of January 1963, three Black, two Indian, and six white children had been sent to adoptive families; only one of the Black children had been placed in a white home.[28]

Ultimately, however, PAMY helped to expand eligibility criteria for white adopters. The *Minneapolis Tribune* reported in July 1963 that public adoption agencies had begun allowing "suitable" single women to adopt in order to find permanent homes for nonwhite children. Widowed or divorced economically solvent working women with access to childcare were deemed suitable, but the child's own mother, who may have been able to parent if provided sufficient resources, was not. Project leaders also reported that some white couples made specific requests to adopt Black children, motivated by a desire to help rather than by desperation to build a family. In December 1963, a *Minneapolis Star* headline captured the main story of PAMY: "Placing Negro Children in White Adoptive Homes is Urged." From 1962 to 1965, the program and its state-run successor placed twenty African American children in white families, signaling a trend toward transracial adoption as a solution to the "over-supply" of nonwhite children in state custody.[29]

PAMY officials' conclusion that "the community was ready to accept Negro-white adoptions" echoed that of other child welfare officials across the country, as did its turn away from finding Black homes for Black children and toward transracial placement. According to historian Matine Spence, dedicated efforts to recruit African American adopters gave way to an emphasis on white adoptions of Black children because leaders of the National Urban League (NUL), which played a central role in defining adoption practice in its collaboration with the Child Welfare League of America (CWLA), believed that integration of the races would best demonstrate African Americans' rightful place in American culture. Instead of working to transform requirements that made adoption inaccessible to many Black would-be parents—a medical diagnosis of infertility; age limits, income requirements, and housing standards; stay-at-home mothers; costly agency fees—the NUL and CWLA started a trend toward "color-blind" placement that held firm even when agencies began loosening some of the other restrictions.[30]

Throughout the 1960s, then, increasing numbers of Black children went to white adoptive homes, peaking in 1970–71 along with the overall rate of adoption. Despite the fact that these Black-white families made up a tiny proportion of all adoptions in the United States—less than two percent—and numbered 12,000 to 15,000 before 1975, they took on great symbolic significance, occurring as they did alongside heated debates about the meaning of racial justice for African Americans and the nature of Black-white relations within the civil rights movement and American society. Similarly, the rise in white-parent/Native-children adoptive families occurred in the context not just of changing adoption practice but also of the evolving relationship between Indigenous peoples and the white-dominated state.[31]

After World War II, federal policy toward Indigenous peoples shifted away from promoting tribal sovereignty to eliminating tribes as political entities standing in the way of acquisition and development of tribal land. Declaring its intent to reduce tribal dependency on federal largesse and grant Native Americans the full rights of US citizenship, Congress announced in 1953 that it would terminate more than one hundred tribes through forced assimilation. While Minnesota's tribal nations were not terminated, Congress also turned over to some states, including Minnesota, criminal jurisdiction as well as financial and legal responsibility for tribal matters that had once been under federal jurisdiction. In these PL-280 states (so called because they fell under the purview of Public Law 83–280, which effected this jurisdictional transfer), state officials realized that they would bear the burden of providing education and ADC benefits to Indigenous mothers and children for whom they were now, to their dismay, responsible. The Bureau of Indian Affairs (BIA) began shuttering its boarding schools (which had been used to deprive Native children of their culture, to devastating effect on Native families) and turning over to the states responsibility for the dependent children living in them. Historian Margaret Jacobs argues that, instead of taking advantage of the opportunity provided by the closing of boarding schools to restore and preserve Native families, PL-280 states turned increasingly to transracial adoption as a means of assimilating Native children into white culture and reducing state expenditures for assistance to poor Native families. In 1958, the BIA's Welfare Branch and the CWLA established the Indian Adoption Project (IAP) to find white adoptive homes for Indigenous children, effectively outsourcing the task of termination-by-assimilation to those families.[32]

Arnold Lyslo, head of IAP, spent the next several years creating both the supply of and the demand for "adoptable" Indigenous children. Drawing on the white, middle-class, nuclear family model, Lyslo and his colleagues declared poor Native families living on reservations as unhealthy, Native unmarried mothers as inherently unfit, and Native children lovingly cared for by extended family members as at risk. He urged social welfare officials to extend their services to Indigenous unmarried mothers living on reservations and in cities, encouraging them toward maternity homes and adoption. In addition to thus bolstering the numbers of Indigenous children "available" for adoption, Lyslo and the IAP embarked on a public relations campaign to raise interest among the many white couples waiting to adopt. The IAP appealed to liberals' desires to "rescue" children from the "plight" of Native American hardship in general and the psychological problems of unmarried mothers in particular. Just as the CWLA and National Urban League were promoting "color-blind" placements of Black children, the CWLA and IAP explicitly advocated for the adoption of Native children by whites.[33]

Margaret Jacobs writes that Lyslo's marketing of the IAP was "wildly successful" and that, by 1968, there were more homes waiting for Native children than there were children identified as adoptable. Over the course of its ten-year existence, the project placed 395 Native kids in white families. When combined with state, church, and agency programs (and sometimes brazen seizures of children by individual social workers) that also facilitated transracial adoption of Native children, IAP efforts led to the astonishing fact that Native kids were nineteen times more likely to be adopted away from their families than other children and that one-quarter to one-third of all Indigenous kids had been separated from their families by the mid-1970s.[34]

In some ways, white and nonwhite single pregnant women alike were victims of the biases inherent in the "best solution." Judged against a family ideal that lay beyond their reach, they were deemed unfit to be mothers and pressured to release their children for adoption. Yet white, Black, and Indigenous women were directed to similar ends—separation from their children—

in different ways, for different reasons, and with different consequences. "Race, reproduction, and the politics of [Black] unwed mothers were *the* shoals on which the progress of the civil rights movement foundered," notes Laura Briggs. In 1961, 24 percent of children in the welfare system were Black; by the end of the twentieth century, 42 percent of children in foster care were Black, though they made up only 17 percent of the overall population of young people. And as Margaret Jacobs writes, "the consequences of removing Indian infants from their mothers not only violated the individual rights of women, as it did with so many white unwed mothers, but also undermined the viability of Indian tribes and violated their rights to exist as a group." Policies and practices toward unmarried mothers and their children were part of the larger struggle of powerful white officials to maintain racial hierarchy based in political and economic power.[35]

Mom's—and Jack's—race rendered her baby, once relinquished, immune to concerns about finding a home, but race defined my mother's and sister's experience as significantly, if differently, as it did that of any nonwhite woman or child. Indeed, white single pregnant girls and women became important suppliers of babies for the booming adoption market. In the United States, the number of families formed through adoption tripled in the first two decades of the postwar period, rising from 50,000 in 1944 to 152,000 in 1966; the number would peak in 1970 at 175,000. Throughout this period, however, the proportion of children adopted by biological kin hovered at just over or under 50 percent, and, in 1950, half of all adopted children had been born to married parents. Nevertheless, babies born to white unmarried mothers constituted a significant portion of adoptable children. According to Rickie Solinger, by the late 1950s, a pervasive "relinquishment culture" led to surrender rates of up to 90 percent in some maternity homes, and in 1962, children born to unmarried women constituted 80 percent of all nonfamily adoptions. From 1945 to 1973, Ann Fessler reports, 1.5 million babies were relinquished to nonfamily adoption.[36]

My sister was one of them.

JANUARY 14, 1961

Everything had seemed so clear, so obvious, six months ago. Then, her pregnancy was the problem that adoption would solve, the baby an abstract idea only hinted at through nausea and fatigue.

Now, as she awaits the arrival of her baby—the one whose feet kicked at her belly, whose hiccups made her laugh, whose being she feels inside her own—clarity has given way to worry.

During the day, she plays cards and smokes and swaps stories with the other girls. She scrubs the floors and dusts the furniture.

But in the still of the night, she worries.

She worries that her labor will begin in the wee hours and that no one will come to help. She worries about the pain of bringing a baby into the world and the pain of letting that baby go.

She tosses and turns as she thinks of Angie, who is keeping her baby, with or without her boyfriend's help.

She imagines telling her caseworker that she has changed her mind, her parents that she's coming home, her grandmother that she has erred, her brothers and sisters that they are now aunts and uncles.

She imagines going back to Blaine, squeezing into an already-full house with a baby, quitting school. She feels the sidelong glances from the neighbors, the sting of their wagging tongues.

She cannot do it. She is not brave enough.

She thinks of Gerri, her silence, her bravado, her wails.

She imagines saying goodbye to her own baby.

She worries that she will not be strong enough. ●

Letting Go

It's one thing to make a plan, another to see it through. Even if Mom had decided on adoption for her baby before she met Patricia Peart from Anoka County, and even if she truly believed it to be in her and her child's best interest, saying goodbye to a baby she had nurtured for nine months was not easy. She suffered this emotional pain in silence, just as she had the physical pain of labor. Indeed, she and other Booth girls were the often-voiceless, anonymous young women at the center of a cultural storm, their decisions the linchpin of the entire "best solution."

But what must it have felt like to let a baby go? Though many studies and memoirs and oral histories contain accounts of birthmothers' painful release of their children, two interview collections are particularly meaningful to me for their connections to Booth St. Paul. The first, of course, is the set of interviews I conducted with the former Booth girls whose stories are woven throughout this book. Their power resides in my personal connection to these women, the ability to see in their faces and hear in their voices the lasting effects of long-ago events and to ask them the questions I wish I had asked my mother. They are powerful, and they allow for reflective insight developed over the intervening years, but they rely on memory of events that occurred decades in the past.

The second source provides a contemporaneous glimpse into the lives and thoughts of Booth girls just before or just after they surrendered their babies. In October 1963, Gisela Konopka and her assistant, Vernie-Mae Czaky, interviewed thirty-three teenage residents at Booth about the events that had led to their pregnancies, their thoughts about the world they lived in, and their plans for their and their babies' futures. Eighteen of them said they planned to have their babies adopted, twelve implied as much, and three indicated they were going to keep their babies. Though these girls were at Booth two years after Mom had left and were two to seven years younger than she had been when she had her baby, they spoke with similar pain and passion about the emotional costs of unwed motherhood and the "best solution." "I want to keep my child so badly but I have no place to go," a sixteen-year-old Caucasian girl from Olmsted County told Czaky. "I want my baby, I want it so much! But I can't support it and I have to give it away," explained a teenager from Mower County. "I feel guilty especially because I have to give away the child. I just can't see someone else care for it, wash it, watch it grow, take its first steps! Yet everybody thinks it's right to give the child away."[37]

Seven girls had already delivered by the time they spoke to Czaky. Sometimes this made them waver in their adoption decision; sometimes it made them more resolute. "Before the baby was born, I thought adoption would be best because I can't support it or anything," said a nineteen-year-old Caucasian girl from Blue Earth County, who was herself an adoptee. "After the delivery, I saw the baby before he was cleaned up and again after he was cleaned up. He had dark features and hair like me. It was hard for me to give him up," she continued in a heart-rending explanation of why she was still proceeding with the adoption, one that touched on all aspects of the "best solution." "I realized he would have a happy home. The social worker said I have many years ahead of me. There is this one family where I worked that were married five years and can't have any kids. How happy they would be if they could have one." A nineteen-year-old French-German-"Indian" girl from Hennepin County seemed not to waffle at all, despite the urging of her parents and new boyfriend to keep her baby. "I will not do it. I am not ready for it and I think that this would not be a good basis for marriage," she said. "I don't know what kind of life I have ready for [a child] and a child should have love and a good home."[38]

Other young women seemed to take solace in the idea of releasing their babies. "I thought I would never make it," a young white woman from Ramsey County said. "I was so desperate I thought I would kill myself. Then I went for help. I saw a psychiatrist. I did it completely on my own. After I have now decided to give up my baby, there is a comforting thought. I can start a renewed life. Perhaps I gained by this experience." Another white nineteen-year-old seemed to subscribe to the notion that surrendering her baby would allow her to build a future free of any encumbrance. "I want a happy family. I don't want to start with any of this," she said. "I don't want any dirty diapers. I couldn't handle it. I want to start with a clean slate."[39]

Whether they despaired at the prospect of losing their children or found hope in the possibility of a better future for their babies and themselves, Booth girls' responses to their situation were infused with the logic of the "best solution." But even those who seemed most resolved to adoption when they were pregnant showed signs of emotional distress once they had delivered. The young woman who rejected dirty diapers in favor of a clean slate had become "somewhat subdued" after she had her baby, according to case notes prepared by Booth's caseworker Evelyn Headen. "All of us noticed this," Headen wrote with a tone of bewilderment. "She was no longer talkative." For all the effort that went into managing the "social problem" of unwed motherhood—the oversight, the intervention, the casework counseling, the planning, the nudging or pushing toward adoption—the experts paid surprisingly little attention to the effect that surrendering a child might have on a new mother. Karen told me in 2017 that no one from Booth or the county had helped her deal with the loss of her son in 1962; casework counseling stopped once she left Booth, her baby in the custody of the state.[40]

More than fifty years after she had helped Booth girls make plans for themselves and their babies, Margaret, the Ramsey County social worker, acknowledged that no one had thought about the lifelong repercussions an adoption decision might have. "I've often wondered about how they survived," she said sadly, "when they couldn't talk about it; that was a piece we never really discussed. . . . We didn't talk about, 'How are you going to feel twenty-five years from now? Are you still going to be carrying this load?'"

As my interviews and Mom's writings attest, former Booth girls did indeed carry their load far into the future.

They told me that my baby girl was perfect in all ways, but I didn't dare compromise my resolve to put her up for adoption by looking at her or holding her or even beginning to think of her as mine. So, they took her away while I lay aching and bloody in that yellow room, tamping down my sadness and guilt and clinging with small comfort to the fact that I had endured the pain without making a sound.[41]

SANDY #1

Sandy, however, clung to more than a brave performance during labor. She clung to her child, one of the 30 percent of mothers who left Booth with their babies.

On April 7, 2016, I found a message in my email inbox with the subject heading "Twice a Booth Girl." Sandy had read a short article I'd written for the *Minneapolis Star Tribune*'s "10,000 Takes" series about my mother's Booth experience. "I haven't heard 'Booth Hospital' since 1957 when I was there," Sandy wrote in her email. She gave me a brief summary of her complicated relationship to adoption, then, "By the way, I am 81." We exchanged several more emails, and, in June 2017, I drove to her home in Glenwood, Minnesota, to hear her story in person.

Sandy likes to say she was delivered by Dr. Will, the physician from Bertha, Minnesota, who met her and her mother at the train station in nearby Wadena when they arrived in January 1936. Sandy's mother, a gentle schoolteacher of Swedish descent, had made the trek from central Minnesota to the Children's Home Society in Minneapolis to pick up and bring home the nine-month-old girl who would make her and her Norwegian husband a family. For more than a decade, Sandy absorbed her adoptive mother's loving warmth, a necessary counterpoint to her adoptive father's stoicism. Her mother died from cancer when Sandy was just fourteen years old, leaving her in the care of a disinterested father and his sister. It was this, she said, even more than the fact of being adopted, that most significantly affected her as she grew up. "I lived in the house with these cold Norwegians, and they ignored me totally." While her father tended to the drugstore he owned and operated in town, Sandy tended to the activities of small-town life. She played in the school band, joined the girls' half-court basketball team, got together with the other "town kids" to ride bikes or play Monopoly. "It was a typical small town where bad things happened and nobody bother[ed] to worry about it and good things happen[ed]," she said. "The not-so-good things were hidden in Bertha and weren't talked about."[42]

Those not-so-good things were bad indeed. When Sandy was about eleven, an older boy from town abused her sexually. "We had a skating rink across the street from where I lived," she recalled. "There was a warming house there. I don't know how it all came about but I ended up with one of the older guys. [He] got me in there and got me doing sex things with him." He was the first boy who forced her to do things she didn't understand, but not the last. Sandy didn't understand what was happening or that she was being exploited. Sex was not a subject of discussion at school or church or in polite conversation, and her mother, who Sandy believes would otherwise have taken the situation in hand, had already taken ill. "It was just a normal thing I thought. Then I didn't have the home life to tell me any different, which happens. It doesn't mean you're not a nice person or not good or anything—just small-town USA."

When Sandy graduated from high school in 1953, her father gave her a car—"that's what you get when you don't have a relationship"—and she moved to Minneapolis, happy to leave small-town life behind. She shared a house with a girlfriend, took a job at Schmitt Music downtown, and immersed herself in the local music scene. She met a man at the Flame Ballroom on Nicollet Avenue. She'd been married and divorced by that time, but she still knew nothing of the biological elements of reproduction, nothing about birth control. "I was a brilliant person but I didn't know anything about pregnancy, babies, or anything." She harbored no shame about her sexual activity, believing it was just the natural progression of a relationship. When it finally dawned on her that she was pregnant, Sandy told her boyfriend that he owed her nothing but financial support. He took her up on the offer and returned, unbeknownst to her at the time, to the other woman he'd gotten pregnant and whom he eventually married. Sandy checked herself into Booth.

Sandy couldn't quite remember how she made the arrangements at Booth, except to say that it was "where they sent you if you were unmarried and going to have a baby." She was there for several months, a twenty-two-year-old, musically inclined, unmarried pregnant adoptee from Bertha. Her boyfriend paid some of her room-and-board fees; Sandy thinks Hennepin County covered the rest. She passed the time socializing with other Booth girls, doing puzzles and playing the piano, attending Salvation Army meetings, and using her car to "come and go pretty much as [she] wanted."

Sandy also warded off efforts to convince her to release her baby for adoption. "The nurses came in, they would say something and the . . . case worker there would have these conversations with you and tell you all the bad things about keeping a baby and all the good things about giving it up for adoption—you know, the prejudices." But she resisted. Despite knowing nothing about babies, despite—perhaps because of—her own unsatisfactory family history, despite the pressure to relinquish, Sandy decided to keep her baby. "The more they pushed towards adoption, the more I said, 'No, I'm going to keep him.'"

Sandy gave birth to her son at the University of Minnesota on Thanksgiving Day 1957, and when she left Booth eight days later, she took him with her.

It wasn't easy, raising her son alone. Though the intervening years have clouded Sandy's memory of the exact sequence of events, she remembered that they lived for a time with a wealthy family for whom she worked as a nanny. "I really didn't know how to take care of kids," she said. "I figured you have to put something on them to keep them dry and have to feed them and—I didn't sit and read books. I . . . just did the natural human thing." After that, she lived in a "big house in Mounds View" where the neighbors helped care for her son. It was during this time that she started dating someone new and got pregnant again. This time, she didn't go to Booth; she stayed with a foster family during her pregnancy. This time, she didn't insist on keeping her baby; she delivered her baby at Fairview Hospital and released her for adoption to Children's Home Society. The social workers didn't want her to see her baby, she said, because they thought she'd change her mind about relinquishing. But Sandy was steadfast. "I said, 'No, I want a picture of her and I want to see her, hold her. I can handle it.' So, I did." And then she let her daughter go.

Why release this baby after having kept the other? "Because I knew that I wasn't giving [my son] a good young life and I wanted her to have a good young life." There was no pressure, "no duress" involved in her decision. She wanted her daughter to have a life she knew she could not provide.

Things get a little blurry again after that in Sandy's memory. Her second baby was born in 1960, then she went home to Bertha for a while because she had taken ill, leaving her son in the care of "those people in Mounds View." She spent some time at the family lake place, started classes at the College of Medical Technology in Minneapolis, met a man at a downtown piano bar. When they married in 1962, her new husband adopted her son, and they became a family. They had four more children, three girls and a boy, and two miscarriages.

Sandy reunited with her birthmother and four biological siblings in the late 1970s. Children's Home Society (CHS) played intermediary between Sandy and her mother for a while, passing letters from one to the other, then helped the two connect by phone. Eventually, Sandy and her husband drove to Iowa to meet Sandy's mother face-to-face. "You grab each other and you look and . . . then you look and you grab each other," she said, describing the moment that wove Sandy into another whole family, with sisters and brothers and nieces and nephews. "Boy, have I got a big family down there now, all over the place." When her husband died, after forty-seven years of marriage, Sandy found two more sisters, this time on her biological father's side. A lonely only child from Bertha ended up with six siblings she had never known she had.

She also ended up with all six of her own children in her life. When Sandy left word at CHS in the late 1970s that she wanted to find her mother, she also left word that she would welcome contact with her adopted-away daughter. Years later, after she found her own birth family, that daughter came calling. Sandy learned that her daughter had grown up on a farm, just as she'd hoped she would. She learned that her daughter had two also-adopted siblings. She learned that her daughter is an adoptive mother herself. Sandy introduced her adopted-away daughter to the mother from whom she herself had been adopted away, a weaving together of complicated family threads.

As our interview drew to a close, I asked Sandy where this all fit into her life now, her time at Booth, her experience as an adoptee and a single mother and a birthmother and a mothering mother and an adoptive grandmother. What sense does she make of it all? "It's been an interesting life," she said, "and ironically, I don't have any regrets. You'd think I would, but I don't because I just—I don't know—I have a pretty good faith and I figure, well, what is, is. [That's] my thing, that's me: what is, is." Then she noticed a photograph on the wall behind me.

"That picture there behind you . . . grab it."

I took it off the wall and handed it to her. It was a photograph of her and her husband with her birthmother and siblings. She pointed out each one to me.

"We do, in some pictures, look a lot alike, me and my mother."

Then she asked if I'd gotten what I wanted out of the interview. Yes, I told her. She asked about the other women I'd interviewed, if they too had relinquished their babies for adoption, if they too had "all these other adoptions in their family." Some do, I said, and told her about Gay—birthmother, mothering mother, adoptive mother. I reminded Sandy of my personal connection to the project—my mother, my son, how adoption has both divided and united my family.

"Now that you're mentioning it," she said, "it seems like adoption begets adoption somehow." ▪

> *The day I had to sign the papers, the social worker told me that a wonderful young couple were waiting for my baby. So, I signed, just as I had planned. But my resolve was no stronger than Gerri's, and I ended up in the smoking lounge, just as she had, crying until it was time to pack for home.*[43]

On January 20, 1961, Patricia Peart took Lynette from Booth and placed her in a foster home to await adoption.

On January 25, 1961, Mom left Booth to start her life anew.

He has a cracker in one hand and a long, yellow plastic spoon in the other. He wears a long sleeved blue plaid shirt over a Minnesota Twins T-shirt, blue jeans, and tiny red leather shoes with a monkey face sewn on top. He is casually munching on the cracker and waving the spoon until he sees the crowd assembled at the airport gate to welcome him to his new home, his new family: two grandmas, four aunts, three uncles, five cousins. The kids hold a sign, backward, that says "Tu home welcome."

Tu goes still and silent, glancing warily at these new faces, leaning into my arms, then tolerating gentle holds from the grandmas, eyes trained on something in the distance, countenance sober.

Exhaustion.

Bewilderment.

Good-natured forbearance.

Gaiety.

Tu exhibits all of these in what must be a bone-rattling upset of his world. Just over twenty-four hours ago, he had been breathing in the heavy air and familiar scents of Vietnam. Just over two days ago, he had celebrated Christmas in Hanoi with new parents, ice cream, a Snow White balloon, and a Santa hat. Just over two weeks ago, he had slept peacefully through his first journey outside of Ben Tre. Just over a month ago, he had been eating and sleeping and playing and growing in the familiar company of his friends and nannies at the care center. Just over sixteen months ago, he had been found abandoned at the Hanh Phuc lying-in hospital, two days old and six pounds heavy.

Now, suddenly, he is in snowy Minnesota surrounded by Finns and Norwegians and a big house that goes from noisy excitement to preternatural quiet as it empties of the grandmas and aunts and uncles and cousins.

Then it is just the three of us.

It is a relief to be home. I can feel my body relax as it settles into the comfort of familiar surroundings.

And yet, everything is different, too. A high chair is now stationed at the kitchen table. Our Toyota has a car seat. The sink is already filled with sippy cups and partitioned plates and long plastic spoons from Vietnam. A baby gate blocks the entrance to the stairs, and a playpen stands in the winter sunlight streaming into the family room. The room under the eaves sports

Winnie the Pooh curtains on the window, a braided baby blue rug on the floor, and a wooden crib along the wall. The closet and dresser are filled to overflowing with stuffed animals and baby blankets and onesies and T-shirts and pajamas, baby shower bounty.

I knew, before we left for Vietnam, that everything would be different when we got back. The transition isn't as sudden for us as it is for Tu, of course, and it is of our own choosing, where he had no say in the matter at all. Still, it's a big change. Just over a month ago, Steve and I were spending the evenings watching *Scrubs* and doing crosswords and sudokus as we endured the interminable wait for travel approval. Just about five months ago, we received the first photos of the little boy who would become our son. Just over sixteen months ago, as hospital staff halfway across the globe found a baby boy, we took the first steps toward adoption. It was just over three years ago that we didn't hear a heartbeat on an ultrasound screen, four years ago that I had major surgery in hopes of relieving pain and preserving fertility, sixteen years ago that we two became one through marriage, Steve with visions of children dancing in his head, me without.

And now, here we are, the two of us with a little walking, talking, laughing, eating, peeing, pooping, wailing stranger in our house, making a go at becoming a family.

It's a change for Mom, too, but one she seems to embrace. She is there at the airport to greet us. She helps host the gathering at our house, which she has prepared for our arrival, stocking the cupboards and vacuuming the floors and setting up the playpen. She has us over for dinner that night.

She records all of this in her journal in a mix of anxious and eager anticipation.

"I hope to see Kim & Tu & Steve every day so I can overcome my nervousness at being able to have him attach to me," she writes.

Just about two years ago, a woman in Vietnam learned she was pregnant. Just over sixteen months ago, she said goodbye to the baby she had nurtured in her body for nine months, held in her arms for two days. Just one day ago, her boy was taken halfway across the world to be raised by strangers.

6
FRESH START

During the first year of my child's life, I had all the nightmares and regrets I thought I deserved, but I learned to seal off the painful memories and tuck them into a place where they wouldn't destroy me. It took a while. There were times when my grief and guilt overwhelmed me, and I fought hard to resist the urge to rush to the Lutheran Social Service and beg them to give my baby back to me.[1]

AND SO THE WEIGHT OF SILENT, invisible grief settled in as Mom set off into the "fresh start" promised by the "best solution." She did all the things a restored young white woman was supposed to do: she returned to college, met and married a fine man, bore two children legitimated by matrimony, played the part of a happy homemaking, then working mother. And yet these hallmarks of a well-adjusted life were built on an edifice of secrecy. The burdensome gap between outward appearance and inner turmoil that had shaped her growing-up years, with shiny floors and tidy counters masking her parents' marital discord, took on new dimensions for Mom as she constructed her adult life, each new milestone a nail holding up the wall she was erecting around her past.

It is here, of course, where our stories and our memories converge, Mom's and mine. I was born in 1968, seven years after she had said goodbye to Lynette, five years after she married my father—the only person other than my grandparents and aunts and uncles who knew about her first baby. My arrival, and my brother's two years later, would have signified a healthy moving on to all those social workers who had assured relinquishing mothers that they would find happiness in future children. I know she did; I know Mom loved me and Eric. She took delight in our achievements, however modest, and soothed our wounds, however minor. She put our needs before hers, working only part-time through most of our elementary school years. She did everything a good mother of the 1970s was supposed to do: hosted slumber parties and taffy pulls, led Brownie troops and coffee klatches, carted us to gymnastics practices and baseball games and music lessons. She was an organizer, an event planner, a social butterfly; she was *involved.* She socialized with our friends' mothers, volunteered in our sports clubs, served on the PTA, and faithfully attended every parent-teacher conference.

Yet these images of Mom basking in the glow of radiant motherhood are counterbalanced by those featuring her tempestuous moods, short-tempered irritability, and anger that erupted into top-of-her-lungs shouting matches and slammed doors. She was notorious for her prickly insistence on keeping the house neat and being a poor sport in board game competition, once wiping a chess board clean of its pieces with an angry swipe of her arm. She bristled at bad table manners and grew positively inflamed at the sound of someone chewing their food. One night, during a suppertime argument—I don't recall now whether it was with me or Eric or my father or the whole lot of us—she chucked a stoneware dinner plate across the kitchen like a Frisbee, putting a dent in our gold refrigerator and spraying her hot dish and broccoli across the floor. Then, as she often did, she retreated into her bedroom, simmering in a hot silence while the rest of us cleaned the kitchen and tiptoed around the house. Occasionally, after her passions had cooled, she would apologize for her outbursts, but just as often she would emerge and carry on as if nothing had happened. In either case, the three of us breathed sighs of relief, happy to put the ugliness behind us.

Such contrasting behavior is certainly not unique to my mother, and Dad, Eric, and I were not innocents in these conflicts. Most people show the two sides of their Janus faces, especially in the most intimate and challenging relationship that is family. Our individual personalities, predilections, and psychologies affect our parenting practices, as do community standards, cultural traditions, and societal biases. But in addition to all of these, Mom had been a Booth girl, and I wonder how that identity and the experiences it entailed affected her subsequent parenting of me. How was her mothering style shaped by the shame, fear, relief, guilt, anger, and secrecy that surrounded her first experience of motherhood?

It may be impossible to answer that question with any confidence, to pull out individual threads from the weave that made her the mother she was, but there are questions that may yield insight. What did Mom do after she left Booth? How did she attempt to make a "fresh start," to get on with her life after letting her baby go? How and why did she live with her secret for more than three decades? What changes were brewing that eventually led to the unearthing of her secret past? The answers to these questions lie in the interplay between the events of her personal life and those of a generation of women who, like her, were struggling with the clean slate they were supposed to have earned by releasing their children. Mom was navigating the turbulent waters of motherhood and family responsibility at the same time that adoption researchers began studying the long-term effects of relinquishment and birthmothers began claiming the right to speak their own stories and reform adoption laws and practices.

Grief and Secrecy in Adoption

The first year of my baby's life, I was beset by doubts. I worried about her constantly, but no information could be had in those days of confidential adoption processes. I wanted her back, but to no avail. The people at the social service agency wouldn't even talk to me. I wondered what kind of parents had taken her, if they actually lived up to the description I'd been given. But, I had no right to ask, no right to care, no right to know. So, I worked. I found a job. I found an apartment. I returned to the University. And I kept my secret.[2]

Almost as soon as Mom returned home to Blaine, she tried to get away again, and not just across county or state lines. On February 18, 1961, she applied to the International Cooperation Administration, a federal agency that became the Agency for International Development later that year, for a one- to two-year secretarial job in Bangkok. She backed out of the position a month later, instead taking a job with Gold Bond Stamp Company, the start of what would become a long professional association with Minnesota businessman Curt Carlson. She went back to school and resumed her social life. She and her brother Earl joined the Minnesota Tip Toppers, a social club for tall men

Mom, at left, in the Miss Tall Minnesota competition, 1962.

In May 1962, shortly after starting as a secretary at Gold Bond's public relations office, Mom visited the construction site for the company's new home office and filed a humorous pictorial report: "I thought I'd go out and start breaking ground for more filing space."

and women. Once again, her slim, dark-haired beauty attracted attention, earning her second place in the 1962 Miss Tall Minnesota pageant and some modeling work at Gold Bond, where she worked first as a secretary and then as public relations coordinator.[3]

On the surface, at least, it appeared as if Mom was indeed picking up where she'd left off, moving past the pain and shame surrounding her unwed pregnancy. But, as she attested those many years later, thoughts of her baby were never far from her mind. Her busy-ness concealed a disquiet that grew from an ambiguous loss, her child disappeared but not dead, her motherhood disrupted but not recognized, her grief acute but invisible. No condolences were offered, no kindly gestures, no ceremonies or rituals or sympathy cards.

So Mom and many other women who had surrendered their babies—especially those who had felt the most powerless—buried the entire experience. An expanding body of literature describes their experiences. They masked it with achievement and success and doing, doing, doing or with withdrawal and self-medicating and self-sabotage. Some sought solace in a series of unsatisfying relationships, others in hurried marriages, still others in isolation. They thrilled at the prospect and arrival of more children or shuddered at the very thought. Some dwelled in anger, some in guilt, some in depression. Grief settled in their bodies, seeping out in headaches and infections and illness. It complicated already-complicated relationships with their parents, strained their marriages, loomed over their subsequent children. They ruminated about their lost kids, fantasized about them, sent love and prayers and regrets into the cosmos in hopes that they would land in a faraway crib or be carried on the breeze riffling a child's hair.[4]

For a good number of years, they did all this out of view of the professionals who had studied and scrutinized and counseled them when they were pregnant. It wasn't until the early 1970s, with the launch of the Adoption Research Project, that researchers began asking about these women's postrelinquishment experiences. A resulting report, issued in 1978, described birthparents as "existing on two levels. They are functioning well within an existing marriage or family, but they harbor deep, unresolved feelings and sharp memories of the bearing and the relinquishing of a child." Most therapists were unschooled in understanding the long-term effects of adoption, especially on birthmothers, so they provided little guidance to a woman seeking help in managing symptoms she herself may not have linked to her experience of lost motherhood. Mary, one of the women I interviewed, had been seeing a therapist for nearly ten years before she mustered the courage to divulge the fact that she had surrendered a child decades earlier. Once they had released their babies, women like Mom and Mary were left to manage their profound loss in profound isolation.[5]

If the loss of her baby weren't enough, circumstances at home likely deepened Mom's distress during this time. Mom's younger sister Diane graduated from high school in the spring of 1961, then disappeared with a man of dubious character, whom she had met at a traveling carnival. My grandmother, distraught at the prospect of another family upheaval, eventually tracked down Diane and tried to get her to return home, relenting only when presented with the couple's marriage certificate. The union didn't last long, however. The "no-good guy"—Diane's words—disappeared again shortly after Diane got pregnant; as with Jack, that was the last anybody ever saw of him. Pregnant Diane moved back to the house on Tyler Street and stayed there until she delivered her baby, a girl, in April 1962. Though she was not, technically, an unwed mother, Diane was a single mother, one made so first by abandonment and then by divorce. For five years, until she married the man who would give her child his name, she raised her daughter in my grandparents' house with their assistance.[6]

Two daughters, two scandals.

Two babies, two absconding fathers.

One baby lost, one baby kept.

"How hard that must have been on your mother," Diane said to me years later.

Even if my grandparents welcomed Diane and her baby because they could not bear the thought of losing another grandchild, the situation must have exacerbated whatever tensions or conflict had already existed between Mom and her mother. It must have been salt in Mom's unacknowledged wounds and made worse the realization she had been excised completely from her daughter's life. Mom didn't approach the adoption agency for information about Lynette because, as she wrote later, "they wouldn't have talked to me anyway. Adoption laws were strict and secretive in those days."[7]

That they were. By the time Mom released her baby girl in 1961, most adoption records were secret and confidential, which meant that even those directly involved in an adoption had to get a court order to obtain information about their own cases. In Minnesota in the early 1960s, this applied to two of the three main sources of information about any adoption case: adoptees' birth certificates and court records of adoption hearings. Once the court had finalized the adoption of Mom's baby, the state issued a new birth certificate in Lynette's new name with her adopters listed as parents of record. The original birth certificate (OBC) with Mom's name was sealed away in the tightly controlled archives of the Minnesota Department of Welfare, along with "all papers pertaining to the new certificate of birth," a policy established by state law in 1939. Closing these birth records meant that Mom could not access any information about her child's new identity and that Lynette, or whoever she had become, could not access any information about her own previous identity.[8]

If Mom had attempted to learn something of her daughter's placement from court records, the second major source of information about adoption cases, she would have faced a similar firewall. The 1917 Children's Code laid the groundwork for limiting access to adoption court records by closing them to *public* view, but in 1945 state law extended the prohibition even to members of the triad. No one—not Mom, not Lynette, not Lynette's new parents—could view "files and records of the court in adoption proceedings" without a court order.[9]

The only hope Mom may have had in obtaining information about Lynette's whereabouts or well-being would have lain with the adoption agency, the third major source of adoption records. Laws that limited access to birth and court records had said nothing about agency records, thus leaving decisions about what information to disclose to whom to the discretion of agency social workers. A long period of relatively liberal disclosure practices began to change after World War II as social workers started tightening control over information about adoptions. In an era when childless couples often turned to private networks to find adoptable children, social workers extended the promise of secrecy to attract unwed mothers and adopters to agencies run by professionals, the former ostensibly wishing to avoid revealing herself publicly, the latter hoping to avoid messy entanglements with natural mothers who might compete for their children's loyalty. Lynette's new parents had likely been given some basic, nonidentifying family and social history about Mom, but if Mom had attempted to learn anything about her baby's well-being or whereabouts, Patricia Peart, her Anoka County adoption caseworker, would likely have offered only general reassurances at best. In 1982, Minnesota law sealed adoption agency records as well, making it impossible for any member of the triad to access any of the three major kinds of adoption records without a court order.[10]

Some of the same factors that accounted for the postwar shift in approach to unwed mothers and their "illegitimate" offspring helped turn the tide toward secrecy in managing adoption case records. These included increasing numbers of younger single pregnant women from the middle class whose reputations would be ruined by the taint of illegitimacy; the influence of a popular psychoanalytic theory that cast adoptees' and adoptive parents' curiosity about birthparents as pathological and abnormal; and professional social work standards that, in this case, emphasized client confidentiality. These combined forces led some social workers to withhold case records or even to provide falsified, sanitized information, whether to shield adoptive families from difficult truths about the children's families of origin or to mollify birthmothers' doubts about having let their children go. Ann Fessler reported that a number of women she interviewed eventually learned that agencies had provided "trumped-up" portrayals of the families waiting to adopt their children.[11]

So Mom made her fresh start, her secret guarded by law and custom, her wonderings about her first daughter unsated.

First Comes Love, Then Comes Marriage . . .

There was one person with whom she shared her secret, however: a short, dark-haired man she met in an evening French class at the University of Minnesota in the fall of 1961. A Finn born and raised in Brooklyn, New York, Matti (shortened to the Americanized Matt) Wikstrom had moved to Minneapolis with his older brother to study political science at the university and to be near friends. Mom and Earl were socializing with their fellow tall folk in the Tip Toppers club, but my father was too short to be part of that scene. At five foot ten, Mom had a good three inches on him, but Dad was not cowed by Mom's superior height. He was smart and athletic, conservative in behavior but liberal in kindness. Though it would later become somewhat of a sticking point, his straitlaced lifestyle—he didn't drink or party and believed in saving sex for marriage—held a certain appeal for Mom at the time, her life having been upended by those behaviors. "Matt . . . was always neat, pressed down, compact," Mom wrote in 1995. "His clothes smelled like fresh air and sunshine, and that's what he was like to me, coming off a period in my life when I had been in too many smoky rooms with too many smoky people." Dad was a reliable man with a bright future and deep adoration for Mom, one he proclaimed frequently and unselfconsciously. "Sharon," he wrote her from Brooklyn on Christmas

Mom and Dad are married, 1963; Mom's mother, Thelma (Iverson) Moore, and grandmother Carrie (Waller) Iverson at left. Dad's mother, Laina (Hokkanen) Wikstrom, is at right.

Day 1962, "I haven't been able to tell you lately that I love you. But I do, and most certainly." Then, a day later in another letter, "I miss you, I love you. . . . 6 words sums up all."[12]

I don't know how or when my mother told my father about her first baby, but the revelation did not diminish his commitment to her. On July 19, 1963, Sharon Moore became Sharon Wikstrom.[13]

Thus began a tumultuous but sturdy thirty-three-year marriage that eventually made Mom a legitimate, socially sanctioned mother of two.

It could have gone like this:

They arrive at the hospital, she in contracting waves of pain and ambivalent anticipation, he in solicitous excitement. You're doing great, Sharon, he says. You are as beautiful as ever, Sharon, he says. Good luck, and I'll see you and our baby soon. I love you.

She moans softly, not wishing to call undue attention to herself. She is polite to the nurse who wheels her away from her happy husband. She should be—is—glad for his presence, grateful that he was there in the dark hours of the morning when her labor began. And yet she breathes a guilty sigh of relief at leaving behind his eagerness, his adoration.

The walls of this delivery room are a clean, sterile white.

Breathe, breathe, the nurse says. (*Breathe, breathe, another nurse once said.*)

Now push, the doctor says.

She does, and it is done, and she has her baby in her arms, her husband by her side, her parents looking on.

The nurse congratulates her, the doctor shakes her husband's hand, her father beams with pride, her mother coos at the baby.

More visitors come, her sisters and brothers and her husband's brothers, aunts and uncles and friends. Good cheer and love in abundance. Delighted chuckles at a big, bald-headed baby. Imagine that, they say, becoming a mother on Mother's Day. What good fortune.

She is exhausted, and relieved, and bewildered.

I was already a mother, she thinks, and she closes off a tiny part of her heart to this new baby, holding it in reserve for her other, her lost baby.[14]

Or, it could have gone like this:

She and her husband hold hands until the nurse wheels her away. Good luck, he says. I'll be here, he says. I love you, he says. I love you, too, she says. Come soon, she says.

When it is over, she welcomes her husband's embrace, shares in his wonder at their big, bald baby girl. She warms at her father's instant adoration of his granddaughter, the joy in her mother's eyes.

She absorbs her visitors' goodwill, feels it filling a mysterious cavern inside her. Yes, she says, it is so wonderful to become a mother on Mother's Day. I am so happy she is here, she says. My daughter, she says, and she opens her heart to her baby, believing herself complete.

But the body knows.

Later, in 2001, Mom wrote me a letter telling the story of my birth:

> *You were born at 5:00 A.M. at the Unity Hospital in Fridley. It was a bright blue day in May, and [you] came into this world without too much pain and with a great deal of anticipation. Your dad was so proud he nearly burst the buttons on his shirt. . . .*
>
> *We brought you home to our apartment and to a whole raft of eager relatives, my dad and mom chief among them. Everyone doted on you from the very first day of your existence. I, on the other hand, was overwhelmed by you and your baby needs. The fun times when you'd cuddle up or smile back at me or splash around in your bath were matched minute for minute by the need to constantly supervise you, to stay up with you late at night, to figure out how to handle a constant and dependent companion when I'd been an independent person for 23 years.*[15]

However ambivalent or excited Mom had been to become a mother, it was a tough adjustment for her. The work life she had enjoyed, the studies she

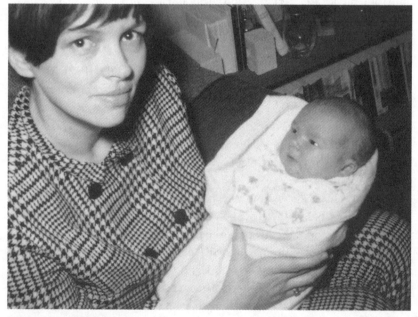

Mom and me, 1968.

had resumed, the independence she had relished all gave way to a forced deference to someone else's needs. She and Dad bought a house in Crystal, a suburb northwest of downtown Minneapolis, and struggled to get by on one income. Dad needed their only car to get to and from the university, where he was completing his master's degree in public administration and working in the Office of International Programs, leaving Mom to build a life for herself in the neighborhood, one that she initially accepted only begrudgingly. "I made friends with all the other young mothers in the neighborhood, but the conversation about cleaning aids and baby formulas and husbandly antics bored me to death, that and the constant competition and comparison of our offspring and their accomplishments."[16]

Over the next couple of years, however, as I became more independent and she more comfortable in her routine, she began to enjoy the rhythms of life, especially when she and Dad bought a used car that afforded her more freedom. My brother Eric was born in June 1970, a blond-haired, blue-eyed, easygoing baby the opposite of me in every way but his even more commanding size (eleven pounds to my ten). She recalled the next several years as happy ones, filled with family gatherings and family outings and long summer afternoons at the Crystal pool. "I still love the smell of suntan lotion and chlorine and the noisy reverberations of kids laughing, lifeguards on the PA, and music from the loudspeakers under the hot summer sun," Mom wrote of these years. "Sometimes we'd stay until the sun started to go down in the western sky, and I'd watch the dappled waves, always making sure I could spot the two heads that belonged to you and Eric, and feel completely content with the world."[17]

These were good days for me, too. I remember those weekday visits to the pool with Mom and watching Dad's arms, strong and tan, cut through those dappled waves when he joined us on the weekends. The hard times would surface soon enough, but through the mid-1970s, my life was tranquil and happy. There was special excitement afoot in 1976, when our family traveled with Dad's siblings and their families to the Summer Olympics in Montreal. Just over a month after we returned home, Mom had some excitement of her own: an appearance on Phil Donahue's talk show.

Mom had taken on some part-time, at-home typing and editing work for author Arlene Rossen Cardozo, who was making a name for herself by challenging what she saw as the antifamily tenets of the feminist movement while drawing on its ideas about choice and equality. By the time Mom connected with her, she was working on a book called *Woman at Home,* which sought to validate homemaking and mothering as a legitimate choice for women who wanted to be neither Friedan's discontented housewives nor the overburdened "Superwomen" combining career and family. The Woman at Home could cultivate her interests while taking care of children by "banking" her specialty training—using it to generate part-time work that could be completed at home while her children were small, then graduating to part-time work outside the home while children were in school, and finally, perhaps, to full-time work once children left home. When Cardozo was invited to appear on *Donahue,* she invited Mom and two of Mom's friends to join her as exemplars of the Woman at Home ideal. Among the talents Mom had been nurturing while she stayed home to mind me and Eric was composing music for, and playing, the piano. There she was, then, on September 19, 1976, playing one of her compositions on national television.[18]

Birthmothers Make News

Nearly three years later, Mom had leapfrogged ahead of the Woman at Home timeline and taken a full-time job at Carlson Companies to help support the family while Dad pursued his doctorate in educational administration at the University of Minnesota. So it's not likely that she was at home at nine o'clock on a morning in June 1979 to watch another guest on Donahue's show who might have captured her attention.

Sitting by herself on a stage, Lee Campbell listened as Donahue opened the show by taking an applause poll to see how many in the audience agreed that a woman who had surrendered a child for adoption should have the opportunity to find out what had happened to that child. A healthy round of applause ensued. Then he posed a counter position: "Once you surrender a baby for adoption, once you give the baby up, make that decision, sign the papers, that's it. You should stay out of that child's life forever." Another round of slightly heartier applause, with one woman in the audience explaining that "You [birthmothers] tried to do a good thing by giving them away because you thought you couldn't take care of them, now they're all set in their life. Why try to mess it up now?" Another woman disagreed: "I feel that a child just naturally wants to, would be interested in their parent," and, once grown, should be able to reconnect with their mother if both agreed to the arrangement.[19]

Donahue then introduced Lee Campbell and let her tell her story. In

1962, she became pregnant at seventeen, was sent to a home for unwed mothers, and surrendered her baby boy for adoption. She buried the experience so deeply she didn't think about it for ten years, during which time she married and had two more kids. Then, a movie about an adoptee searching for birthparents prompted her to look for her son. Their eventual reunion, she said, brought growth and healing for both of them as well as for her son's adoptive parents and her own husband and children.

Campbell's story about the difficulties surrounding her unwed pregnancy wasn't new to the legions of women like Mom who had lived it themselves, but it was new to many in the viewing audience who hadn't given much thought to the long-term effects of the "best solution" on relinquishing mothers. Her search for and reunion with her adopted-away son was new even to many birthmothers, however, who had believed they were consigned to a lifetime of unfulfilled wondering about their children. And it was new to hear a woman talk about it all so openly, something Campbell had begun doing three years earlier, in 1976, when she founded Concerned United Birthparents (CUB).[20]

Campbell had been attending meetings of the Adoptees' Liberty Movement Association (ALMA), a search-and-reunion organization established by Florence Fisher in 1971, when she decided it was time to bring birthparents out of the shadows of adoption. She began reaching out to other invisible mothers in the Boston area, and in 1976 they formed CUB as a support and advocacy organization for birthparents who had been disenfranchised by secretive, shame-based adoption practices. From the beginning, CUB welcomed all members of the triad and both birthmothers and birthfathers, but its membership and image have been associated primarily with birthmothers. It was CUB that promoted the term "birthparent" rather than "biological" or "natural" parent and used "surrender" to convey the emotional experience of mothers' "decision" to have their children adopted. Both ALMA and CUB drew on the "rights revolution" of the 1960s in creating assertive political identities for once-stigmatized communities and demanding access to sealed information to which they believed they were entitled.[21]

By the time Campbell told her story on *Donahue* in 1979, CUB had established footholds in sixteen other locations; three years later, forty CUB chapters were meeting across the country. The Minnesota chapter had convened in the waning days of 1977 after four birthmothers attended a meeting at Children's Home Society to learn about a new Minnesota law governing access to adoptees' original birth certificates. One of them, Patty O'Gorman, spoke at the meeting about her longstanding desire to form a support group for birthparents. After the meeting drew to a close, three other birthmothers—Deanna Mramor, Kristin Kunzman, and Mary Jo Penne—met with O'Gorman to share their stories and swap ideas for how they might help reform the "laws, policies, and practices that detract from the sensitive, respectful process that Adoption is *supposed* to be!" They held their first meeting on December 11, 1977, and a month later, CUB Minnesota (CUB-MN) declared that its goals were to "fulfill the needs of birthparents individually" and "to humanize the adoption process and strive to eliminate the secretiveness and negativism surrounding birthparents culturally." As Deanna Mramor put it years later, the group's primary function was to "support each other [and] to talk," a revolutionary act given the pressures to remain silent. By the end of 1978, CUB-MN listed twenty-one full birthparent members (including two men), two auxiliary members, and eight nonmember supporters, one of whom—Sandy Sperrazza—would go on to play a major role in CUB-MN and Mom's story.[22]

In order to humanize the adoption process, CUB-MN had to humanize birthmothers. It did so by establishing a speakers' bureau that sent birthparents (mostly birthmothers) to speak at schools, parent groups, and adoption agencies, and by cultivating local and national media attention. In 1979, CUB-MN members were featured in a multipart article in the Minneapolis papers, on KSTP-TV's *Twin Cities Today,* and at meetings of adoptive parent groups. Joan Grabe of CUB-MN was in the studio the day Lee Campbell appeared on the *Phil Donahue Show,* and she talked about her own experiences during the audience participation segment. In the summer of 1980, Patty O'Gorman made the pages of both *Good Housekeeping* and *Woman's Day.* That November, CUB-MN's coordinator, Pam Bolduc, described adoption as "degrading" for birthmothers in a letter to the editor of the *Minneapolis Star,* generating a spirited defense of more current adoption practices in the paper's opinion pages for the next several weeks.[23]

These women—Bolduc, O'Gorman, Grabe, Mramor—didn't want to disrupt their children's families. "Those good people *are* my daughters' parents," O'Gorman (who was also an adoptive mother) told *Woman's Day.* They did want to know, however, that their children were all right. They wanted their children to know that they had not abandoned them, and they wanted to allow for the possibility of contact. They wanted the public to see beyond the stereotype of birthmothers as "either promiscuous or dumb." Most of all, they wanted to dispel the fallacy underlying the "best solution" by giving voice to the lingering grief endured by birthmothers. "Everybody wants to pretend that adoption is a process that ends on Decree Day, happily ever after for all," Gail Hanssen of the national CUB office wrote to CUB-MN's Patty O'Gorman in 1978. "Nobody wants to (God forbid) tell [adopted kids] that we love them still, that for us adoption is never finished." On April 11, 1984, in the middle of Minnesota's newly declared "Birthparent Week," the theme of CUB-MN's open meeting was "Birthparents Care Forever."[24]

Most of these efforts focused on the experiences of white birthmothers, but other activists called attention to the distinct harms caused by transracial adoption. Critics of the practice came to view it as another expression of white power and privilege. Babies taken from structurally disadvantaged communities to grow up in white middle-class families lost not just their personal identity but the connection to their cultural heritage as well, thus placing the future of those cultures at risk at the same time. In 1972, the National Association of Black Social Workers (NABSW) took a "vehement stand against the placement of Black children in white homes for any reason." The organization challenged the assimilationist goals of "color-blind" adoptive placements, arguing instead that "ethnicity" was a vital component of physical, psychological, and cultural identity and that Black families were naturally equipped to fulfill Black children's needs in ways that white families never would be. Useful adoption reform, in the eyes of NABSW, should therefore focus on making the adoption process more accessible to African Americans and redefining the concept of "suitable" homes and families. Although some Black leaders denounced the NABSW's stance against transracial adoption as harmful and regressive, others applauded it for championing the rights of Black mothers who had lost children to the child welfare system. In any case, the statement contributed to a significant decline in the numbers of Black children adopted by white parents.[25]

Similarly, Indigenous activists, social workers, and their white allies in the Association on American Indian Affairs took aim at transracial adoption of Native children beginning in the 1960s. Native American mothers who had lost their children to foster care or adoption played a central role in these efforts as they shared heartbreaking and horrifying stories about the forcible removal of their children in lawsuits, hearings, and media stories. Their activism to restore Indigenous families reflected the broader concerns of the movement for self-determination among Native Americans and of Native women specifically. They acknowledged the real struggles that many Native families faced, but argued that they originated in federal Indian policy rather than inherent cultural defects and that they were best addressed by providing support for parents, families, and tribes rather than removing kids and placing them with white families. The result of this decade-long campaign was the 1978 Indian Child Welfare Act, which gave tribes a say in the disposition of child welfare cases and made it official policy across the country to place Indian children in Indian homes—ideally in their extended family or tribal community—with adoption by white parents considered an option of last resort.[26]

Mom may not have been attuned to the debates surrounding transracial adoption, but I imagine she was cognizant of the increasing visibility of white birthmothers throughout the 1970s and early 1980s even if, as far as I can tell, she had no contact with CUB until after my sister found her in 1994. She may not have been following developments in Minnesota law regarding adoption and birth records, but Mom and Dad took the Minneapolis newspaper, so it stands to reason that she saw articles about CUB and ALMA. She may have been too depleted by her responsibilities as a new mother to read the two-part story about adoption that appeared in *Life* magazine in June 1968, just a month after I was born, but I'm almost certain it was in our house. Dad had a voracious appetite for such news magazines, including *Life*. He had probably been drawn to the main focus of the issue— the assassination of Robert Kennedy—but maybe Mom read the eight-page article on adoption in the still of a long, dark night after her restless baby finally fell asleep.[27]

She must have felt these stirrings, these winds of change.

Change was afoot for Booth St. Paul, too.

A Fresh Start for Booth

In August 1971, the *Minneapolis Star* published a two-part series on how unwed mothers' increasing tendency to keep and raise their babies was, in the words of staff writer Joe Blade, "wreaking havoc on the adoption process." From 1966 through the first half of 1971, the percentage of single mothers who relinquished their babies had declined from 50 percent to 20 percent. Decreasing social stigma, laws protecting pregnant and parenting girls and women in school and at work, 1960s youth culture, and a skepticism about psychoanalytic explanations of single pregnancy had led to an imbalance of demand and supply in the adoption market once again, prompting local agencies to expand their search for "adoptable" children while contracting their definition of "acceptable" adopters.[28]

Blade pointed out another consequence of these changing social mores: a decline in occupancy at local maternity homes, including Booth Memorial Hospital. Although the controversial campaign to expand its facility had culminated in the opening of a new, million-dollar wing in 1969, Booth ran into trouble almost immediately thereafter. Occupancy had been declining for a number of years, a fact Booth administrator Major Mary White attributed to the disruption caused by the construction project. But in June 1970, a committee appointed by the Community Health and Welfare Planning Council of the Greater St. Paul Area reported that referral agencies were reluctant to send girls to Booth because of their concerns about insufficient staffing and outdated programming. It chided Booth for having proceeded with its expansion against the recommendation of the Metropolitan St. Paul Hospital Planning Council and suggested that Booth outsource all delivery services, expand its educational offerings beyond the high school level, and offer services for nonresidents. It recommended that the United Fund continue its current level of support of Booth for another year to allow for such adjustments.[29]

Unsurprisingly, Major White was not happy with the report. On July 16, 1970, she wrote to the president of the Greater St. Paul United Fund and Council to assure him that changes were already underway at Booth and to ask that the report be withheld from the news media until she and her colleagues could present "a more detailed statement of our comments." Nevertheless, on July 26, 1970, a headline in the *St. Paul Pioneer Press* blared "Booth Hospital Found Wanting After Study."[30]

On February 13, 1971, Booth closed its hospital facility and began sending all of its residents to the University of Minnesota hospital for delivery. It maintained ten beds for its maternity residence program, dedicating the other forty to a new program called the Brown House, which housed girls referred by the Ramsey County juvenile court and children in need of temporary shelter. White blamed Booth's failure to rebound on the negative publicity generated by the 1970 report, but also acknowledged that "cultural and social changes" had contributed to its problems. Two years later, on June 30, 1973, when its final six-month funding allocation expired, Booth ceased its unwed mother program altogether to concentrate exclusively on caring for a new generation of girls who, White told the *Pioneer Press,* "need help in turning themselves around and really coping with life." Thus, like many such maternity homes across the country, Booth remade itself to meet the new needs of a new era. In 1974, Booth Memorial Hospital became the Salvation Army Booth Brown House.[31]

In its seventy-five years as a rescue home and maternity home and hospital, sixty of them on Como Avenue, Booth had served 13,500 unwed mothers.[32]

Parenting and Parkinson's

I don't know if Mom was aware of these changes or not, but she certainly had plenty of other things demanding her attention, not least of which was me and Eric. I didn't sense at the time, and don't see from my vantage point now, the overindulgence or overprotection that some birthmothers have described of their relationship with subsequent children. If anything, Mom tilted toward the other end of the parenting spectrum, more akin to the birthmothers who said they had difficulty attaching to their next babies or sank into depression after their arrival or guarded their intimacy. Mom was not one to express or display affection. She did not communicate her love in sweet words or tender hugs; Dad did that. Instead, it seemed she held me at emotional arm's length even as she performed the role of super-mom. I didn't feel this distancing as a lack, only as standard operating procedure in our family.[33]

The irritability and stoicism Mom exhibited may have been her nature or her family inheritance, but they may also have been her way of maintaining the precarious emotional balance she had established after losing one child and having two more. By 1978, however, these issues had taken a back seat to another walloping blow, one that would command Mom's attention and resources for the next eighteen years.

1978

Parkinson's disease, the doctor says.

She sits back in her chair, glances at her husband. They both stare at the doctor.

It explains the stiffness, the numbness, the dizziness, the doctor says.

They say nothing.

The doctor continues, using words they've never heard—progressive neurological disorder, dopamine, tremor, bradykinesia, levodopa.

What about the depression? she asks the doctor, thinking of the times she'd come home from work to find her husband sitting on the couch, silent and sullen. His unfinished dissertation. His trouble finding and keeping a job. His monthlong hospitalization at a mental health center.

Is that the Parkinson's, too?

Probably, the doctor says.

She feels guilty for having thought him lazy, overly concerned about phantom ailments. For the arguments about unwashed dishes and unmade suppers. For the resentment at his increasing reliance on her income. For, even now, worrying about her own future as much as his.

It will get worse, the doctor says. There is no cure.

She hears the doctor's words, but does not, cannot, really understand.[34] ●

Dad was forty-two years old when he was diagnosed with Parkinson's, Mom thirty-eight. His disease altered the course of their lives, our lives, in profound ways. Dad never completed his doctorate, instead taking a job sorting mail at the downtown Minneapolis Post Office, a position he would hold for ten years. Mom became the primary, then sole, breadwinner in our family, her career at Carlson Companies fueled in equal measure by talent, ambition, and necessity as my once athletic and sharp-witted father disappeared into his illness. He was either so stiff he could barely move or so medicated he could barely control his movements. He fell, forward and backward and sideways, bruising his head and his legs and his ribs. His temperament became as mercurial as Mom's, a function of both the disease and the drugs he took to control it. When his body moved more fluidly, his mood declined; when he was his usual kind and chipper self, he was trapped in a stiff, trembling, unstable body. He suffered hallucinations and paranoid thoughts. One night, I found Dad having a late-night bowl of cereal in the kitchen, talking to himself in an eerie, rhyming chatter. By the time I graduated high school in 1986, we were a family in disarray, carrying on the best we could.

Then, in 1989, Dad lost his driver's license and his job at the post office. Mom was working, Eric was in college, and I had moved out of the house by then, so Dad was at home alone during the day. Mom enrolled him in an adult day care program after she came home from work one day to find him sleeping on the couch as a forgotten pan smoldered on the still-lit gas stovetop. At first, he went one day a week, then three, then all five as he lost his ability to function independently at home, stymied by daily tasks such as turning on the television or brushing his teeth. One day, the shuttle that brought him home from day care left before he had entered the house. He fell on the driveway and, unable to get up, lay there until the neighbor came home and rushed to his assistance.

By this time, Mom had become director of corporate communications at Carlson. In the best of circumstances, she'd have been exhausted by the demands of her job. But it wasn't the best of circumstances, and her emotional and physical reserves were at an all-time low, as she recalled in 2001:

> It was hard to get up early, help him get dressed, sit him down at the kitchen table with his breakfast in front of him, and then rush to get dressed for my own work day. It was hard to be on call all the time when he couldn't get up out of a chair unaided, when he became incontinent, when even I couldn't understand what he was saying or what he wanted. . . . I was tense and overwhelmed.[35]

The "fresh start" that Mom had been promised in 1961, which led her to marry a man who smelled like sunshine, had, by 1989, evolved into the layered realities of a complicated life, one defined as much by my father's illness as by my mother's first pregnancy.

KAREN

Mom wasn't the only birthmother who found the "fresh start" promised by the "best solution" to be wanting. So did Karen.

Karen heard that I was looking for former Booth girls to interview and reached out to me in March 2017. Four months later, on a hot July day, I pulled into the driveway of her quiet suburban home. We sat at her dining room table and talked for more than an hour. She told me about her family, her pregnancy, her time at Booth, her labor and delivery. We had just started talking about her life after Booth when she suggested we take a break. She had prepared a lovely midmorning snack, fruit and bars and iced tea. We relaxed and ate and talked about other things. Then, appetites sated, legs stretched, and minds relaxed, we resumed the interview, Karen picking up where she had left off, much as she had tried to do after she left Booth without her son in 1962.[36]

* * *

Karen grew up in post–World War II north Minneapolis with two older brothers, a hardworking mother, and a "nice, easygoing" father with a drinking problem. When her mother could no longer tolerate the trouble alcohol brought, she put her husband out and raised the three kids by herself. She relocated the family to Brooklyn Center, then Northeast Minneapolis, pulling Karen from one high school to another. Karen was a good kid, involved in her school and her Lutheran church, but this uprooting disrupted Karen's life more than the alcohol ever had, contributing, she thinks, to the "not-so-great decisions" that ultimately led to her pregnancy. Still, she understands her mother's need to strike out on her own, find better work, earn her GED, establish some independence and security. And her mother offered nothing but sympathetic support when Karen got pregnant.

But that support could not take a public face. This was still the era when good girls didn't, so when Karen got pregnant at seventeen after a short relationship with a nineteen-year-old boy whose best pregnancy-prevention advice had been to "go home and take a bath," the story was that Karen had taken a job in Yellowstone National Park to earn money so she could pay off a debt. Never mind that there may have been jobs in Minneapolis that could have served the same function; never mind that this sudden employment interrupted her final year of high school; never mind that the story cast a thin veneer on reality. In 1962, it was better to tell a face-saving lie than admit the truth. "It was just a shameful, terrible thing at that time," Karen said. "You just didn't do that." Her baby's father disavowed his role in the situation and disappeared. In the spring of 1962, Karen disappeared into Booth.

Booth was not a "horrible experience" for Karen. She liked the Salvation Army staff and her Hennepin County social worker. She finished her high school coursework at Booth and strolled to the nearby store in the company of other pregnant girls, all of them wearing fake wedding rings. A couple of her trusted friends from high school, girls who knew her secret, would come and pick her up, drive her around town, share the latest gossip. Her mother would visit, too, and sometimes she would visit her mother at home, crouching down in the car as it approached the driveway, then sneaking from the garage into the house through the breezeway so that none of the neighbors would discover their deceit. Then, after a few weeks at Booth, Karen moved in with a kind family who paid pregnant girls to help with the ironing and the cooking and the childcare. She returned to Booth in August, just a couple of weeks before delivering her son in the sweltering, late-summer heat, the sounds of fairgoers' fun echoing in the distance.

Karen knew she could not keep her baby. The options for young women in midcentury America—even the well-behaved ones—were limited: secretary, teacher, or nurse if one must pursue work; wife and mother regardless. Marital pregnancy was often grounds for dismissal from employment; nonmarital pregnancy was grounds for public shaming. She couldn't go on the public dole having been raised in a "very anti-welfare" family. Keeping her son could have been "disastrous"; she wasn't ready to be a mother. Besides, said the social worker, she would have other babies, later, when she was married. Her best, her only option was to let him go. At Booth, she tried to be "the best possible person I could be in hopes that would help my son find a good home." She didn't name him or hold him, reserving those honors for the parents who would raise him. Karen left Booth without her son; the wilting flowers her mother had brought after his birth were a sad reminder of joy denied.

No one helped Karen prepare for life after Booth. "You walked out the door and there was nothing for you," she recalled. No hovering social workers, no concerned counselors. Nothing. "You will go on with your life and everything will be just fine." For a while, it seemed to be.

Just a few months after her son was born, Karen took a clerical job on the news floor at the *Minneapolis Star and Tribune*. She learned a lot, making the most of the opportunity to work with "well-educated people, interesting people." She also appreciated the fact that her boss had hired her despite her checkered past. The Yellowstone story had started to wear thin by the time Karen interviewed for the clerical job, and so, despite the admonitions to keep quiet and pretend it had never happened, she "broke down and started crying" and confessed the truth. "They hired me anyway," she said with a chuckle. But, for the most part, she held her tongue about her son.

In 1965, Karen married, eager to start a family under the proper circumstances this time. Seven years after that, when her husband admitted he did not want children, Karen divorced. Another lost future. One suicide attempt, then another, then counseling. Karen married again, had a miscarriage, started abusing alcohol, divorced again. Loss compounded by loss compounded by loss. But then she started going to Alchoholics Anonymous. She quit drinking. She was "getting healthier and feeling better" about herself. She was starting to come to terms with the idea that she would never have another baby when she met a "fantastic" man who had two teenage children. They married in 1983, and she became a stepmother. "My life changed for the better," she said. "It was a really good relationship, a good solid experience."

After her life had settled into stability, Karen initiated a search for her son, inspired by a story she saw on "*Donahue* or one of those shows." She started attending CUB meetings and listening to birthmothers talk about finding their adopted-away children, and she realized that she could look for her son, too. At first, she reached out to him through the agency that had facilitated his adoption. His response: not interested. Then she worked with a private searcher, learned her son's identity, and in 1988 sent him a letter directly. This time, he responded. "He wasn't really thrilled, but he was decent about it," Karen recalled.

For years, Karen and her son had a halting relationship by phone and letter. They never spoke in person. He refused to share photos of himself as a child. Once, though, a sympathetic acquaintance told Karen to come to a church function that her son would be attending; Karen stood at the back of the room, incognito, absorbing her first glimpse of her son since 1962. When Karen heard that he was to graduate from the seminary, she and her mother attended the public ceremony, never making themselves known. She learned about happenings in his life—his first assignment as a pastor, his wedding—from others, friends and mutual acquaintances. Frayed by his repeated rebuffs of her attempts to know him, Karen eventually wrote him a letter to tell him she was "stepping away" but would be open to further contact should he desire it.

Any chance for more than a distant relationship with her son came to a crushing halt in 1995, however, when he was killed in a car accident. Karen learned about it from a friend who saw the obituary in the paper. Her son and his family had been living out of state at the time, but there was a memorial service at his hometown church in Minnesota. Karen went with a friend, once again slipping in without making her presence known. "I didn't want to cause any grief," she said. "I know it was such a horrible time for everybody anyway." It was there, at her son's funeral, that she first saw any photographs of him as a little boy. Loss compounded by loss, but this time, a gain, too: after the service, Karen's son's wife reached out and let her into her and her two daughters'—Karen's biological grandchildren's—lives. Her real relationship to the girls was concealed for the first few years they were in contact in deference to her son's parents, who wanted nothing to do with Karen, but now all is in the open. She sees in her granddaughters reflections of herself. "Here I lost him, but I gained all these other things," she said.

What does it all come to? What sense can be made of these experiences of repeated loss and uneasy reunion, of secrecy and revelation, of shame and restoration? "I think it makes me a pretty tolerant person and makes me aware that we never know what other people are experiencing," said Karen, "and so I hesitate to make judgments about what people are doing in their lives." If she feels lingering disgust with her son's father, who continues to deny his paternity, she harbors no particular ill will toward those who shepherded her through her pregnancy—her mother, her social worker, the staff at Booth. She understands that, given the times, people did what they thought best, for her and her baby. Still, she says, good intentions "can demolish a lot of people's lives and families."

As for adoption, Karen believes the records should be open and available. She doesn't buy the argument that keeping them sealed protects birthmothers' privacy. "Probably 85 to 95 percent of women are certainly willing to share their information . . . or would really desire to have a reunion with their children," she insisted. "I'm not anti-adoption, but I would like to see those things changed. I think it's healthier if they could be more open and not lock people out. I mean, I left [Booth] thinking I would never be able to know what ever even happened to my son and I didn't—until he was twenty-six years of age—know what happened to him or what his life had been like." ■

> *I knew I was too immature to give my child a home, much less the kind of home I wanted her to have. In my heart, I kept the faith that she would have everything with adopted parents, everything that I, as a weak and worthless girl, could not give her. I didn't realize for many years that she might have wanted me anyway, in spite of all my short-comings.*[37]

For more than thirty years after she left Booth without her baby, Mom did her best to put her past behind her, focusing on her marriage, her career, her other two kids. Still, thoughts of the baby girl she had relinquished bubbled to the surface, especially in the early post-Booth years, family outings to Como Zoo stirring images of a cold January spent in a maternity home on Como Avenue in 1961, the smell of hot exhaust triggering nausea reminiscent of a bus ride down Central Avenue in 1960. In later years, my father's illness consumed most of her energy. In her darkest moments, she gave in to bitterness and regret, tormenting herself with imponderable what-ifs. What if she hadn't fallen for an unworthy man in 1960? What if she had kept her baby, raised her in California or in Minneapolis? What if she hadn't married a man so filled with promise but so doomed to peril? What if the twin engines of her emotional turbulence had never started spinning?

But what if, in their eventual convergence, these two definitive experiences would provide her a measure of grace she could never have imagined?

I barely recognize myself in this new life.

Steve is new to parenting, too, but he returns to work after we get home, bridging the Before Tu and After Tu eras.

My new life is immersive and isolating. I am not unhappy, quite, but I feel like a stranger in my own skin. The rhythm and content of my days are not my own. I wake when Tu rises, eat when he eats, rest when he naps. Some things are pleasant surprises—that I find Elmo adorable, that I can walk the dog and push a stroller at the same time, that I can do this at all. There are times when I am overcome with an aching, physical love for this little boy who won't take a nap unless I drive loops around the city, who loves reading *Five Little Monkeys* and *Over the Moon,* who falls asleep in the sled as I drag it through foot-deep snow on the golf course, chin on chest, one mittened hand hanging over the edge tracing a winding trail behind us.

In the spring, I agree to teach a weekend class in hopes that it will anchor me to my former self. Tu starts attending a preschool three days a week. He is sociable, used to being around other kids from his earliest days. He makes no protest. I am relieved.

I wonder if I am having problems with attachment.

What would Tu's Vietnam mama think if she knew of my unease?

We meet with the social worker to discuss Tu's adjustment to his new life. We write reports for our agency that are then translated into Vietnamese and sent to a care center in Ben Tre. We read books about Vietnam and adoption and look at photos from the time we became a family and tell Tu his adoption story over and over. We spend three days at culture camp surrounded by families who look like ours to balance the days we are surrounded by families who don't. We try to address Tu's needs as a toddler, as an adopted toddler, as a transracially, transnationally adopted toddler.

It is overwhelming, and I am falling short in every way. I have no idea how to do this, despite the training and reading and support groups. I marvel, in alternating bouts of envy and suspicion, at other families who seem to embrace it all with such ease.

Tu seems happy and healthy.

He is small on the American growth charts, but progressing. He likes rice and fruit and sweets. He has a hard time falling and staying asleep, but it's getting better. He is outgoing and friendly.

And yet, there are signs, evidence of the loss this little boy has suffered. He is not prone to fits of bad humor, but he occasionally slips away into a terror tantrum. He cries, then sobs, then wails and thrashes, his eyes trained on sights we cannot see, his ears longing for words we cannot speak, his body aching for a touch we cannot provide.

We can only bear witness.

We can only create space for his pain.

We can only hold him tight with love, aware of its insufficiency.

I write letters to Tu's Vietnam mama, the woman who brought this boy into the world.

I tell her about him, about who he is becoming, about his life so far away from hers.

I store them on my computer in hopes that, one day, we will know where to send them.

Mom absorbs Tu into her life wholeheartedly, becomes central to ours. She feeds him, bathes him, plays with him, indulges him. She lives just a few miles from us in St. Paul now, eleven years into her widowhood, and has stocked her house with toy cars and diapers and children's books and sippy cups. She picks him up from preschool, takes him to the zoo and the beach and the mall and the museum. She brings him to his first movie (*Alvin and the Chipmunks*), helps him make his first batch of cookies (chocolate chip), gives him his first taste of pop (Diet Coke). She does all this in between her days at work, now winnowed down to three, now at the University of Minnesota.

This woman, who worried about being able to form a bond with her new grandchild.

This woman, who once turned up her nose at the drudgery of childcare.

This woman, who once lost a baby to adoption.

This woman has become an extraordinary grandmother to another woman's lost baby.

And this is how I do it. This is how I survive these long, unsettling months, how I adjust to my new life.

My mother mothers me into motherhood.

I ask Mom if she would be willing to write Tu a letter—for later and for him alone, birthmother to adoptee—that might help answer questions he is too young to imagine now but that his body is already asking.

She agrees.

7
REUNITED

Matt was sick for a long time with Parkinson's disease. Two years before he died, Lynette came into our lives. She was 33 years old, and I was 54. She was beautiful, with burnished blonde hair and blue eyes, just like our son Eric's. She was small and slender, just like our daughter Kimberly. Her adoptive parents had never called her Lynette, but renamed her Kimberly, never dreaming that she would have a half-sister who would be given the same name seven years later.[1]

NINETEEN NINETY-FOUR was a watershed year for Mom. She had spent much of the previous fifteen years shouldering her considerable responsibilities at work, managing my father's doctor's appointments and medications, and assuming the role of caregiver and household director as my father lost his ability to feed, clothe, and bathe himself; to walk without assistance; and to communicate intelligibly. One morning, as he sat at the kitchen table trying to eat the breakfast Mom had set out for him, Dad tipped over in his chair and smacked his head on the floor. Mom could barely help him up in his limp and disoriented state. She finally had to admit that he needed more care than she and adult day care could provide. In October 1994, Mom made the painful decision to admit my father to North Ridge Care Center in New Hope.[2]

As Mom faced the reality that the nursing home was yet another step toward a final loss, she demonstrated a new tenderness toward my father. She became more patient, more willingly solicitous of his needs. She didn't share many of her internal struggles with me, so I hadn't known that she was in therapy and taking antidepressants until she told me one day on our way to visit Dad. She also offered a rare nugget of advice. People too often mistake romance for love, she said, confusing starry-eyed, butterflies-in-the-stomach sensations with the clear-eyed, calm-headed commitment that is the love that sustains a marriage.

Mom probably shared these insights that day not just to tell me something about herself, but to tell me something about myself. Steve and I had married in June 1990. Mom and Dad both rallied to the occasion: he over-medicated and agitated but physically able to walk me down the aisle, she doing her best to enjoy the day while keeping an eye on him. Mom had witnessed my own uneasy transition into marriage and saw in my often-cranky temperament echoes of her own. Though she didn't say it outright, she likely was trying to spare me the years of struggle, internal and external, that she had endured. Her words have stayed with me, but the example she set made an even greater impression. For the last eighteen months of my father's life, Mom was at the nursing home with him nearly every night. She would go home after work, change clothes, grab a quick bite to eat, then spend the evening in the company of her fifty-eight-year-old husband and the eighty-something-year-olds who surrounded him in the dementia ward. She tended to his physical needs; she played host to the friends and family who stopped by, attempting to translate Dad's confused mumbles into some sort of conversation; she made his half of the room he shared with another slipping-away man as comfortable and familiar as possible. She got to know the staff and the residents and the residents' families. In order to execute her physical caregiving duties to the fullest, she even took the official nurses' aide training course, stopping just short of completing the certification exam. Placing him in a nursing home wasn't an abrogation of my mother's commitment to my father; it was an expression of it.

The year Mom seemed to settle into herself was also the year her first daughter came back into her life. One closed door from her long-ago past was being pried open just as the door to her immediate past seemed to be swinging shut. Mom's reunion with Kim answered some long-standing questions—What had become of her daughter? Had she enjoyed the good life promised by the "best solution"?—but it raised new ones as well. What shape would their relationship now take? How would Kim be integrated into Mom's life and vice versa? How would reunion affect their other family relationships? Kim's return transformed Mom's private, individual past into our family's public, shared future, a reminder that the effects of adoption extend far beyond the limits of the triad. Though I was witness to and participant in Mom's reunion with Kim, I still wonder: was it enough to salve the wounds Mom had suffered in silence for so long?

LATE JUNE–EARLY JULY 1994

The phone rings, but she's tired, worn too thin to have a friendly chat or fend off a salesperson. She lets the answering machine pick it up.

She escorts her husband to the bedroom, helps him change clothes, gives him his last pills of the evening. She removes his dentures, watches his lips and cheeks cave in around his gums. He lies back uneasily, stiffly, and she hoists his legs up and around so his head can find the pillow. His eyes are already closed.

She goes to the kitchen, retrieves a piece of store-bought cake from the fridge, and settles in front of the TV to relish the momentary peace, knowing her husband will wake once, twice, three times in the night, calling out for help. She falls asleep, the half-finished dessert on a plate on her lap.

She doesn't think to check the answering machine until a couple of days later. It's a voice she doesn't recognize, an old classmate wanting to catch up. She deletes it without taking down the woman's phone number. She doesn't have room for anyone else.

Then, near the end of the long Fourth of July weekend, there's another blinking light on the answering machine. She erases a message from a credit card company, makes a note to return a call to her sister. She's about to delete the next message from someone named Sandy, barely noting that the voice is the same one from the message she deleted a few days ago.

Then, her heart nearly stops.

Lynette is in town, Sandy says on the recording. She'd like to see you. ●

Lynette's Return, or Meeting Kim Sr.

Mom was notorious for not answering her phone. "Just because someone wants to talk to me," she would say, "doesn't mean that I have to talk to them." But she had been waiting a lifetime for this call. She called Sandy back right away.

Sandy explained that she was not, in fact, an old classmate, but had been hired by Kim, the formerly and briefly named Lynette, to search for Mom. A clerical error on some long-ago paperwork, a surname that had escaped the clerk's black redacting marker, led to a family obituary, which led to Mom. When the classmate ruse failed to evoke a response from Mom, Sandy decided the only way to capture Mom's attention was by referring to Lynette. Now that she finally had Mom on the phone, Sandy said that Kim would very much like to communicate with her birthmother. Would Mom be open to that?

Mom told Sandy that yes, of course she wanted to talk to her daughter. After another exchange of voice messages, back and forth among the three women, Mom called Kim one morning in July.

For the first time in more than three decades, Mom heard her first daughter's voice, not the wail of an infant, but the voice of a grown woman.

She learned that her daughter had had a good life.

She learned that her daughter had been raised as an only child by loving parents.

She learned that her daughter lived with her second husband in a suburb outside of Detroit.

She learned that her daughter and her husband were leaving for North Dakota the next day and would be driving through Minneapolis.

She learned that she would be meeting her long-lost daughter within forty-eight hours.[3]

Mom was both eager and anxious to meet Kim face-to-face. "My biggest fear," she wrote later, "was that she would be disappointed in me. I had become a white-haired, work-roughened, plain woman, and my chronically ill husband had absorbed most of my strength and resources." She tried to quiet such worries by staying busy. She cleaned the house, got groceries, gathered family photos, and created a family tree so that Kim would know her history, her people.[4]

When Kim and her husband pulled into Mom and Dad's driveway in Crystal on July 5, 1994, Mom didn't wait for her daughter to come and knock on the door. She greeted her, arms open wide, on the front steps.

Mom and my sister Kim, reunited in 1994.

Kim's Story

At our first meeting, I discovered that many of the things I'd always hoped for her had come true. She'd been raised by a well-to-do couple as their only child. She had been greatly loved and given all the privileges that come with a stay-at-home mom and a successful father. She was smart and good-looking and had an easy smile. But there were surprises, too. She was small and slender, not big-boned and tall like me. She was confident and self-assured, not insecure and self-effacing like me. In spite of this, she was so much a member of our family that her presence astounded me. Her looks, her personality, even her handwriting readily marked her as one of us.[5]

In many ways, Lynette/Kim has been looming over this work as a specter, first as a tiny being whose presence made Mom an unwed mother-to-be, then as a much-deliberated-over newborn who was whisked away into another life, and finally as a critical absence that cast long shadows over Mom's "fresh start." But what had happened to that baby girl, the innocent but "illegitimate" child in whose name child welfare experts had crafted the "best solution"? Had she enjoyed the benefits adoptees had been promised?

When I asked Kim this last question in an informal interview in 2019, her answer was clear: yes.[6]

When baby Lynette left Booth on January 20, 1961, she was placed with a foster family while Anoka County caseworker Patricia Peart worked to find a permanent adoptive family for her. "I feel this child has very much potential," Peart wrote on January 31. "This child will be small and very attractive physically. I know of no special attributes the parents should have other than a good education and ability to give this child the educational stimulation it will need to live up to its potential. The parents should naturally love and understand the child and desire to make a good home for it." Some five months later, she placed the baby with "a clear, milky white complexion" and "easy going" personality with Ted and Carolee Thompson, who named their new daughter Kimberly Kay.[7]

Ted and Carolee had been waiting for a baby for two years, having initiated the adoption process in 1959 after their attempts to conceive were unsuccessful. They were delighted to become parents, especially Carolee, who, according to Kim, would have filled her house with children if she'd been able to get pregnant. Ted was a successful businessman, Carolee a stay-at-home, "June Cleaver kind of mom." Though the Thompson family moved from Minnesota to Nebraska to California to Michigan and back to California, following Ted's jobs, Kim considers herself a "Michigan girl." She spent her formative years there before moving to Orange County at age sixteen, a difficult transition for an introverted teen from the Midwest.

Whether in Michigan or California, however, Kim grew up wanting for nothing. "I was just a lucky kid," she told me. "I was an only child, so I never had anything I needed that I didn't get. We had nice houses and just a happy, regular [life]." She would have liked a sibling but had gotten a taste of big-family life by spending time with her best friend in Michigan, who was one of eleven children.

Though her extended family was small—three aunts and uncles and nine cousins, total—it was happy and close-knit. She didn't look like any of them, her straight blonde hair and blue eyes a contrast to their dark curls and dark eyes, but she never felt like an outsider. Her parents had told her from her youngest days that she was adopted; it was a subject of open discussion in her family. She said that being adopted made her feel special. "I've come across other people who felt abandoned," she explained, "[but] for me, it was all positive, like somebody went through a lot of effort and sacrifice to give me life. And when I tell people I'm adopted, they're always interested; they always want to know about it." Once, well into Kim's adulthood, an aunt asked her if she had ever felt out of place in the family. Kim marveled at the idea. "That was the first time the thought had ever occurred to me that I wasn't a Thompson at heart. Even though the blood isn't there, the rest of me is part of that family, just like everyone else."

Still, she wondered about the woman who had brought her into the world. Her parents had shared what little information they had received from Patricia Peart: Kim's birthmother was a college student of Norwegian descent, pretty enough to be a model, who had named her baby Lynette. Every January 16, while she celebrated her birthday with her family, Kim wondered if there was another woman somewhere who took special note of the day. When she was sixteen, she acquired a special empathy for her birthmother when she had a pregnancy scare of her own:

> I just connected in my mind so much with that unknown birthmother, like this is how she felt. I bet she was young, too. . . . My mom and dad and I sat around the table talking about [what to do]. It was very intense. And I felt like I needed to give birth to the baby because having an abortion would be like slapping my birthmother in the face like, This is what I think of your sacrifice that you [made for] me, even though I wasn't against abortions per se. . . . It turned out I wasn't pregnant. Hallelujah! But it made me really relate to Sharon and just appreciate her.

When she turned eighteen in 1979, Kim began looking for information about her adoption and her birthparents. She wrote to Anoka County but was told they had no information to share. At eighteen, Kim was too young to fall under a Minnesota law granting adopted people age twenty-one or older the right to request information contained on their original birth certificate. The county could only retain a copy of her letter in its files, to be shared with her birthparents in the event that they asked after her. Ten years later, when she was married to her first husband and living in California, Kim wrote to the Adoption Unit of the Minnesota Department of Human Services (DHS) and got the same response. She kept a copy of the letter she had written, then forgot about it until 1994.

By that time, Kim had divorced, remarried, and relocated to Michigan. One day, while cleaning her desk, she came upon the 1989 letter to DHS and realized that her contact information was outdated. Perhaps her birthmother or birthfather had tried to find her, only to be sent down a path that dead-ended with an old name and address in California. She wrote to DHS again and, a few weeks later, received an envelope from Anoka County Human Services. This time, it was more than a one-page form letter. This time, it was photocopies of the case records from her adoption that Patricia Peart had completed in 1961. "I just started sobbing uncontrollably in the street at the mailbox because that's how excited I was," she recalled. "I couldn't even finish reading it for a while because I was crying so hard. I was so excited."

Before sending this information to Kim, some Anoka County staff person had taken a black marker and crossed out the last names of everyone mentioned in the reports: Kim's birthmother, birthfather, maternal grandparents, and aunts and uncles. That staff person, however, made a critical mistake on page two of the Referral History Guide, blacking out the word "birth" instead of the birthmother's last name. "Sharon Moore gave ~~birth~~ to an illegitimate child, a female, on 1-16-61 at Booth Memorial Hospital in St. Paul," it reads. "In the best interests of the welfare of the child, she wishes to place her for adoption."

Now Kim had in her possession the full maiden name of her birthmother, as well as the first names of maternal grandparents and aunts and uncles. But she was in Michigan, and the last known location of her birthmother was in the Twin Cities. Kim rifled through the adoption literature she had amassed over the years and found a card for an adoption searcher based in Minnesota. Sandy charged $150 and said she'd search until she was successful. It didn't take long. She found Sharon's parents' obituaries, learned Sharon's married last name and city of residence, and tracked down a phone number. Kim asked Sandy to contact Sharon on her behalf, steeling herself for the possibility that Sharon wouldn't welcome news of her adopted-away daughter.

"If she doesn't want to meet me," Kim told Sandy, "just ask her for a picture because I've never seen anyone I was related to in my whole life."

But, of course, Sharon did want to meet Kim. And so, after her own decades of wondering, in July 1994, Kim walked into the embrace of the first blood relative she had ever met. She described her emotions as she and her husband neared the house in Crystal:

> I've never had such butterflies in my stomach in my life. I was a nervous wreck and it wasn't [because I was] scared. I had talked to her on the phone and I knew she was really nice, but I was just crazy nervous, excited, anxious. I still remember that the streets by your mom's house were in alphabetical order by state. So . . . we're getting closer and closer and finally we get to the "L's," right? I remember Louisiana [Avenue]. And we drive up and before I got out of the car, she came out on the porch and we just gave each other a great big hug. It was just really cool.

Kim and Mom spent most of that day together, their husbands making quick acquaintance, then leaving the women to the moment. For four or five hours, they sifted through photo albums, shared stories, and generally reveled in each other's company. They answered as many questions for each other as they could. Kim learned the story of Mom's pregnancy, how Jack had abandoned her, how she had been sequestered away at home and then at Booth, how she had let her baby go into what she hoped would be a better life. She learned that Mom could not conjure up Jack's last name, however hard she tried. She learned that Mom had divulged her secret to my father from the beginning, but that no one else knew that Mom actually had three children.

Kim also learned that she had two half-siblings who knew nothing of her existence. She didn't want to stir up any trouble for Mom by forcing her to reveal herself to us, but Mom said she was ready.

It was time to bring her children together.

It was time to tell.

Telling: From Triad to Constellation

I had closely guarded the secret of her birth; only my parents and my husband knew. My two other children didn't know, my sisters and brothers and aunts and uncles didn't know, and even my Gramma hadn't known. And in spite of the fact that I considered myself to be a sophisticated and confident woman of the 90s, I was unnerved at the prospect of revealing so much of myself and my past by acknowledging my first daughter.[8]

No wonder Mom was nervous the night we had dinner at the Ground Round in Crystal. Adoption, after all, affects more than the members of the triad. Its reach extends to what is now referred to as the "adoption constellation"—siblings and members of the extended birth and adoptive families, adoptees' partners and children, friends, even the myriad professionals involved in adoption practice, counseling, and regulation.[9]

For all Mom's worry, neither Eric nor I was upset by my mother's revelation. "I'm certainly not angry—what for?" I wrote in my journal the next morning, July 6, 1994. "Not wounded or offended. Just mostly stunned . . . and [feeling] dis-acquainted with Mom." I digested the news about my re-formed family for the next three weeks as I prepared to meet my sister. I took some pleasure in telling the story to friends and colleagues, relishing their reaction to the punch line about our shared names but taking pains to point out that it was Kim's adoptive parents who chose her name, not Mom. I was eager to meet her, and a little nervous, but I had other concerns on my mind. I was struggling in 1994, too. I had become increasingly dissatisfied with my job in a county community corrections department and had been rejected by a couple of graduate programs to which I had applied. When Steve and I made the difficult decision not to move across the country to accept the generous offer from a third, I fell into a deep funk over my professional future. Added to all this, of course, was Dad's seriously declining health. Although I experienced it at a more distant remove than did Mom, I knew the situation was urgent and that he was heading toward full-time institutional care.

So it was that, in that July 6 journal entry, I wrote of the news about Kim, "I could look at this one of two ways: a continuation of the stress of 1994, or the beginning of the 'good things' I've been waiting for. I choose the latter."

On Friday, July 29, I met my sister for the first time.

Steve and I drove to Mom and Dad's place in Crystal that evening, where Kim was already waiting. My heart pounded as I walked through the front door that led directly to the living room. Eric was already there, and Mom and Dad, of course, but I saw no one but Kim. Pretty, thin, taller than me but not as tall as Mom. Straight blonde hair and blue eyes like Eric. Dimples like all of us. She rose from the couch where she'd been sitting and, putting my awkward uncertainty to rest, reached out for a hug.

We visited at Mom and Dad's for a while; then, when it was time for Mom to help Dad to bed, Kim, Eric, Steve, and I went out for dinner at a nearby Applebee's. We chatted about our growing-up lives, about our shared mother and Kim's family, about what we already knew and wanted to know about each other. Kim told us about living in California and working as an elementary school teacher and the Santa Ana winds that had driven her crazy and her Thompson relatives in Minnesota. We told her about growing up in Crystal and family get-togethers with the Moore relatives and our jobs and hobbies. When the conversation slowed and excitement turned to fatigue, we brought her back to her hotel so we could all rest before the next day's activities.

On Saturday, July 30, Kim met her extended Moore family at a picnic at Lake Harriet. She was more excited than nervous, she would recall later, comforted by the ease with which her relationship with Mom was unfolding. On the grassy lawn near the city lake, Kim met her aunts and uncles by blood, Diane and Marcia and Dave. She met her aunts and uncles by marriage, Roger and Bill and Loretta and Joan. She met cousins with dark hair like Mom's and cousins with light hair like her own. But she couldn't meet the people who had the closest connection to the circumstances of her birth. Grandma and Grandpa would not have a chance to find solace in the return of their eldest grandchild, the one whose conception had caused such an uproar, whose loss had caused such pain. Earl would not have the chance to meet his niece, the one born to his adoring sister and his onetime friend. Mom's younger brother Sam, who had been a teenager when Kim was born, was gone, too. But Kim reveled in the family she did meet, smiling and laughing and chatting breezily through the whole windblown afternoon.

Years later, in 2019, Kim recalled that weekend in July 1994. "I was a little surprised at how welcome I was," she told me. "All of Sharon's siblings were just excited to meet me and very nice and treated me like part of the family. . . . It was like a best-case scenario, honestly. And having siblings of any kind—as an only child, that was awesome. I love telling people I have a sister named Kim because they look at me weird . . . and having someone that I look like! Eric and I looked so much alike, and when I see pictures of us when we were little kids, wow! That was the first person I'd ever seen that looked like me."

I had recorded my thoughts about Kim and the weekend as well. "I tell you," I wrote in my journal in 1994, "she's one together person. She has lots of respect [for] and gratitude towards Mom, less so for the mysterious Jack. . . . We'd planned on hooking up on Sunday before she left, but plans didn't work out. . . . Then she was gone. This weekend was like a little teaser. 'Here's your sister. Like her? Good. And good-bye.' Now what?"

Mother and Child Reunions

Now what, indeed. Though a made-for-TV movie might roll closing credits over the scene of our family gathering at Lake Harriet, that was not the end of the story. In many ways, it was just a beginning. For years, Mom had kept a tightly sealed lid on her secret, and then, in the space of just a few weeks at an initiative not her own, it burst into the light. I know she was relieved at its release and thrilled to have Kim back in her life. It seems the revelation also prompted her to make her first, and apparently brief, forays into the world of adoption-related search and birthparent support groups.

I don't remember Mom being involved with CUB-MN in 1994, but after she died, I found among her papers an envelope containing a couple of its brochures, a summary of Minnesota laws governing access to birth and adoption records, and a reprint of a 1986 article from *Public Welfare* about the impact of the "adoption decision" on birth families. Sandy, the searcher who had contacted Mom about Kim, had written a personal note on one of the brochures: "Sharon—Good to talk to you this morning! Sending along some things [about] CUB that you'll enjoy reading. . . . I will be at the Aug. [CUB] meeting. Do try to attend one soon—they're so good! . . . Let's talk or meet for coffee if you like. Again—congratulations! Sandy."

I don't know if Mom ever met Sandy for coffee or attended any CUB meetings; I doubt it. She didn't talk or write about having done so—at least not in any of her surviving writings—and was preoccupied with making plans for Dad's care that summer of 1994. It appears that she had only fleeting, if life-altering, contact with CUB-MN and with Sandy. Sandy, on the other hand, was in the middle of a long tenure with the group by the time she helped connect Kim and Mom. Her efforts were part of a widespread movement to reunite parents and children separated by adoption.

Herself a birthmother who had delivered and surrendered a baby girl in 1961, Sandy Sperrazza had been involved with CUB-MN as early as December 1978, when she was listed as a "non-member" supporter on the organization's membership list. Sperrazza reunited with her daughter a couple of years later, and by the fall of 1984 had become CUB-MN's president, a position she would hold for twenty-eight years. Though CUB did not function as a search organization per se, by the 1980s it had begun advocating for birthmothers' rights to search for their adopted-away children. Like the adoptees' rights movement that had taken hold in the mid-1970s, CUB argued that opening sealed records would allow both adoptees and birthparents to heal from the lifelong, traumatic wound that adoption had inflicted, a position advanced by a 1978 book titled *The Adoption Triangle: Sealed or Opened Records: How They Affect Adoptees, Birth Parents, and Adoptive Parents.* At the very least, CUB activists argued, birthmothers should be able to learn the fate of their children. Ideally, they would be able to reconnect with them once they became adults.[10]

National and local media picked up on the story of long-separated parents and children who had found each other once again, aided by mutual consent registries such as the Minnesota Adoption Reunion Registry and the International Soundex Reunion Registry (ISRR) and the efforts of grassroots activists across the country. Lee Campbell's reunion story reached a nationwide audience with her 1979 appearance on *Donahue*, while Minneapolis newspapers published articles about a 1977 Minnesota law that made it easier for adoptees ages twenty-one and older to access their original birth certificates alongside stories of local women, including CUB-MN's Pam Bolduc, who had reunited with their birth families.[11]

Loosening of regulations controlling access to birth records, activism by adoption reform advocates, press accounts of successful searches, and a growing body of adoptee and birthmother memoirs made reunion seem a real possibility, if not a necessity, for many in the adoption community by the time Sandy Sperrazza took the helm at CUB-MN in 1984. During her tenure, hundreds of birthparents and adult adoptees from across the country whose adoption had some connection to Minnesota contacted the organization for help. In March 1988, for example, a woman wrote after having seen a story on a local news program about a mother reuniting with the daughter she had surrendered for adoption. "I to [sic] did the same because I was single and still am but would like to find my two children, like she said you think about them on there [sic] birthdays and holidays. I felt so bad in doing it but one parent cannot do what a couple can." An adoptee born in 1969 wanted to search for her birthmother in 1993: "I feel that I should do this now before I lose my nerve again. I was adopted from [a local agency] and they told me that they will find my mother but it would cost. And for me, what they want is an arm and a leg. . . . I am married with a seventeen month [old] son, and we couldn't afford to lose that much." Birthfathers also sometimes reached out to CUB-MN. One married father of three children hadn't been in touch with his first child's mother since her sixth month of pregnancy, when she'd broken their engagement. "I am now 39 years old," he wrote, "and I have been haunted by the memories of this past relationship, and constantly wonder about the life of the child I have never seen. Do you have any birth fathers in your group who have had similar experiences?"[12]

Sometimes these letters were addressed to CUB-MN, sometimes directly to Sperrazza herself. If responding on behalf of CUB-MN, Sperrazza would send information about the ISRR or Minnesota law or affidavits of disclosure the correspondents could send to the state. But by the 1990s, Sperrazza had become a well-known independent searcher as well. "Search angels," as these genealogical sleuths were known, were often motivated by their own experiences with adoption reunions and charged little to nothing for their services. They used a variety of ingenious methods and sources to find information that the closed adoption system shielded from view. They scoured reunion registries; church, census, military, and property tax records; birth, death, and marriage certificates; divorce and probate records; phone books and city directories; newspapers and high school yearbooks. (Later, of course, the Internet became a critical tool, as have the current DNA-testing and online genealogy industries.)[13]

In some cases, such as Kim and Mom's, the process went quickly and smoothly and yielded satisfying results. In others, the outcome only produced more heartache. Sometimes adult children refused contact, as was the case for an eighty-seven-year-old woman from northern Minnesota who asked Sperrazza to help her connect with a daughter who had been adopted away in 1926. From January 1993 to September 1994, the woman wrote fourteen letters describing her lonely longing and increasing frustration at her daughter's refusal to respond to her or Sperrazza's entreaties. The final letter in the collection leaves the story trailing off with the woman vowing to write her daughter once more.[14]

Birthmothers sometimes rejected their searching children as well. Their secondhand stories crop up in newspaper articles about adoption records and searchers' reports about abrupt telephone hang-ups and adoptees' heartbroken accounts of their mothers' refusal to acknowledge them. "Dear Child," an anonymous birthmother wrote in a letter to Ann Landers in 1978,

"Don't look for me. Don't find me. Your very search would violate the reasons I gave you up."[15]

This plea echoes the logic of those who claimed that sealed birth and adoption records protect the privacy of relinquishing mothers and that opening those records would constitute a violation of their rights. Certainly, some women were unwilling to identify themselves as birthmothers of adopted children, as this letter-writer makes clear, or uninterested in searching for their adopted-away children, as Pam, whose story is featured in chapter 1, explained. But disinterest in searching for a child did not always mean an unwillingness to be found by a child. Many women, like Mom, didn't search for their adopted-away children because they didn't believe they had a right to do so, didn't want to upset the stability and happiness they hoped their children had found in adoptive families. Yet when those children came calling, buoyed by the gains achieved by the adoptees' and birthmothers' rights movements, these women were just as pleased as the birthmothers who had been actively searching for their children all along.[16]

Reunion is more than the moment contact between parent and child is reestablished, however, and even mutually consensual, eagerly anticipated reunions often proved difficult for both parties, despite the tendency of newspapers, television talk shows, and published memoirs to end their stories at the dramatic climax. Adoptees whose images had been seared into birthmothers' minds as tiny newborns wholly dependent on their mothers for life and identity emerged years later as fully formed adults whose life experiences had been shaped by their adoptive families. Birthmothers brought their own histories, personalities, and families to the equation. Add to this the potential differences in temperament, interest, and expectation, and it's no wonder that reunions did not always proceed smoothly or develop into long-term intimacies.[17]

Whatever benefits or challenges it brought, Mom's reunion with Kim was unfolding against the backdrop of my father's declining health. Just a few months after Kim found Mom, Dad entered the nursing home permanently. It must have been a lot to deal with all at once, this simultaneous coming-back of one beloved and going-away of another, but Mom seemed to bear it all with a new resolve as she marshaled her energies to be my father's best advocate and true companion. Then, in February 1995, her first grandchild was born when Kim gave birth to her son, Christopher. Just over a year later, on March 24, 1996, my father died at North Ridge Care Center with Mom, Eric, Steve, and I huddled around his bed as he drew his last breath.

The house has a different kind of quiet to it than it has for the past two years. A permanent quiet.

She decides to go for a drive.

She drives from Crystal to Blaine, past the house on Tyler Street where she had hidden in the room under the eaves.

She drives through Northeast Minneapolis, past the office where Dr. Goode had told her she was pregnant.

She traces the bus route along Central Avenue where she had fainted on the 5:20 to Blaine.

She crosses the river, winds her way through downtown, finds a place to park near the curved building on the corner of First Avenue and Seventh Street where she had once waited for a bus to California. This time, though, young people dance across the checkered floor, music pulsing from the stage. Cigarette smoke has replaced the odor of bus exhaust.

She sits at the bar for a while, watching the kids and feeling her age. She thinks back to another time she was lonely and afraid as her life veered off one path and down another.

Then, she goes home.[18] ●

Fresh Start Redux

Mom was fifty-six and recently widowed when she took this drive. Her adopted-away daughter had been back in her life for two years, and Eric and I were well into our lives as independent adults. The aches and pains of age were starting to settle in, and not long after my father's funeral, she had one of her arthritic knees replaced. Her longtime job at Carlson Companies had become increasingly tenuous, and she was considering leaving it. This was a major transition period for my mother, so she journeyed back to another time she had faced an uncertain future.

My father's death brought pain and grief to my mother, to be sure, but also a measure of relief. For the first time in many years, she had the time and energy to focus on herself. In 1997, Mom returned to the University of Minnesota as a part-time student to complete the degree that had been interrupted by her 1960 pregnancy. Instead of journalism, however, she enrolled in the creative writing program. It was during this time that she wrote "Greyhound" and "Birth Rite," the most direct and enduring testimony of her first experience of motherhood. It was also during these years that her relationship with Kim evolved and assumed the shape it would hold until Mom's death in 2009.

> *After the initial exuberance of our reunion wore off, we settled into a cordial relationship. She is definitely a member of my family, so much so that it still amazes me. And although I've come closer to accepting the realization that what I did for her was the best I could do, the odor of bus exhaust or the glare of shiny linoleum floors can make me feel uneasy and apprehensive. Then, I have to find a place to retreat, a place like that small upstairs bedroom at home.*[19]

Mom's brief description of her by then five-year relationship with Kim as "cordial" echoes those of many reunited birthmothers. By the time Kim found Mom in 1994, adoption researchers had begun studying the long-term outcomes of reunions. Ten studies published between 1992 and 2018 offered a generally reassuring assessment of mother-child reunions. According to this body of work, both adoptees and birthmothers reported overall satisfaction with the experience of reunion, whoever initiated the search, as they adjusted their expectations and attempted to define the terms and nature of their contact. Most maintained a long-term relationship of some kind, whether through frequent in-person interactions or sporadic communication. Whatever the interaction with their birthmothers, adoptees did not abandon their adoptive families and, in fact, often claimed that the experience had enhanced their relationship with the parents who had raised them. Overall, the researchers argued, "the great majority of all parties [adoptees, birthparents, and adoptive parents] reported the experience of contact and reunion to be happy and satisfying." The rates were especially high for birthmothers, 94 percent of whom said they were pleased at the contact with their offspring.[20]

These observations seem to apply to Mom and Kim's relationship. But what of the disappointments and stresses the literature also described? Even "successful" reunions such as theirs sometimes brought emotional upset for birthmothers as old feelings of shame and guilt resurfaced. In 2014, a small Canadian study found that birthmothers experienced grief during the reunion process as they embarked on the complicated task of building a relationship rooted in both connection and separation. "The women had to 'let go' of the latent dream of reuniting with their baby and accept the adopted adult who he or she had become. Relinquishment of that image became a major loss that also needed to be grieved and mourned."[21]

I don't recall having anything more than superficial conversations with Mom about what it meant to have Kim back in her life. She communicated with Kim more often than I did, each of them paying occasional visits to the other's homes. Mom met Carolee, Kim's mom, on one of her trips to Michigan, a meeting Kim later described as smooth and happy. Mom and I would update each other on our respective interactions with Kim, sharing the latest news about her and her husband's jobs or Christopher's most recent accomplishments or her scrapbooking projects. Often, the conversation would turn to how Kim was similar to or different from Mom and me, in ways both trivial and profound. We would speculate about how we might all have been different people if Mom had raised both of her daughters. It was as if Mom and I were in it together, trying to make sense of this newcomer who both fit and broke the Moore/Wikstrom family mold.

Kim's reunion with Mom brought her me and Eric as well, a wholly new association unfettered by the past and its potential baggage. The three of us established a cordial relationship, too, one Mom described as "more like (distant) cousins than siblings." Kim found in us another mirror in which she saw reflections of herself. "I see so many similarities in personality between me and you and Eric that are opposite from my adoptive family," she told me. "They're very social and everybody loves them and they make friends with everyone in five minutes. I wish I was like that but I'm not at all. And when I met you guys, it was like, Ah, maybe I fit in this puzzle over here."[22]

If their reunion had answered long-standing questions for Mom and Kim, it was different for me and Eric. We hadn't spent our lives speculating about phantom relatives, searching strangers' faces for a hint of resemblance. January 16 came and went each year just like any other day in the monotonous winter months. As children, we had taken our sibling companionship for granted on the best days and harassed each other mercilessly on the worst. Adding a bonus sibling to our family was a pleasant surprise and made for some interesting conversation with friends and acquaintances, but it was not fraught with the weight of years' worth of wondering as it was for Kim and Mom.[23]

Thus proceeded our lives post-reunion. After we all found our footing on the terrain of our new family landscape, we settled into its routines: emails and birthday cards and phone calls with an occasional visit thrown in here and there. It seemed to me as if we had simply absorbed Kim and moved on.

Mom with Eric, me, and our sister Kim, 2007.

Still, there is evidence beyond my recall of the impact of Kim's coming back on Mom's life. The road trip. The essays. Photocopies of the "Girls in Trouble" series from the 1959 *St. Paul Dispatch* Mom had tucked away in a green pocket folder. In that same folder, a collection of newsletters from the late 1990s that had been published by the Salvation Army Missing Persons Service, which, for a time, had helped reunite former Booth girls with their adopted-away children. Mom never mentioned any of these things to me, but sometime after Kim's return, she became a born-again hugger. The woman who had embraced her Norwegian stoicism, who hid her tears behind shut doors, who rarely admitted out loud that she loved anyone, suddenly began hugging us at every opportunity. Eric and I joked that she had pulled a bait and switch, raising us to be reticent about such expressions of affection only to foist them upon us in our advancing age. I wonder, though, if her newfound—and still modest—emotionalism sprang from the same deeply buried well that had held her secret. Mom didn't articulate such things to me, so I am left to speculate, to try to piece things together through research and reading and listening to the stories of other onetime Booth girls.[24]

Women like Pam, who would welcome contact from her daughter but hasn't the energy to initiate it.

Like Karen, whose son limited their relationship to the occasional letter and died before she could meet him in person, in the clear light of day.

Like Gay, who lived to love her first adopted-away daughter and that daughter's children, and to see her second adopted-away daughter come back, leave again, die young.

Like Gayle, whose relationship with her son has ebbed and flowed through joy and wonder and frustration.

Like Mary, who found true and abiding love with her son and his family.

Like Sandy #1, whose reunion with her own birthmother led to her reunion with her birth daughter and a multigenerational combining of families separated by and constituted through adoption.

And like Sandy #2.

SANDY #2

Sandy's daughter contacted me first. She emailed me in August 2017 and said she'd been born at Booth St. Paul in 1958 and happily reunited with her mother in 1995. She put me in touch with her mother, and on September 29, 2017, Sandy arrived at my house for an interview.[25]

There were many details of her long-ago pregnancy and delivery and surrender that Sandy couldn't remember. Perhaps she'd hidden them from her conscious mind, the way she'd hidden her pregnancy from herself, her parents, her friends. "I put a lot of that out of my mind," she said. "It's really kind of like a blank."

One thing was clear, however: the reunion with her daughter has been joyful.

Sandy grew up in a working-class neighborhood in 1950s St. Paul. Her mother, a Catholic Minnesota native, worked at the Swift & Company meat-packing plant and was the "nicest person you would ever want to meet." Her father, a Jewish immigrant from Poland, worked as a laborer and was quick to show his disapproval. He moved the family from place to place, mostly within the St. Paul city limits, but once, briefly, to Arizona, too. It was hard for Sandy, having to fit in at one new school after another; one year, she attended four different schools between September and May.

Things got better once she settled in at Washington High School, where she was a cheerleader, vice president of the student council, and member of the bowling team. "The fifties were a good time," she said. "I just remember being very happy and hanging out with my friends and going ice skating and roller skating and going to the Prom [Ballroom] dancing. We just had things to do all the time. We'd walk to the drive-in theater, which was miles away, and find people we knew that were there and sit in their car just, you know, sit outside. It was always fun."

Sandy had a boyfriend for a couple of years in high school. They'd hang out with their friends and spend time at each other's homes, but they didn't have sex. Though she doesn't remember talking about sex or dating with her parents or getting any sex education in school, Sandy believed sex before marriage was wrong. Mostly, she and her boyfriend just made out, but one time he "got frisky" and she said no. Sometime after that, Sandy couldn't say for sure how long, he broke up with her and started dating a girl who didn't say no. Then, in her junior year, when she was sixteen, she started dating another boy, a senior. This time, Sandy didn't say no, either.

Here's where Sandy's memory gets fuzzy. She doesn't quite remember how long they dated. She doesn't quite remember the circumstances in which they had sex, or for how long, or how often. She doesn't quite remember why they broke up. "The only thing I remember is standing in the doorway of the house that we lived in on Albemarle [Street] and him going out the door and me throwing his ring," she said.

Whatever the cause of their breakup, it happened before Sandy knew she was pregnant. Then she missed a period. And another one. Her clothes got tighter. She knew what was happening, but she pretended it wasn't. She wore girdles and big shirts to conceal her expanding belly. Then, "One day at school, one of my teachers asked me if I was pregnant and I broke down and cried and said, 'Yes, I am.'" Her mother was empathetic, her father angry. In those days, pregnant teens were banished from their schools, safeguarding the other students from their bad influence. So Sandy met with a tutor at home a few times, but she was already in her third trimester. After school ended that spring, at her father's directive, she entered Booth to await delivery of her baby.

She knows she arrived at Booth on June 25, delivered a baby girl on

July 22, was rushed to the University of Minnesota hospital because she was hemorrhaging, returned to Booth on July 23, went home on July 30. She knows this not from memory, but because she later obtained her records from the Salvation Army. But in her mind, there are only images, snapshots of those weeks she spent at Booth. Dusting the wooden spiral staircase. Watching TV in the lounge with other Booth girls. Her parents driving over for a brief visit, bringing watermelon but refusing to come inside. A "dungeonous" area where she delivered her baby. Seeing a strut on the Raymond Avenue bridge as the ambulance sped her from Booth to the hospital. "I think those months leading up to going [to Booth] were freaking me out and then going there freaked me out," she said. "I think after leaving and then going back to school, I put that time slot out of my mind totally. Like it's buried somewhere. I would love to know more but I just can't pull it out. No matter how hard I try, I don't remember details of it."

The records show that her baby was placed in foster care pending adoption through Jewish Family Services, the agency's religious affiliation perhaps a sign that her father had had a hand in making the arrangements. But Sandy knew none of that at the time, or at least doesn't recall it now. "I remember after seeing [my baby after she was born], I wanted to keep her, but I just put it out of my mind because I knew it wasn't a possibility. I was seventeen years old and had to finish school, had no money, and no job." So she abided by the plans others had made. She has vague memories of calling her baby's father from a phone booth, probably sometime after she left Booth. He said he wanted to be involved, to help. She said it was too late.

Sandy went back home, started her senior year at Mechanic Arts High School that fall, graduated in 1959. She got a job, married in 1962, kept her secret from her husband and their two boys. They moved to northern California in 1970, then back to Minnesota; to Oklahoma, then back to Minnesota; to southern California. Then Sandy came back to Minnesota alone and stayed. By the time she and her husband divorced, one of their sons was an adult, the other a teen who split his time between his parents' homes. She met another man, made a life with him in St. Paul, immersed herself in art and design and antiques dealing.

Through all of this, Sandy squirreled away thoughts of her first child, allowing them into her consciousness only sporadically. One time, she received a mysterious phone call from someone she didn't know. The details have faded, but it seemed to have something to do with the child she had surrendered. The exchange got her thinking about her daughter. Where was she? Was she okay? She didn't attempt a search; she knew information was hard to come by for a birthmother, and she didn't want to disrupt her daughter's family—or her own.

Then, in 1995, Sandy received a letter in a large manila envelope, a letter she was waiting for. Her daughter had contacted a woman at the adoption agency who contacted Sandy's nephew, who told her how to reach Sandy, who said she'd welcome the opportunity to hear from her daughter. So her daughter sent a letter directly to Sandy at home. They exchanged a couple of letters, until one day, while Sandy was writing one of those letters, her phone rang. It was her daughter. Neither of them wanted to wait any longer. They set up a meeting at a restaurant in St. Paul. Sandy got there first. "I sat at a table and she came in the back door and she peeked around the corner," she remembered. "I waved at her because I was sitting right within eye contact. She had this big smile on her face and I got up and we hugged and we've been best friends ever since."[26]

Sandy took comfort in hearing that her daughter had been raised by a "wonderful" family who took "amazing care" of her and her also-adopted sister. But she also saw how much her daughter was like her, despite the years they'd spent apart. "I was happy and fortunate that she had such a great upbringing and a family to take such good care of her, but then to meet her and realize that because of our genes, we're so much alike—it was like I raised her or something because she's just like me." They saw themselves in each other's faces and expressions and interests. They both had been raised in families with Jewish heritage, but neither of them practiced the faith. They shared a passion for art. They marveled at the fact that they had crossed paths over the years, Sandy having patronized a store her daughter had managed, her daughter having received as a gift one of the designer belts Sandy had crafted and sold at a local clothing store.

The impact of Sandy's daughter's return rippled beyond their two lives and into their respective families as well. Both Sandy's parents and her daughter's adoptive parents had died by this time, but Sandy met her daughter's husband and four-year-old son the very day they reunited. Later, her daughter met Sandy's siblings. "They loved her the minute they met her," Sandy said, "just like I did, because she's extraordinary." Sandy's sons embraced their newfound sister right away, welcoming her into the family. Sandy told her ex-husband about her daughter, too, and he met her as well. Sandy and her current partner hosted her daughter's family and in-laws for Christmas. It was a flurry of new-family activity.

Then things settled down, the big family gatherings tapering off to occasional get-togethers as excitement gave way to life's normal rhythms. Some years into their reunion, Sandy helped connect her daughter to her birthfather after having seen him at a class reunion. The three of them had lunch once, then again. She still doesn't recall how their relationship ended, and though she seems not to harbor any particular ill will toward him, she has long recognized the unjust midcentury dynamics that blamed girls but excused boys for unplanned pregnancies. "I feel that it really was unfair for women, the way they were treated and that nothing was ever said about the men being the problem. It was always the women."

But what's important now is that her daughter is in her life. They remain close and see each other often. When the 2020 coronavirus outbreak forced the new practice of social distancing on them, they stayed in touch through daily phone calls. "I wouldn't change a thing," Sandy said in 2017. "If that [unplanned pregnancy] had never happened, great, you know, that I didn't have to go through that. But the result of going through it is [my daughter] and that's worth it."

And her daughter's name?

Joy. ■

Reunion has brought an enduring and satisfying relationship to Sandy's and Joy's lives. "Sandy and I are most fortunate," Joy wrote in that 2017 email, "in that we have become the best of friends."

What about Kim? What has reunion meant to her?

I asked her if she found what she was looking for when she embarked on a search for her birthmother.

"Oh yeah," she told me in 2019. "It's not like I wanted to move in and be really annoying, but just to know that there's this whole family here, yeah, it was just right."

I never asked Mom if she found what she was looking for when she reunited with her first daughter. The essays she wrote in the late 1990s suggest that she had, but also that the circumstances surrounding her first experience of motherhood had left a permanent mark.

> *I cherish [Kim's] presence in my life, even though it has forced me to let go of some long-held illusions about who I really am.*
> *The real anguish of her birth and her loss has been all but erased*

from my memory. I think Gramma's quiet way of dealing with such trials was instilled in me, for better or worse. It's her example that helps me endure the pains of living with the knowledge that things will get better by and by. But endurance is not everything, and my habit of suffering out my doubts and fears in silence and secrecy takes a toll. My reticence is rooted deep and tangled and strong, and just when I think I have weeded out my fear enough to confide in someone, a green tendril of doubt shoots up to remind me of who I am and what I have done and what I too often have left undone. [27]

I don't know what it is Mom felt she had left undone. I do know that she had kept a secret for thirty-three years, one that had cast her apart from friends and family and neighbors, even as it cast her together with thousands of other women similarly shunned by polite society. Denying such a figurative experience must also have led to an inner cleaving, a division of self, one part of her carrying on and maintaining appearances and doing all the things expected of a wife, mother, and worker, the other lying dormant but powerful, stirred by the random passing of a bus or the annual turn of a calendar before being tamped down once again. Kim's return unearthed Mom's secret, let it grow and blossom in the light of day as it twined itself around her visible life. However imperfect the resolution, reunion gave Mom a measure of restored peace for the last fifteen years of her life.

We're on the road. The car is stuffed with swim gear and snacks and suitcases and sunscreen. Mom, Tu, and I are meeting Kim and Christopher for a long weekend at a water park in the Wisconsin Dells.

Kim and I have already played aunt to each other's sons with birthday cards and phone calls and Christmas gifts. I visited Kim and her husband in Michigan once when Chris was just a little boy, and they have come to Minnesota to visit both of Kim's families, the one defined by nurture and the one defined by nature. For years, I kept a voice message from Chris on my phone, his singsong little boy voice exclaiming, "Happy Buff-day, Aunt Kim!" Kim welcomed Tu into his adoptive family, her birth family, with a hand-made alphabet book. She readily agreed to write him a letter, one only-child adoptee to another, that I have placed in safekeeping for him along with the one from Mom.

But this is the first time we will spend concentrated time together as a family. Mom has made the arrangements and paid for the hotel, eager to show her two daughters and two grandsons a good time.

The hotel is not one of the shiny behemoths that lure tourists from across the region. Its water park facilities are modest, paint peeling from the bottom of the pool. Mom notices the worn carpet in the hallway and starts calling the hotel the "Wretched Resort," disappointed in her choice.

Tu, who will turn three in a few weeks, loves it. He shrieks with laughter as he goes up and down the slide in the little kids' pool, thirteen-year-old Christopher patiently splashing along with him, Mom, Kim, and I watching from deck chairs.

Up and down, up and down in the hot sun.

Mom and Tu and I share a large two-room suite on Thursday night. By the time Tu and I wake on Friday morning, though, Mom is gone, decamped to a room of her own.

"I don't want to keep you two awake with my snoring," she explains.

(In her journal she writes, "Had a pretty terrible night . . . Felt squeamish & my chest [esp. on my right side] was aching like crazy.")

We venture into town to visit an animal park with a kid-sized train that circles the kid-sized property. The giraffes lick our hands with their scratchy purple tongues. Tu thrills at it all; Christopher endures; the three of us try to keep both of them entertained and happy.

That night, we order pizza and gather around the TV in our suite to watch the opening ceremonies of the Beijing Olympics. Mom is subdued, doesn't eat much, goes to bed early. Kim, Chris, Tu, and I snack on popcorn and Hershey's kisses as the Chinese begin the games with a spectacular display of discipline and might.

("I started feeling crummy around suppertime. . . . Had another restless night. . . . Achy rib-cage again.")

Mom begs off of a few activities again on Saturday. I'm tired, she tells us, you go on. Kim and I take the boys into town for ice cream, then to Noah's Ark, a water park more suitable for a thirteen-year-old than the one at the Wretched Resort. When we reconvene for dinner, the boys squabble, worn out by too much sun and too much together time.

We wake on Sunday morning feeling both regret and relief that the weekend is coming to an end.

("Today is breakfast and then home! Felt better last night, but still know I need to see a doc right away!")

Mom and my sister Kim, 2008.

Mom and Kim and I manage the boys' bickering over pancakes and bacon. We snap some photos in the restaurant parking lot, various arrangements of Mom and her daughters and grandsons. Then we part ways, Kim and Christopher heading east, the three of us west.

("Right side was aching away.")

("It's been nice spending some time with Kim. We have more in common than not, and I hope it reassures her—rather than discourages her—to realize she's got us (me) as her forebear.")

I imagine Tu posing for pictures with his Vietnam mama, wonder if there are brothers and sisters and aunts and uncles and cousins and grandparents—a father—who would welcome Tu back to his family.

> *Wednesday 9/3/08—6:35 P.M.*
>
> *Today, I learned that I have terminal cancer—pancreas of all things, metastasized to my liver. Surgery can't be done, and the prognosis is not good. Six months or so, it seems. Surely didn't see this coming, and it's hard to absorb.*
>
> *. . . I'm now struggling with the hardest part of all this—telling the kids and then having to leave them. When I hold my breath and stop crying over this, I realize that this happens to all people, and that all people suffer the same pain at leaving the ones they love.*

BEGINNINGS AND ENDINGS

December 2008

My biggest wish for you, my dear Kim, as you know, is that you are happy and find fulfillment. . . . Right now, you are doing everything perfectly, taking Mister Tu on with your own unique, loving, and determined style. There's little doubt he is his own little man, but the person he grows to be will carry a large part of your being around in his heart and soul, too. What you endured, body and soul, to make sure he is part of our lives is a gift we can never repay you for, nor really even understand completely. Did I ever really say thank you??

Recounting my own life's path, I hope to have shown you that love is not perfect. That it grows out of faith and hope, but also out of perversity and sin and uncertainty and weakness. That it sustains us when we are down and demands us to give when we feel we have nothing left to give. And through this most wonderful of God's gifts, we receive the same in return . . . it gives us companions to find our way through this world with, even though our gait be uneven and our music out of tune. With slow and unsteady steps, we acquire a marriage partner, then blessing upon blessing and if we are lucky, our own children and grandchildren. In these blessings exists great peace . . . turmoil, yes, to be sure, but peace also.

How much I love you, my dear Kimberly!! Wish I could stick around to see more of what happens to you and Steve and Tu and Eric and Kim and Christopher, but it's a good long life I've had and I am more than grateful for the years I've been given. No matter where you are, I'll be with you too: in the way you look at the world, in the ways you react, in your anger and your laughter. And when you are tired or lonely or afraid you'll know I'll be there somewhere, having experienced these burdens many times myself.[1]

Us: Sunday, February 8 – Monday, February 9, 2009

My mother lies in a hospital bed in her second-story bedroom. She has stopped eating and drinking. Her eyes are not quite open, but they are not quite closed. The head of the bed is raised to a forty-five-degree angle to ease her breathing. Her feet and fingers are cold. The skin at her temples seems to glow blue beneath her thin white hair. Eric sits at the head of her bed; I perch on its side. We watch and wait.

After she takes her final breath, when it becomes clear that her chest will not rise again, I look at the clock, feeling it important to note as many details as possible. 12:14 AM Monday, February 9, 2009. The Julia Roberts movie *Dying Young* plays quietly on the small TV near the clock.

The undertakers come and carry Mom away from the house and into the hearse. A red shroud covers her body. It is cold outside. It is after 1:00 AM. I wonder if the neighbors notice any of this movement in the night.

I wonder if anyone else realizes the world as I have known it has just ended.

I began this project in 2012, three years after Mom's death. My first book had been published the year before, and I was beginning to think about what would come next. I wanted to work on something that would imbue my professional work with personal significance. I also had been a mother for five years, but I was still grappling with my maternal shortcomings. Though I was deeply grateful to have my son, I felt ambivalent about the meaning of motherhood in my life. Many mother-friends reassured me that they, too, fell victim to short-temperedness and other failings, but I secretly believed that my deficits were somehow deeper, more entrenched than theirs.

I suppose there's a conceit in thinking my struggles were unique in the world of mothering, but a trusted health care provider who knew me well once mentioned, in the context of another discussion, that perhaps I hadn't received the kind of nurturing I'd needed as a child. I don't know if that's true—I didn't then and don't now feel any sense of deprivation—but it reminded me of a question another practitioner had put to me years before, while we were undergoing infertility treatments. "Was your mother under any particular stress while she was pregnant with you?" she asked, suggesting that perhaps Mom had transmitted some of that stress to me, which was contributing to our difficulties in getting pregnant. The idea seemed too far-fetched to consider at the time, but I thought of it again in 2012 as I was trying to come to terms with my identity as a motherless mother. I began wondering if Mom's past—her first, hidden pregnancy—was affecting my present.

By that time, the intensity of my grief about Mom's death had lessened enough that I could think, talk, and write about her beyond the limits of those painful but poignant last months of her life. With space for new intellectual work opened by the completion of my previous project, my personal reflections about Mom took on new meaning as I realized the depth of my missed opportunity. It wasn't only that I'd failed to ask her about having been a Booth girl, but that I'd not asked how she felt, as a birthmother, about my becoming an adoptive mother. The letter she wrote me before she died, quoted above, and her immersion in my life with Tu seem to be expressions of unqualified support, but we never talked about it, despite the fact that we shared the experience of having mothered through the losses and gains of adoption. As Sandy #1 pointed out and, with Gay, exemplified, adoption seems to beget adoption.

So I tried to make up for what *I* had left undone by combining my personal quest with historical inquiry and using the tools at my disposal—historical archives, oral history interviews, Mom's writings, personal experience, and imagination—to try to know Mom, and thereby myself, better.

Did it work? How has studying the history of single pregnancy, maternity homes, and adoption in mid-twentieth-century Minnesota affected my understanding of Mom? How did knowing Mom shape my interpretation of the historical record? What have I learned?

I learned that Mom, like all of us, was not the sole author of her life. Some of her most intimate moments had been shaped by historical forces far beyond her ability to control and, perhaps, even her awareness. Cultural beliefs, institutional policies, and professional practices regarding sex, pregnancy, and adoption—all of them inscribed through ideologies of race, class, and gender—turned her into the Booth girl she became and shaped her experience of motherhood, marriage, and family for the rest of her life.

If Mom was not a free agent with exclusive control over her life's path, however, neither was she an automaton entirely subject to external forces. History (with a capital "H") cannot explain the entirety of a person's life. The specific circumstances of her individual life and her unique personhood weave Mom's story in and out of the overarching narrative. I believe Mom felt she had no real option but to surrender *and* that she wasn't ready to parent. I think she longed to have her baby back *and* that she believed that letting her baby go was the best she could do given the circumstances. I believe that the experience deeply affected the rest of her life *and* that it wasn't the only factor in the challenges and heartaches she later encountered. I believe that she shared many experiences and beliefs with the activist birthmothers of CUB *and* that she was not entirely comfortable with its single-minded mission. I believe that she welcomed Kim back into her life with love *and* that Kim's return reinforced the bond she felt with me and Eric. I believe that she lived in the in-between, the murky gray middle of the road, the both/and instead of the either/or.

It is this nuanced relationship between the aggregate and the individual that oral history so usefully demonstrates. The seven former Booth girls I interviewed brought their personal stories to the collective tale as well, each illuminating, in concert or in contrast, aspects of Mom's own. In Pam, I heard echoes of Mom's good-girl naivete and inability to contemplate searching for a lost daughter in the midst of life's other crises. Gayle's relationship with her parents paralleled Mom's in its father-daughter affection and mother-daughter conflict; her decision to release her baby mirrored Mom's in both its resolve and its consequences. Like Mary, Mom was neither a teenager nor a legal adult when she got pregnant and hid herself from public view—Mary with the assistance of her baby's father, Mom at the behest of her parents. Gay and Sandy #1 were probably most unlike Mom, Gay in her teenage defiance and vocal advocacy for birthmothers, Sandy in her willingness to flout convention and keep her baby, both of them in their subsequent unmarried pregnancies. Yet all three of them saw their families grow through, not just shrink by, adoption. As was the case for Mom, Karen's experiences as a Booth girl inform her empathy for others and her critique of the sexist double standard and support of reproductive rights.

Sandy #2, her joyful reunion with her daughter a heightened version of Mom's with Kim, reminds us of the fallibility of memory, as do Mom's written recollections of her time at Booth. The factual errors Mom made—about the year she joined Tip Toppers or the name of the adoption agency—don't negate the power of the story as a whole. Even the glaring absence of memory, as in Sandy #2's case, or the mistaken or misrepresented recall of the past tells us something important. In the unlikely event that Mom had left home regularly during those months she spent in the room under the eaves, her later portrayal of it as a period of extreme isolation suggests that that's how she experienced those months emotionally and psychologically. Even if I had taken the opportunity to have long conversations with Mom about her Booth girl experiences, she'd have been calling up the story through the vagaries of memory, subject to the same limitations and failings. Still, the story-truth, to use novelist Tim O'Brien's language, tells us more about lived experience than the literal, factual happening-truth ever can.[2]

So yes, the study and practice of history has helped me better understand my mother. The exploration of her relationship to motherhood has also led to some interesting observations and uncomfortable questions about my own. If I was looking for a project that hit close to home, I certainly found it.

Us: February 14, 2009

We sit in the front of the church. Eric, me, Steve, and Tu. Kim, Mark, and Christopher. All of Mom's children, together, to say goodbye.

Tu sits quietly for a while, then, as the pastor speaks, he starts whispering, "Dead. Dead, dead, dead."

This little boy, not yet four years old, has lost another woman who loved him dearly.

When the service is over, we follow Mom's coffin down the aisle, past rows of mourners into the frigid cold where the hearse awaits.

The bells peal; the sky sparkles a brilliant, cold blue.

Dead. Dead, dead, dead.[3]

Tu was three and a half years old when Mom died. I tried to keep her alive in his memory for as long as possible. We talked about the things they did together, drove past her house, visited the cemetery, remembered her white hair and brown eyes and glasses. He's almost fifteen as I write this, though, and his conscious recall of Mom is fading ever further, his memories constructed mostly through stories and photos. He hasn't read the letter she wrote him, birthmother to adoptee, but it may be time. I leave that decision to him.

Kim and I are still in touch. We had to establish new terms for our relationship in Mom's absence. I went to Michigan for Christopher's high school graduation, and Kim is always the first one to send Christmas and birthday gifts to Tu. She and I spent a weekend together in Chicago one fall, just as I was beginning work on this project and starting to envision it as a book. I asked her how she felt about it, if she'd be comfortable with my telling a story that is, in many ways, more hers than mine. She offered her support without hesitation and has continued to do so over these many years, sitting down for an interview, sharing her records and recall, patiently answering my questions about obscure details, reviewing drafts of my writing. In the summer of 2018, she had exciting news: she had learned Jack's last name through some research on Ancestry.com. For reasons that are not mine to tell, she has not made contact with him, though she has found some satisfaction in learning at least a bit about her paternal biological roots.

I've been a mother for fourteen years at this point, and the challenges of parenting have changed as Tu and Steve and I have grown up together. I'd once thought I'd be a better mother to a teenager than to a toddler or grade-schooler, better able to communicate with and understand a young adult, but now I'm not so sure. Tu is by turns agreeable and combative, thoughtful and thoughtless, innocent and wise, delightful and awful, all of which is appropriate to his age. The disturbing fact is that I vacillate between those extremes as well, despite my age. I wonder, though, how much of his adolescent angst and development is shaped by his having been adopted. Many researchers and professionals argue that adoption is the defining factor in any adoptee's experience, affecting everything from self-image and brain development to personal relationships and academic performance. I'm not sure if or to what degree this is true for Tu, though I know it is impossible to separate the fact of his adoption from who he is and who he will become, just as it is impossible to separate the fact that I became a mother through adoption from the mother I have become.

Tu, eight years old, is restless. He can't fall asleep in his bedroom, so I let him camp out on the floor in ours. He rustles his pillows and blankets while I read in bed. Steve is watching TV downstairs.

He sighs, then says, "Sometimes it feels like I'm missing a home, like I have another home in this world."

I put my book down. "You mean Vietnam?"

He nods.

"Hmm," I say, leaving him space to continue.

"I miss Vietnam. That's why I like to sleep with my blanket, even if I get hot. It was hot in Vietnam."

"Yes, it was," I agree.

He pauses.

"Sometimes it feels like someone put me in a car and drove and drove all the way over here and gave me to you guys."

"I bet it does," I say.

He waits, then asks *the* question for the first time.

"Was my Vietnam mama mad at me? Is that why she didn't keep me?"

My heart breaks into a thousand pieces, but I answer calmly. "No, honey, she wasn't mad at you." I want to assure him that she loved him and wanted to give him a better life, that she loves him still and misses him every day, but stories of found mothers who reject their adopted-away offspring and stories of birthmothers who long for their lost children and stories of baby-finders and women who give up their infants under duress or for money run through my mind in a jumbled mess. I am confused and don't know where the truth lies, so I am as honestly reassuring as I can be.

"I guess we don't know exactly why she didn't keep you, but it wasn't anything you did. She was not mad at you. I bet she loves you and misses you."

This settles his mind enough for him to drift to sleep.

I dream that night that I am pregnant. I can feel the baby grow and move inside me. It is so real, so visceral. I see the baby emerge from my body, a bloody, squalling thing that I love instantly and completely. I reach down to take him in my arms when someone else's arms reach in and tear him away from me.

"He is not yours," the faceless baby-stealer hisses at me. "Forget about him."

I startle awake, heart pounding and body heavy with an aching absence, wondering about a woman halfway across the globe whose child is snoring peacefully on the mattress on the floor beside me.

I stand on the opposite side of Mom in the adoption gain-loss equation. Though the pain of infertility is real and deep, the irreconcilable fact is that adoption "solves" it only by capitalizing on another woman's (and man's) loss and that it is those privileged by class, race, and nation who most often benefit in the process. Mom and other Booth girls were deemed by their white middle-class culture to be unfit mothers by virtue of their marital status and, often, age and economic dependence. Although single motherhood does not carry the same stigma it once did, and though adoption practice now favors open relationships among members of the constellation, many critics of adoption argue that it is, in all but the most extreme examples of abuse and neglect, a system that continues to disenfranchise women of lesser means who lack the resources that would enable them to either parent their children or make a genuinely free choice to have them adopted. And that's just the critique of domestic, same-race adoption. Add to that the complex structural inequalities that shape transracial and transnational adoption, and the injustice deepens. Many Black, Brown, and Indigenous women in the United States and across the globe have lost their children because politicians and policy makers have exploited them and their communities in service of racist economic and political ends. Instead of devising solutions that would help mothers raise their children with dignity or remedy the underlying inequities, too often child welfare officials have turned to adoption as the solution, placing those children in white, middle-class families . . . such as mine.

I neither pretend nor intend that this book is an exploration of the history or dynamics of transracial/transnational adoption. A topic so complex demands full treatment, and others are doing this important work. Scholars and writers have provided powerful critiques of the global adoption market that are informed by the voices and experiences of adoptees, especially those born in Korea. But it is important to acknowledge that, as much as Mom's personal experiences as a birthmother had been shaped by the historical forces of her era, so, too, are mine as the mother of a transnationally and transracially adopted son. In 2006, our adoption of Tu was one of 20,675 such cross-border placements to occur in the United States, a slight decline from the historic peak of 22,989 in 2004. More than 5,600 of those adoptions were of children born in Vietnam. In 2001, Vietnam ranked third, behind

China and Korea, among Asian countries that sent children to families in North America. By 2018, however, transnational adoption had declined by a whopping 82 percent from its 2004 peak as the provisions of the Hague Convention, designed to preserve biological kinship and cultural identity and to prevent child trafficking, tightened control of the intercountry transfer of children.[4]

As I write these final words in the spring of 2020, in the year of the coronavirus pandemic, Minneapolis, St. Paul, and cities across the country have erupted in righteous fury over the latest in a long history of police killings of unarmed African American men. George Floyd's brutal death at the hands of Minneapolis police officers on May 25 has sparked protest among Black Americans who daily live with the consequences of entrenched, systemic racism. But it has also triggered an outpouring of support from a good many white people and widespread acknowledgment of "white privilege," a concept I first encountered in graduate school in the mid-1990s. Though mentioning George Floyd and Black Lives Matter might seem a detour from the topic at hand, it is white privilege that weaves them together.

Steve and I, like the majority of those who bring a child from another country into their families, are white, middle-class, US citizens with the means, however cobbled together, to afford the costly adoption process. It is no coincidence that most transracially and transnationally constituted families are headed by people like us. The power differences that distinguished Booth girls from the adoptive parents who raised their children are in our case magnified by race- and nation-based inequities. If I must grapple with the imbalance that defines adoption in general—one mother's loss becoming another mother's gain—I must also acknowledge that my family has been made possible through an interlocking system that has granted me far more rights than it has my son's Vietnamese mother.[5]

I had a sense of this as we made our way through the adoption process and traveled to Vietnam, but mostly I was focused on the deficits that we, as white Americans, would bring to our role as parents of a Vietnamese child and how we might mitigate them as effectively as possible. Though we had turned to adoption in order to build a family that we could not create biologically, not to "rescue" a child, we believed that Tu and the other children in his care center were in genuine need of homes and families. This project has helped me see the ways in which such "need" has often been created or exaggerated by a system prepared to offer adoption as a solution that benefits people like us and serves political and/or economic ends far beyond the radar of most adoptive parents. As a historian and daughter of a Booth girl, it is easy to condemn these dynamics. As an adoptive parent, it is more difficult, but perhaps more urgent, to do so. In the best-case scenario, if undertaken in an environment as attuned to the rights of birthmothers (and fathers) and children as it is to those of adoptive parents, adoption is an imperfect but valuable response to real need. Those of us who stand to gain the most from it must work to minimize the loss suffered by our children and their mothers. I am still working out how to do so, how to live justly when I have benefited from injustice.

This too, however, is work to be undertaken elsewhere, and likely for a lifetime. For now, I will say only that I am deeply grateful to have Tu in my life. I love him dearly if not always well. He has his own story to tell, and it is his alone to tell. It will evolve as he grows from adolescence to adulthood, in the process acquiring the capacity to examine his life through the wider lens of history. I am eager for it and hope he knows I stand ready to help him discover it and to hear it, in all of its pain and anger and happiness and love.

In the meantime, I will practice my mothering and will do so with the insights gleaned from this project. I will remember the onetime Booth girls who shared their joys and sorrows with me as I reached across time and space to learn about my mother's past, their generosity all the more remarkable for its willingness to cross the birthmother–adoptive mother divide. Their voices will help me try to imagine my son's mother, the one about whom we know nothing and for whom we have fruitlessly searched, even as I realize that my ability to do so is limited by differences of culture, of language, of economic power, of experience. The lessons I have learned from the archives, and the other historians who have mined them, remind me that everything has a context, even the most important relationships that grow in the most intimate spaces, including mine with Mom and mine with Tu. I shall try to live by Mom's example of loving deeply, if imperfectly, as I make my way down the thorny path of motherhood.

Us: February 9, 2010[6]

Dear Mom,

Today it is a year since your death. Steve and Tu and I drove by your house, and Tu said, "I'm sad Grandma had to move out of that house and into the ground." "Me, too," I said. We still talk about you often.

Tu is doing well. He's getting big and sassy and funny and smart, as you would expect. He enjoys swimming and skating, but not soccer. He hasn't bitten anyone at school for a couple of months now, knock on wood. He is learning to write words and spell a little. He loves reading some of those old kids' books of mine that you saved, from *The Snowy Day* to *Puss in Boots* to *Jack and the Beanstalk*. We have survived, I have survived, without you here to help care for and love him, sometimes just barely.

I love you and I miss you and I hereby allow you to exist as a happy memory, a secret smile, a familiar gesture. I see you in myself and Eric, and in Tu. You live on in your words, your writing. I take from you your sense of humor, and compassion, and modesty, and impatience, and insecurity, and tendency toward isolation. I feel you in the legacy of love you left behind. I see in your flaws and failings and strengths and successes the full measure of your humanity. On this day, this anniversary, I love you as much as ever I did, and I also begin to let you go.

Love,
Kim

ACKNOWLEDGMENTS

There's a document on my laptop titled, simply, "People Who Helped," and it is to them I would like to offer my heartfelt thanks.

This book, if not the events it describes, began in the archives as I delved into the history of Booth Memorial Hospital. I relied on the expertise and guidance of the staff at the Gale Family Library at the Minnesota Historical Society; Erik Moore at the University of Minnesota Archives; Susan Mitchem and Tyler Boenecke at the Salvation Army National Archives; Major John Price, Major Gloria Stepke, and Nanci Gasiel at the Salvation Army Central Territory Historical Museum; and, especially, Linnea Anderson at the University of Minnesota Libraries' Social Welfare History Archives. Salvation Army officers and staff at what is now the Booth Brown House opened its doors to me three times. Major Arnel Ruppel, Katharine Adams, Jessica Nelson, and Steven Godfrey helped me imagine my mother as a Booth girl who once scrubbed the floors on which I stood some fifty years later.

I am also indebted to organizations and individuals that supported my research. The Minnesota Independent Scholars Forum (MISF) secured two Minnesota Arts and Cultural Heritage Fund grants, the first of which funded my visit to the Salvation Army National Archives in Alexandria, Virginia, the second of which allowed me to conduct oral history interviews with former Booth girls. Thank you to David Megarry, Michael Woolsey, and Barb Sommer for overseeing these grants. St. Catherine University also provided assistance through its 2015 Summer Scholars program. My student/colleague

Amanda Campbell brought unique insight to the study of "unwed mothers" in mid-twentieth-century Minnesota. She has her own adoption-and-mothering story to tell, and I eagerly await its emergence.

The Abigail Quigley McCarthy Center for Women at St. Kate's gave me the chance to discuss my work in a collegial environment, as did the MISF, the Ramsey County Historical Society, and the Minnesota Correctional Facility for women in Shakopee. The conversations that followed these presentations deepened my thinking, as did feedback offered by fellow writers. My longtime writing group—Jennifer Reinhart, David Good, and Steve Plasch—read the earliest drafts of this work, while Andy Silberman reviewed the manuscript in its entirety. The late Cheri Register helped me conceive this project from the beginning, while Ann Regan, my editor at the Minnesota Historical Society Press, helped me see it to its end. Ann offered just the right balance of support and critique, nudging me to think more deeply when it would have been easier, but less honest, not to.

I offer my humblest thanks to the women who agreed to share their own Booth stories with me. They welcomed me to their homes and hearts, and I found pieces of my mother in each of them. Thank you also to my friends who have also become parents through adoption, among them Margaret Weeks, Cindy Janssen, Senia and Kai Tuominen, and, especially, Stacie Johnson. Thank you, too, to my friend and boxing trainer, Sarah Mickelson, who has shared her insights as a Korean adoptee raised by white parents in Minnesota.

Finally, and most importantly, thank you to my family, extended, nuclear, and adoptive. My Iverson / Moore relatives—especially Irene (Iverson) Pehling, the late Diane (Moore) Pletcher, Marcia (Moore) Kellerman, Dave Moore, and Kari (Pletcher) Erickson—have willingly sifted through old memories and lent important insights about our family dynamics. I would not have considered turning my family's private past into a public narrative without the consent of those who share most intimately in it: my brother, Eric; my sister, Kim; my husband, Steve; and my son, Tu. Each of them has offered unqualified support from the beginning, when this book was just a kernel of an idea. I am especially grateful to Kim, who has graciously and unhesitatingly opened herself, her memories, and her family story to me. I am especially hopeful that Tu will find something useful in learning more about the grandmother he hardly remembers, the one who loved him so readily and so completely. May he find, in her story, clues about his first mother's own. I hope that someday she can share it with him herself.

NOTES

Notes to "A Note about Language"

1. Marietta E. Spencer, "The Language of Adoption," 1978, box 2, Concerned United Birthparents, Inc. Minnesota, University of Minnesota Libraries, Social Welfare History Archives (hereafter, CUB-SWHA); Marietta E. Spencer, "The Terminology of Adoption," *Child Welfare* 58, no. 7 (July-August 1979): 451–59. For use of market language in adoption, see, e.g., "187 Babies in State Placed by 'Gray Market,'" *Minneapolis Star*, January 31, 1952, 29; Clark E. Vincent, "The Adoption Market and the Unwed Mother's Baby," *Marriage and Family Living* 18, no. 2 (May 1956): 124–27, available: http://www.jstor.org/stable/348636; Diane Turski, "Why 'Birthmother' Means 'Breeder,'" 2002, Healing and Restoring Families Dismembered by Adoption website, http://adopting back.com/.

2. Gail Hanssen, national CUB, letter to Patty O'Gorman, CUB-MN, June 19, 1978, box 2, CUB-SWHA; CUB Communicator, July 1978, available at CUB History Channel, cubirthparents.org; "Honest Adoption Language," The Baby Scoop Era Research Initiative, https://babyscoopera.com/adoption-language/honest-adoption-language/; Melissa Rizzo Weller, "'I Guess They're All Real Moms Then': Constructing Motherhood Through Language in the Adoption Community," *Adoption Quarterly* (2019): DOI:10.1080/10926755.2019.1675836.

1. Jane Jeong Trenka's *The Language of Blood* (St. Paul: Minnesota Historical Society Press, 2003) is a memoir of a Korean woman who had been adopted and raised by white parents in Minnesota. Cheri Register's *Beyond Good Intentions: A Mother Reflects on Raising Internationally Adopted Children* (St. Paul, MN: Yeong and Yeong, 2005) seeks to educate adoptive parents about how to acknowledge racial difference in families constituted through international adoption.

2. Statistics from "Historic Booth Hospital," on the Salvation Army Booth Brown House website, https://centralusa.salvationarmy.org/northern/BoothBrown House/historic-booth-hospital/; extrapolated from the Salvation Army, "Service to Unmarried Parents and Their Children, 1961," 1962, 2, Women's Social Services—Rescue Homes (Unwed Mothers), Salvation Army National Archives, Alexandria, VA (hereafter, SANA); Ann Fessler, *The Girls Who Went Away: The Hidden History of Women Who Surrendered Children for Adoption in the Decades Before* Roe v. Wade (New York: Penguin, 2006), 8.

3. Kim Heikkila, "My Mother 'Got in Trouble' in 1960s Minnesota," *Minneapolis Star Tribune*, April 30, 2016; Kim Heikkila, "'Brighter and Better for Every Person': Building the New Salvation Army Rescue Home of St. Paul, 1913," *Ramsey County History* (Spring 2016): 3–11; Kim Heikkila, "'Everybody Thinks It's Right to Give the Child Away': Unwed Mothers at Booth Memorial Hospital, 1961–1963," *Minnesota History* 65, no. 6 (Summer 2017): 229–41.

4. Many others who have connections to Booth St. Paul have contacted me as well, through social media and email. Though I was unable to conduct formal interviews with them or include their stories in this book, I am deeply grateful for their willingness to share their stories with a virtual stranger and hope to devise an ongoing project to collect such accounts.

5. National Center for Education Statistics, Indicator 7, "Births to Unmarried Women, by Age and Race," 26, available at nces.ed.gov; Robert D. Grove and Alice Hetzel, "Vital Statistics Rates in the United States, 1940–1960," US Department of Health, Education, and Welfare, 1968, Table 29, 186; Rickie Solinger, *Wake Up Little Susie: Single Pregnancy and Race Before* Roe v. Wade (New York: Routledge, 1992), 203. As Solinger points out, at least until the mid-1970s, most Black babies were born to married mothers: Rickie Solinger, *Beggars and Choosers: How the Politics of Choice Shapes Adoption, Abortion, and Welfare in the United States* (New York: Hill and Wang, 2001), 94. The NCES figures and Solinger's *Susie* focused on Black and white women. Grove and Hetzel's statistics about Minnesota did not distinguish among nonwhite women, but given the racial composition of the state in 1960, "nonwhite" probably refers to Black and Indigenous women.

6. Solinger, *Wake Up Little Susie*.

7. Tessie Liu, "Teaching the Differences Among Women from a Historical

Perspective: Rethinking Race and Gender as Social Categories," *Women's Studies International Forum* 14, no. 4 (1991), reprinted in Vicki L. Ruiz and Ellen Carol DuBois, eds., *Unequal Sisters: A Multicultural Reader in U.S. Women's History* (New York: Routledge, 2000): 627–38, quotes, 637.

8. Solinger, *Wake Up Little Susie*, 24. See also Laura Briggs, *Somebody's Children: The Politics of Transracial and Transnational Adoption* (Durham, NC: Duke University Press, 2012); Margaret D. Jacobs, *A Generation Removed: The Fostering and Adoption of Indigenous Children in the Postwar World* (Lincoln: University of Nebraska Press, 2014); Dorothy Roberts, *Killing the Black Body: Race, Reproduction, and the Meaning of Liberty* (1997; reprint, New York: Vintage Books, 2017); Dorothy Roberts, *Shattered Bonds: The Color of Child Welfare* (New York: Basic *Civitas* Books, 2002).

9. Solinger, *Wake Up Little Susie*, 51, 203. Kathy Stolley notes that 19.3 percent of white women relinquished premaritally born children from 1952 to 1972, a considerably lower percentage than that cited by Solinger and others: Kathy S. Stolley, "Statistics on Adoption in the United States," *The Future of Children* 3, no. 1 (Spring 1993): 26–42, figure cited 32–33. Solinger's figure may pertain specifically to white women who gave birth in maternity homes, as it is in accordance with statistics provided by the Salvation Army for its network of such facilities; this would not account for the majority of white women who did not reside in maternity homes, some portion of which opted to keep and raise their babies. Moreover, Stolley's statistic encompasses the period of highest rates of surrender as well as the period of sharply decreasing rates of surrender among white single mothers in the 1960s. Its comparably low surrender rate may also include white women who gave birth premaritally, kept the child, and married thereafter. In any case, the percentage of Black women who surrendered premaritally born children from 1952 to 1972 was a mere 1.5 percent: Stolley, "Statistics on Adoption in the United States," 32–33.

10. Jacobs, *A Generation Removed*, 93; Minnesota Compass, Population by Racial and Ethnic Group, Minnesota, 1960–2019, available: http://www.mncompass.org /demographics/race#1–5523-d; Roberts, *Shattered Bonds*, 249.

11. My comments about policies and practices governing nonwhite single pregnant women will attend primarily to Black and Indigenous women. In 1960, Minnesota's population was 98.2 percent white, 0.7 percent Black, 0.5 percent Native American, and 0.1 percent Asian (the 1960 census did not take note of nonwhite Hispanic people: Minnesota Compass). Though no comprehensive population records from Booth St. Paul exist, it was, per national Salvation Army policy, a nominally integrated facility. The few references I have found to nonwhite women in residence at Booth, however, have been of "Negro" and "Indian" women.

1. Sharon Moore Wikstrom, "Greyhound," unpublished, undated manuscript, written sometime in the late 1990s, 5–6.

2. Sharon Moore Wikstrom, "My Brother Sam," unpublished family story, November 1995, 5, in my possession. Sam, the shortened name by which my uncle Sterling was known, was the fourth of the six Moore children. He died in 1991, after which my mother wrote an account of his life as she recalled it.

3. This family history is culled from various of my mother's writings, including "Little Man," July 2003; "My Brother Sam"; an untitled, incomplete memoir, March 1993; "The Moore Family of Arkansas," unpublished family history, June 1999; "Carrie's Story: A Time to Speak," December 1994.

4. These figures are taken from Iverson Maternity Home Registers, 1943–1958, Minnesota, Division of Hospital Services, Maternity Hospital Records, Minnesota Historical Society (hereafter, MNHS), and from an essay written by my mother's cousin: Rick Iverson, "Carrie," unpublished, undated manuscript, 16. Although I have a copy of this essay from my mother's possessions, it is also archived at MNHS, along with other records of the Iverson Maternity Home.

5. Quote and account of this event from Sharon Wikstrom, "Birth Rite," undated, unpublished essay, perhaps written for her coursework at the University of Minnesota in the late 1990s, 5–6.

6. See, for example, "Kinsey Reveals His Findings on Behavior of Women," *Minneapolis Star,* August 20, 1953, 25; Beth L. Bailey, *Sex in the Heartland* (Cambridge, MA: Harvard University Press, 1999).

7. There was one exception in the Iverson Maternity Home patient records: a register from 1951 listed only the mother's name, with no "Mrs." preceding it. Her name and the doctor's signature were the only pieces of information contained on the register. There was nothing further about her or her marital status, or a husband, or the birth of a child—information the state required Carrie Iverson, as the licensee of the maternity home, to collect. If this woman perchance had delivered a child out of wedlock, Carrie also would have been legally obliged to record the birth as such and forward that information to the state public welfare department. For state-mandated record and reporting requirements in effect during the time Carrie operated the Iverson Maternity Home, see Minnesota Statutes 1927, section 4553 and 4556; Minnesota Statutes 1953, section 258.08, https://www.revisor.mn.gov/statutes/.

"Moral ostracism" from memo to Budget Committee and Social Planning Committee from staff at Greater St. Paul Community Chest and Council, June 16, 1947, United Way of the Saint Paul Area (Minn.) Organizational Records, box 47, folder: United Way Agencies: Booth Memorial Hospital, 1947–1949, Minnesota Historical Society (hereafter, UWSP-MNHS). This memo was part of a larger analysis of the funding the St. Paul Community Chest provided Booth relative to that received by Booth residents' home counties. The local chest was concerned that it was being unduly charged for caring for girls who lived beyond its service boundaries. Statistics from memo to Miss Chase from Jean Roberts, August 25, 1947, Minnesota Department of Public Welfare, Division of Social Welfare, Central Files, box 23, folder: Unmarried Mothers, MNHS.

8. Dr. Alfred Kinsey and his associates questioned 5,940, mostly white, mostly urban, American women. "Kinsey Reveals His Findings," 25; Victor Cohn, "Here Are Dr. Kinsey's Findings About Women; Indiana Professor Publishes Results of 15-Year Sex Research," *Minneapolis Morning Tribune*, August 20, 1953, 1, 12; "Here's State Reaction to Dr. Kinsey's Report," *Minneapolis Sunday Tribune*, September 20, 1953, 3: articles from the *Star Tribune* cited here and below available at startribune.newspapers.com. For an analysis of how the discourse surrounding the Kinsey reports reflected broader concerns in American culture, see Miriam Reumann, *American Sexual Character: Sex, Gender, and National Identity in the Kinsey Reports* (Berkeley: University of California Press, 2005).

9. See Beth Bailey, *From Front Porch to Back Seat: Courtship in Twentieth-Century America* (Baltimore, MD: Johns Hopkins University Press, 1988), 77–82, for a discussion of the distinguishing sex-based features of youth culture, and the role the mass media played in shaping them, in the early to mid-twentieth century. Jean James, "Teen-Agers Told of Love Pitfalls," *Minneapolis Morning Tribune*, February 3, 1950, 15; Josephine Lowman, "Teen-age: Time for Gayety, Not For 'Going Steady'" and "Love Can Be an Illusion, Young Told," both in *Minneapolis Star*, August 1, 1950, 17; Jhan and June Robbins, "The Truth About Teenagers; A This Week Report," *Minneapolis Star and Tribune*, March 9, 1952, 7–9, and "The Truth About Teen-Age Morals," March 16, 1952, 12–13; Geri Hoffner and Victor Cohn, "Teens in Trouble" series, *Minneapolis Morning Tribune*, March 10–14, 1952; quote from Robbins, March 9, 1952, 7.

10. Pitirim A. Sorokin, "The Case Against Sex Freedom," *This Week Magazine/Minneapolis Star and Tribune*, January 3, 1954, 7, 16, 19; Paul A. Landis, "Your Dating Days" series, *Minneapolis Morning Tribune*, February 28–March 5, 1955; Victor Cohn, "What Can Parents Do?" series, *Minneapolis Morning Tribune*, September 5–18, 1956; Howard Whitman, "Keeping Our Sanity" series, *Minneapolis Star*, March 18–30, 1957; "Our Crisis in Morals" series, *Minneapolis Star*, October 20–November 4, 1958; "Truth From Youth" series, *Minneapolis Sunday Tribune*, January 25–March 8, 1959, statistics from "Truth From Youth: What Teen-Agers Say About Necking, Drivers Licenses, and Dating," January 25, 1959, 1, 5, and "Truth From Youth: 61 Pct. of Teen-agers Say Adult Criticism Isn't Justified," February 1, 1959, 6. The *Sunday Tribune* ran another "Truth From Youth" series in 1960 as well. See also John D'Emilio and Estelle B. Freedman, *Intimate Matters: A History of Sexuality in America,* 3rd ed. (1988; reprint, Chicago: University of Chicago Press, 2012), part iv.

11. Elaine Tyler May, *Homeward Bound: American Families in the Cold War Era* (New York: Basic Books, 1988), 127–28; Paul H. Landis, "Your Dating Days: Should Teen-Agers Go Steady? Many Youths Never Date at All," *Minneapolis Morning Tribune*, February 28, 1955, 9, and "Your Dating Days: When Is Petting a Sign of Love?" *Minneapolis Morning Tribune*, March 1, 1955, 8. These and four other articles that ran in the series

were excerpted from Paul H. Landis, *Your Dating Days: Looking Forward to Happy Marriage* (New York: McGraw-Hill Book Company, 1954). See Bailey, *From Front Porch to Back Seat,* 87–95, for a discussion of how market-based ideology was used to control young people's sexual behavior and the degree to which it "equated value with woman's virtue" (94).

12. Statistic cited in Landis, "Should Teen-Agers Go Steady?" 9. He also notes that 50 percent of high school boys rarely or never dated.

13. From an unpublished, handwritten journal entry/essay written by Sharon Moore Wikstrom, titled "In Search of the Invisible Woman," ca. 2000, hereafter referred to as "Invisible Woman"; Wikstrom, "Greyhound," 6; "E-Day Royalty," *Minneapolis Morning Tribune,* May 6, 1960, 18.

14. Wikstrom, "Invisible Woman."

15. Bailey, *Sex in the Heartland,* 83–84; Alan Petigny, *The Permissive Society: America, 1941–1965* (Cambridge: Cambridge University Press, 2009), 161–62; statistics for Spring Lake Park High School based on my unscientific analysis of data from the 1957 commencement brochure and fiftieth reunion scrapbook.

16. Nevitt Sanford, "Is College Education a Waste of Time for Women?" *Ladies' Home Journal,* May 1957, 198, cited in Rebecca Frances Isaacs, "The Feminine Mystake: Betty Friedan and the Dogma of Domesticity in 1950s America" (MPhil thesis, University of Birmingham, 2010), available: https://etheses.bham.ac.uk//id/eprint/2910/; Cedric Adams, "In This Corner," *Minneapolis Star,* September 6, 1957, 1B; Wini Breines, *Young, White, and Miserable: Growing Up Female in the Fifties* (Boston: Beacon Press, 1992), 73–75; May, *Homeward Bound,* 78–79; Ellen Carol DuBois and Lynn Dumenil, *Through Women's Eyes: An American History with Documents, Volume Two: Since 1865,* 3rd ed. (Boston: Bedford/St. Martin's, 2012), 605; Betty Friedan, *The Feminine Mystique* (New York: W. W. Norton and Co., 1963), ch. 7. See also Isaacs, "The Feminine Mystake," ch. 1; Joanne Meyerowitz, "Beyond the Feminine Mystique: A Reassessment of Postwar Mass Culture, 1946–1958," in *Not June Cleaver: Women and Gender in Postwar America, 1945–1960* (Philadelphia: Temple University Press, 1994), 229–62; Eva Moskowitz, "'It's Good to Blow Your Top': Women's Magazines and a Discourse of Discontent, 1945–1965," *Journal of Women's History* 8, no. 3 (Fall 1996): 66–98.

17. James P. Mitchell, "First Jobs of College Women: Report on Women Graduates Class of 1957," US Department of Labor, Women's Bureau Bulletin No. 268, 1959, 20, available: https://fraser.stlouisfed.org/docs/publications/women/b0268_dolwb_1959.pdf. The percentage of women graduating with degrees in journalism was the smallest of all fields listed. Theta Sigma Phi was established at the University of Washington in 1909, and in 1972 changed its name to Women in Communications, Inc. (WICI). In my late teens and twenties, when Mom was working in the marketing department at Carlson Companies, she spoke often about her involvement in WICI.

18. GPA information is taken from a resume she prepared sometime after August 1964.

19. Wikstrom, "Moore Family of Arkansas," 208–9; Wikstrom, "Invisible Woman."

20. Dr. Marion Hilliard, "A Woman Doctor Talks About Sex Education," *Minneapolis Morning Tribune*, October 9, 1957, 12. This article was a condensed excerpt from Hilliard's book, *A Woman Doctor Looks at Love and Life* (New York: Doubleday, 1957).

21. "Ministers Dispute Catholic Stand on Sex Training," *Minneapolis Star,* November 20, 1950, 19; Herman M. Jahr, MD, "The 'Facts of Life' Problem," *This Week Magazine,* August 21, 1955, 14–15; "Thousands Now Look to the Church for Sex Guidance," *Minneapolis Morning Tribune,* August 4, 1952, 1, 8 (this article was a condensed version of Eric Northrup's "The Clergy's New Task: Sex Education," that would appear in the August 12 issue of *Look* magazine); Alfred Kinsey in Victor Cohn, "Kinsey's Goal: Happier Marriages," *Minneapolis Morning Tribune,* August 23, 1953, 6.

22. See Susan K. Freeman, *Sex Goes to School: Girls and Sex Education Before the 1960s* (Champaign: University of Illinois Press, 2008) for more on the development of public school sex education curricula; William S. Jarnagin, "Objects to Prelate's Ruling on Sex Classes," letter to editor, *Minneapolis Morning Tribune,* December 17, 1949, 4; Albert E. Wiggam, "Explore Your Mind," *Minneapolis Morning Tribune,* October 9, 1951, 14, June 4, 1952, 14, and September 8, 1952, 43.

23. Jeffrey P. Moran, *Teaching Sex: The Shaping of Adolescence in the Twentieth Century* (Cambridge, MA: Harvard University Press, 2000), ch. 5; Cohn, "Kinsey's Goal: Happier Marriages"; Freeman, *Sex Goes to School,* 9, 51. For a more detailed description of the film, produced by the E. C. Brown Trust in Oregon, see Freeman, *Sex Goes to School,* 48–52, 76–79. *Human Reproduction,* 16mm, 21 min. (New York: McGraw-Hill, 1947). The film was a companion to Harold S. Diehl's *Textbook of Healthful Living* (New York: McGraw-Hill, 1945).

24. "City Schools Began Using Movie in '49," *Minneapolis Sunday Tribune,* August 13, 1950, 6; Wiggam, "Let's Explore Your Mind," *Minneapolis Morning Tribune,* July 27, 1948, 9; Bernard Casserly, "Nokomis Parents OK Sex Film for School," *Minneapolis Star,* April 4, 1949, 1; Lillian L. Biester, William Griffiths, and N. O. Pearce, *Units in Personal Health and Human Relations* (Minneapolis: University of Minnesota Press, 1947). Even if there had been a coordinated education program, many Catholic students would have been prevented from participating in light of Archbishop John Gregory Murray's insistence that public school sex instruction violated church law and that parents had a duty to remove their children from such courses: "Archbishop in Warning; Bars Catholic Children From Sex Education Classes," *Minneapolis Star,* December 12, 1949, 25.

25. Jane Browne to Mary Brown of the Star and Tribune, February 28, 1956, box 19, folder 10; "Educational Programs," June 18, 1957, 4, box 17, folder 13; "Dating / Courting / Marriage," brochure for course cosponsored by Fireside Luther League and Hennepin County League for Planned Parenthood, 1956, 2, box 17, folder 10—all from Planned Parenthood of Minnesota records, sw0024, University of Minnesota, Social Welfare History Archives (hereafter, PPM-SWHA).

26. Interviews BH-230, BH-236, BH-238, BH-240, BH-241, quote from BH-236, box

19, folder 2: Adolescent Girl in Conflict: Individual Interviews—Booth Memorial Hospital (Unwed Mothers) 1963, Gisela Konopka papers, University Archives, University of Minnesota Libraries (hereafter, Konopka papers); Fessler, *The Girls Who Went Away*, 37–40, quote 38–39.

27. Wikstrom, "Invisible Woman."

28. Wikstrom, "Invisible Woman"; Breines, *Young, White, and Miserable*, 47, 58; Wikstrom, "Moore Family of Arkansas," 209–11.

29. Wikstrom, "Invisible Woman."

30. Quote and contents of this section from Pam, interview with author, July 13, 2017, Booth Memorial Hospital Oral History records, sw0349, University of Minnesota Libraries, Social Welfare History Archives (hereafter, BMHOH-SWHA).

Notes to Chapter 2: "California Dreaming"

1. Wikstrom, "Greyhound," 5, 8.

2. This scene is based on Sharon Wikstrom, "A Letter to Kim," May 12, 2001, 20, and "A Letter to Kim from Mom," December 2008, 5; Referral History Guide, completed by caseworker Patricia Peart, January 31, 1961, 3—all in my possession.

3. Elaine Tyler May, *Barren in the Promised Land: Childless Americans and the Pursuit of Happiness* (New York: Basic Books, 1995), 128–38, "reproductive mania" quote on 133; Sandra L. Colby and Jennifer M. Ortman, "The Baby Boom Cohort in the United States: 2012 to 2060. Population Estimates and Projections," *Current Population Reports*, P25-1141 (US Census Bureau, May 2014), 2, available: https://www.census.gov/prod/2014pubs/p25-1141.pdf; "American Generation Fast Facts," CNN library, September 14, 2018, available: http://www.cnn.com/2013/11/06/us/baby-boomer-generation-fast-facts/; Petigny, *The Permissive Society*, 113–15, 130–33; Fessler, *The Girls Who Went Away*, 30–32. The pregnancy rate was higher for single African American girls, but the numbers were rising more dramatically among young white women: Stephanie J. Ventura and Christine A. Bachrach, "Nonmarital Childbearing in the United States, 1940–1999," *National Vital Statistics Reports* 48.16, Department of Health and Human Services, Centers for Disease Control and Prevention, October 18, 2000, 2, 10, 17, 20, available: http://www.cdc.gov/nchs/data/nvsr/nvsr48/nvs48_16.pdf; "Vital Statistics of the United States, 1961, Volume I—Natality," National Center for Health Statistics, 1961, 1–3, 1–14, 2–91, available: http://www.cdc.gov/nchs/data/vsus/vsus_1961_1.pdf; Solinger, *Wake Up Little Susie*, 13; "Trends in Illegitimacy, United States, 1940–1965," Vital and Health Statistics Series 21.15, February 1968, Table D, 8, available: www.cdc.gov/nchs/data/series/sr_21/sr21_015.pdf; untitled memo, 1961, box 47, folder 4, UWSP-MNHS.

4. Andrea Tone, *Devices and Desires: A History of Contraceptives in America* (New York: Hill and Wang, 2001), 98–107, 114–15, 200; Petigny, *The Permissive Society*, 110–12; Mary, interview with author, July 19, 2017, BMHOH-SWHA.

5. Tone, *Devices and Desires*, 117, 151–56.

6. Kirsten M. J. Thompson, "A Brief History of Birth Control in the US," Our Bodies, Ourselves website, December 14, 2013, available: https://www.ourbodiesourselves.org/book-excerpts/health-article/a-brief-history-of-birth-control/; Steven M. Spencer, "The Birth Control Revolution," *Saturday Evening Post*, January 15, 1966; Minnesota Statutes 1891, chapter 86, title 10, section 6234; Minnesota Statutes 1965, chapter 617, section 251, https://www.revisor.mn.gov/statutes/; Sam Newlund, "Birth Control Curb Repealed by House," *Minneapolis Tribune*, May 7, 1965, 18. Minnesota's statute had not criminalized the *use* of contraceptives, and authorities had not actively enforced the law for some time, but common practice still funneled birth control to married women.

7. May, *Homeward Bound*, 151; Carl T. Rowan, "Moral Issue Disagreement Causes Debate," in "How Many People?" series, *Minneapolis Morning Tribune*, February 15, 1960, 22; quotes from "The Churches Speak Up on Birth Control," Planned Parenthood Federation of America, ca. 1961, box 21, folder 14, PPM-SWHA. Tom Davis argues that a broad cross-section of clergy—the most notable exception being the Catholic Church—had come to support Planned Parenthood and women's reproductive rights by the mid-twentieth century: see Tom Davis, *Sacred Work: Planned Parenthood and Its Clergy Alliances* (New Brunswick, NJ: Rutgers University Press, 2005), esp. 41–46.

8. Bailey, *Sex in the Heartland*, 124. In 1918, the New York State Court of Appeals decided in *The People of the State of New York v. Margaret Sanger* that doctors could prescribe contraceptives to married couples in order to prevent disease. Letter from Donald W. Cowan, director, University of Minnesota Student Health Services to Professor Noel Perrin, Dartmouth College, December 23, 1969, box 11, Health Service 1969 folder, Vice President of Student Affairs records, University of Minnesota Archives (hereafter, VPSA-UMNA); Donald W. Cowan, "Bulletin to Staff re: Policy on Contraceptives," September 27, 1965, box 11, Health Service 1964–1966 folder, VPSA-UMNA; Delores Lutz, "Birth Control Plan Announced," *Minnesota Daily*, October 30, 1969, 1, 14; Delores Lutz, "At University Health Service, Single Coeds Refused Contraceptives," *Minnesota Daily*, January 15, 1970, 1–2; memo from Paul Cashman to University of Minnesota President Malcolm Moos and Donald K. Smith, January 3, 1970, box 11, Health Service 1970 folder, VPSA-UMNA; memo from Donald W. Cowan to Paul Cashman, October 25, 1971, box 11, Health Service 1971 folder, VPSA-UMNA.

9. Mary Losure, "'Motherhood Protection' and the Minnesota Birth Control League," *Minnesota History* 54, no. 8 (Winter 1995): 359–70; Elaine Tyler May, *America and the Pill: A History of Promise, Peril, and Liberation* (New York: Basic Books, 2010), ch. 2; Bailey, *Sex in the Heartland*, 105–9; Linda Gordon, *The Moral Property of Women: A History of Birth Control Politics in America* (Champaign: University of Illinois Press, 2002), ch. 11 and 12; Rickie Solinger, *Pregnancy and Power: A Short History of Reproductive Politics in America* (New York: New York University Press, 2005), 163–73, 186–200; transcript, Twin City Roundtable on KUOM, June 10, 1956, quotes on 7, 11, box 17, folder

9, PPM-SWHA. Jane Browne said that allowing couples to control the spacing of their children would also help prevent unwanted children from becoming delinquents.

10. Clinic questionnaires, November–December 1958 and March 1959, box 21, folder 10; volunteer notebooks, State Fair 1959, n.p., folder 15, State Fair 1955, n.p., folder 12, and "State Fair Log, August 23rd through September 1, 1958," 5, folder 14—all in box 18, PPM-SWHA.

11. Planned Parenthood of Minneapolis annual reports, 1957 and 1958, box 21, folder 2; patient letters, 1950s, box 20, folder 19; clinic questionnaires, 1958–59, box 21, folder 10; "Churches Speak Up"; "A History of Planned Parenthood of St. Paul," 1970, quote on 4, box 26, folder 1—all in PPM-SWHA.

12. Solinger, *Pregnancy and Power*, 163–73, 186–200; Roberts, *Killing the Black Body*, ch. 2, esp. 76–79, 82–88; Gordon, *The Moral Property of Women*, 289–90.

13. Roberts, *Killing the Black Body*, 90–95; Gordon, *The Moral Property of Women*, 342–47; Jacobs, *A Generation Removed*, 91–93. For more on eugenic sterilization in Minnesota, see Molly Ladd-Taylor, "Coping with a 'Public Menace': Eugenic Steriliza-tion in Minnesota," *Minnesota History* 59, no. 6 (Summer 2005): 237–48.

14. Roberts, *Killing the Black Body*, 95–96; Gordon, *The Moral Property of Women*, 343–44.

15. Spencer, "The Birth Control Revolution"; Wikstrom, "Greyhound," 7.

16. May, *Barren in the Promised Land*, 18 and ch. 4.

17. May, *Barren in the Promised Land*, 164, 166–68; Serena H. Chen, MD, and Edward E. Wallach, MD, "Five Decades of Progress in Management of the Infertile Couple," *Fertility and Sterility* 62, no. 4 (October 1994): 666–73, available: www.fertstert.org /article/S0015-0282(16)56987-8/pdf; Kara W. Swanson, "The Birth of the Sperm Bank," *Annals of Iowa* 71 (2012): 241–42, available: https://doi.org/10.17077/0003-4827.1645; Margaret Marsh and Wanda Ronner, *The Fertility Doctor: John Rock and the Reproductive Revolution* (Baltimore, MD: Johns Hopkins University Press, 2008), 106–8, 166–68.

18. "Selective breeding" quote from Swanson, "Birth of the Sperm Bank," 246; Gene Newhall, "Test Tube Baby Bills Drawn Up," *Minneapolis Star*, February 28, 1949, 1; "'Test Tube' Baby Ban Supported: Catholics Back Bill to Outlaw Practice," *Minneapo-lis Morning Tribune*, March 23, 1949, 7; "'Test Tube' Babies," editorial in *Minneapolis Star*, March 24, 1949, 24; William Thorkelson, "Church Study Asked on Planned Parent-hood," *Minneapolis Star*, November 13, 1952, 1, 8; "Catholics Are Warned," *Minneapolis Star*, June 14, 1958, 7. For more on the history of artificial insemination, see Kara W. Swanson, "Adultery by Doctor: Artificial Insemination, 1890–1945," *Chicago-Kent Law Review* 87, no. 2 (April 2012): 591–633, available: https://scholarship.kentlaw.iit.edu /cklawreview/vol87/iss2/15.

19. For more on race and reproductive technology, see Roberts, *Killing the Black Body*, ch. 6, figures cited on 250–53. Roberts accounts for this disparity by pointing to the high cost of ART, systemic biases against diagnosing and treating infertility in Black women, and reticence among Blacks to seek medical assistance in light of past abuses.

20. Kenneth Eric, "The Unwed Mother," *True Love*, November 1961, 54, in the files of the Women's Social Services—Rescue Homes (Unwed Mothers), SANA.

21. Minnesota Territory Statutes 1851, section 100.11; Minnesota Statutes 1957, sections 617.18–19, https://www.revisor.mn.gov/statutes/; Solinger, *Beggars and Choosers*, 41–43, 53–55; Solinger, *Pregnancy and Power*, 211; Roberts, *Killing the Black Body*, 101.

22. Solinger, *Beggars and Choosers,* 49–55 and the rest of ch. 2, quote on 52; Eric, "The Unwed Mother," 54; "The Terrifying Ordeal of an Unwed Mother," *True Confessions,* November 1949, 14, in the files of the Women's Social Services—Rescue Homes (Unwed Mothers), SANA; "Machinist Held on Suspicion of Abortion," *Minneapolis Sunday Tribune,* June 29, 1958, 18; "Dentist Accused of Operation," *Minneapolis Star,* July 16, 1958, 6A; "City Dentist Pleads Guilty of Malpractice," *Minneapolis Morning Tribune,* September 19, 1958, 25; "Duluth Woman Faces Court on Abortion Death Charge," *Minneapolis Morning Tribune,* March 16, 1960, 11; "Woman Kills Self Before Court Hearing," *Minneapolis Morning Tribune,* June 28, 1960, 33.

23. Solinger, *Beggars and Choosers,* 49–51.

24. Quote from Interview BH-222, Adolescent Girl in Conflict: Individual Interviews—Booth Memorial Hospital (Unwed Mothers) 1963, box 19, folder 2, Konopka papers; Mary, interview with author, July 19, 2017, BMHOH-SWHA. For other examples of young pregnant women's thoughts of suicide, however temporary or elaborate, see Linda I in Fessler, *The Girls Who Went Away,* 313; Jean Thompson, *The House of Tomorrow* (New York: Signet/Harper & Row, 1967), 11; Lorraine Dusky, *Hole in My Heart: A Memoir and Report from the Fault Lines of Adoption* (New York: Leto Media, 2015), 33; "The Terrifying Ordeal of an Unwed Mother," 6. Most of the women in Fessler's book, as well as in Linda Back McKay's *Shadow Mothers: Stories of Adoption and Reunion* (St. Cloud, MN: North Star Press, 1998) and the women I interviewed, did not mention having contemplated suicide. Alex Barno, "Criminal Abortion Deaths, Illegitimate Pregnancy Deaths, and Suicide in Pregnancy, Minnesota, 1950–1965," *American Journal of Obstetrics and Gynecology* 98, no. 3 (June 1, 1967): 358–60. Barno noted that nine married women had also died from illegal abortions. Eight of the total of twenty-one died from self-induced abortions, though the marital status of these eight women was unreported.

25. Ventura and Bachrach, "Nonmarital Childbearing in the United States, 1940–1999," 17, 20; May, *Homeward Bound,* 101–2, 117–22; Table MS-2, Estimated Median Age at First Marriage, by Sex: 1890 to the Present, US Census Bureau, Decennial Censuses, 1890 to 1940, and Current Population Survey, Annual Social and Economic Supplements, 1947 to 2018, available: https://www.census.gov/data/tables/time-series/demo/families/marital.html; the birth rate per one thousand married women aged fifteen to forty-four was 156.6 (Ventura and Bachrach, "Nonmarital Childbearing in the United States, 1940–1999," 17); Amara Bachu, "Trends in Premarital Childbearing: 1930 to 1994," Current Population Reports P23-197 (US Census Bureau, 1999), 2–4; Fessler, *The Girls Who Went Away,* 67.

26. This account of Mom's travel to and arrival in San Francisco is based largely on "Greyhound" as well as my visit to the Powell Street YWCA in 2015 and a few imagined details.

27. Wikstrom, "Greyhound," 11–12. Title VII of the Civil Rights Act of 1964 prohibited discrimination in employment on the basis of sex, among other things. The 1978 Pregnancy Discrimination Act amended Title VII to also prohibit employment discrimination against pregnant women.

28. Regina Kunzel, *Fallen Women, Problem Girls: Unmarried Mothers and the Professionalization of Social Work, 1890–1945* (New Haven, CT: Yale University Press, 1993); "An Organized Approach to Illegitimacy," National Association on Services to Unmarried Parents, September 1963, 1–2, box 47, folder 1, Child Welfare League of America Records, sw0055, University of Minnesota Libraries, Social Welfare History Archives.

29. Laws of Minnesota 1917, chapter 194, sections 2 and 4, 279; Edward MacGaffey, "A Pattern for Progress: The Minnesota Children's Code," *Minnesota History* 41, no. 5 (Spring 1969): 229–36; Michael J. McMahon, *State and County Roles and Responsibilities in the Provision of Human Services: A Review of the Historical Development of Poor Relief and Related Programs in Minnesota* (Special Projects Office, Minnesota Department of Human Services, 2002); Laws of Minnesota 1937, chapter 343, section 7, 466; "A Brief History of the AFDC Program," US Department of Health and Human Services, https://aspe.hhs.gov/system/files/pdf/167036/1history.pdf; Linda Gordon and Felice Batlan, "The Legal History of the Aid to Dependent Children Program," *Social Welfare History Project*, 2011, available: https://socialwelfare.library.vcu.edu/public-welfare/aid-to-dependent-children-the-legal-history/; Department of Services to Children, Ramsey County Welfare Board, *Report of the 1957 Study of the Unmarried Mother*, 1959; Family and Child Welfare Division, Hennepin County Community Welfare Council, *The Unmarried Mother in Hennepin County*, October 1956, 8, 13, box 4, folder 36, Beatrice Bernhagen Papers, sw0134, University of Minnesota Libraries, Social Welfare History Archives. Catholic and Jewish women could have turned to the Catholic Welfare Association or Jewish Family and Children's Service, respectively.

30. Karl W. Windhorst, Hennepin County Attorney's office, letter to Ruth T. Devney, Hennepin County Welfare Board, June 8, 1942, box 177, folder 20, United Way of Minneapolis records, sw70, University of Minnesota Libraries, Social Welfare History Archives (hereafter, UWM-SWHA); *Report of the 1957 Study of the Unmarried Mother*, 15; *Unmarried Mother in Hennepin County*, 16–18; McMahon, *State and County Roles and Responsibilities in the Provision of Human Services*, 8–9.

31. *Unmarried Mother in Hennepin County*, 18–21; *Report of the 1957 Study of the Unmarried Mother*, 16–17; classified ad, *Minneapolis Star*, July 22, 1960, 19B.

32. Paul Ravenscraft, William Cratic, and Stan Stabno, "Punishment No Answer," letter to editor, *Minneapolis Star*, June 27, 1959, 6. Even if she had been able to avoid the welfare system during her pregnancy, once she delivered her "illegitimate" baby, state law mandated that hospitals report all such births to the state welfare department and county welfare boards inform unmarried mothers of available services: *Unmarried Mother in Hennepin County*, 14.

33. Quote and contents of this section from Gayle, interview with author, October 25, 2017, BMHOH-SWHA.

1. Wikstrom, "Greyhound," 14.

2. "WCCO Television Reports: Unwed Mothers," recorded October 26, 1960, aired November 28, 1960, Peabody Awards Collection, 60043 PST 1 of 1, Walter J. Brown Media Archives & Peabody Awards Collection, University of Georgia, Athens, available: https://kaltura.uga.edu/media/t/1_nez1exsh/86446941. WCCO television earned a Peabody Award for the series of which this program was a part.

3. Carl T. Rowan, "Increase in Unwed Mothers Is an Index of the Problem; The Family: A Failure?" *Minneapolis Morning Tribune*, February 25, 1959, 1, 13; "There's Door Open to Happy Future," Dear Abby column, *Minneapolis Star*, February 7, 1959, 4A; *Playhouse 90, In Lonely Expectation*, directed by Franklin Schaffner, written by Mayo Simon, CBS/WCCO television, April 2, 1959; "About Unwed Mothers," talk by the Lamplighters, Central Free Church, April 26, 1959, advertised in *Minneapolis Star*, April 25, 1959: 7A; ad for *Unwed Mother* and *Joy Ride*, *Minneapolis Star*, June 5, 1959, 20A.

4. "The Terrifying Ordeal of an Unwed Mother," 4–6+; Ann Landers, *Minneapolis Morning Tribune*, March 6, 1959, 9; meeting minutes of Committee on Services to Unmarried Mothers, May 28 and June 5, 1956, box 19, folder 3, Community Health and Welfare Council, Hennepin County, sw38, University of Minnesota Libraries, Social Welfare History Archives (hereafter, CHWCHC-SWHA); Mr. Fixit, *Minneapolis Morning Tribune*, May 31, 1952; "Booth Hospital Offers Help—Haven for Unwed Girls," *St. Paul Pioneer Press*, September 25, 1950; "Girls in Trouble—Booth Hospital Offers Security," *St. Paul Dispatch*, October 29, 1959.

5. In 1960, 70 percent of the 558 young women cared for at Booth had been referred by social agencies, 16 percent by doctors or pastors, 12 percent by friends or on their own, and 2 percent from "publicity." See flyer titled "Salvation Army Booth Memorial Hospital," May 1961, box 88, folder: St. Paul: Salvation Army—Booth Memorial Hospital 1942–1971, Minnesota, Hospital Services Division, Health care facilities files, State Archives, Minnesota Historical Society (hereafter, Health care facilities files, MNHS). For examples of informational material, see "How to Help: Unmarried Mothers, Children Needing Adoption, Adoptive Applicants," Minnesota Department of Public Welfare, 1957 and 1961, folder: Adoption and Unmarried Mother Services in Minnesota, Minnesota Department of Public Welfare, Published Records and Reports, MNHS-SA; quote from "The 20th Baby," Salvation Army brochure, no date (but likely 1961), in Women's Social Services—Rescue Homes (Unwed Mothers), SANA.

6. Referral History Guide of Anoka County Welfare Department regarding Sharon Moore (name blacked out) and child Lynette, January 31, 1961. A copy of these forms was in my mother's possession.

7. For more on the gap between sexual behavior and acknowledgment thereof in the 1950s, see, for example, Alan Petigny, "Illegitimacy, Postwar Psychology, and

the Reperiodization of the Sexual Revolution," *Journal of Social History*, 38, no. 1 (Fall 2004): 63–79; Breines, *Young, White, and Miserable*, 89–92; Dear Abby, *Minneapolis Star*, February 7, 1959; Margaret, in Fessler, *The Girls Who Went Away*, 72.

8. Solinger, *Pregnancy and Power*, 149–50; Leontine Young, *Out of Wedlock: A Study of the Problems of the Unmarried Mother and Her Child* (New York: McGraw-Hill, 1954), 36; *The Unmarried Mother in Hennepin County*.

9. Solinger, *Wake Up Little Susie*, 42–49, 191–94, quote from 86 (emphasis in original); Young, *Out of Wedlock*, 120–22. Young's views about Black unmarried mothers are more complicated than is often recognized. She called attention to the dangers of the taken-for-granted "white attitude toward illegitimacy" and argued that illegitimately pregnant Black women deserved the same individualized treatment as white women. She also, however, demonstrated race, class, and cultural paternalism in her descriptions of the "backward" areas of the South in which matriarchal Black families existed (121) and of girls and homes characterized by a "lack of social and moral standards" (88).

10. May, *Barren in the Promised Land*, ch. 5, esp. 154, "'incompetent' female body" on 159, 170, 174, 175; quote about "aggressive" women from W. S. Kroger, MD, "Evaluation of Personality Factors in the Treatment of Infertility," *Fertility and Sterility* 3 (November–December 1952): 542–51, as cited in May, *Barren in the Promised Land*, 172–73. Inexplicably infertile women could attempt to restore their femininity, and hence their chances of conceiving, by quitting work and associating with children, whether through babysitting or—in a myth that retains cultural currency even today—adopting a child, a suggestion that has troubling implications for all members of the adoption triad, not least the adopted child herself. Fortunately, other physicians warned against such facile and unproven admonitions and pointed out that emotional duress was more often the result than the cause of infertility: May, *Barren in the Promised Land*, 175–77.

11. Sara Edlin, *The Unmarried Mother in Our Society: A Frank and Constructive Approach to an Age-Old Problem* (New York: Farrar, Straus and Young, 1954), 12, 93, 95; Young, *Out of Wedlock*, 41–42, 60–61. For an alternative view on the role played by parents in daughters' pregnancies, see Clark E. Vincent, *Unmarried Mothers* (New York: Free Press of Glencoe, Inc., 1961), 118–19.

12. Susan Douglas, *Where the Girls Are: Growing Up Female with the Mass Media* (1994; reprint, New York: Times Books/Random House, 1994), 73–78; Charissa Keup, "Girls 'In Trouble': A History of Female Adolescent Sexuality in the Midwest, 1946–1964" (PhD diss., Marquette University, 2012), 205–9; Goodrich C. Schauffler, "Today It Could Be *Your* Daughter," *Ladies' Home Journal*, January 1958, 43, 112–13; Virgil Damon and Isabelle Taves, "My Daughter Is in Trouble," *Look*, August 14, 1962; Eric, "The Unwed Mother," 51, 53.

13. Betty Leonard, "Social Worker: Unwed Parents Are Not Just Statistics and Sinners," *Minneapolis Morning Tribune*, March 6, 1956, 17; Carl T. Rowan, "These Children Should Be Delinquents—But They Aren't; The Family: A Failure?" *Minneapolis*

Morning Tribune, February 24, 1959, 10; Elizabeth Nowicki, chief social worker at the University of Minnesota hospital, as cited in Falsum Russell, "Girls in Trouble—Varied Reasons Given for Illegitimacy Rise," *St. Paul Dispatch,* October 26, 1959, 18; "Unwed Mothers Increase; Permissive Parents Blamed," *St. Paul Pioneer Press,* October 19, 1962.

14. Eric, "The Unwed Mother," 51; Salvation Army, "Service to Unmarried Parents and Their Children, 1961," 1, 4; Moore, "Unwed Mothers."

15. Minnesota Statutes 1957, sections 257.18–257.30, https://www.revisor.mn.gov /statutes/. See also Mr. Fixit, "Complaint Begins Paternity Action," *Minneapolis Tribune,* February 13, 1966, 16.

16. May, *Homeward Bound,* 127–28; interviews BH-222, BH-239, Adolescent Girl in Conflict: Individual Interviews—Booth Memorial Hospital (Unwed Mothers) 1963, box 19, folder 2, Konopka papers. Gisela Konopka and her assistant, Vernie-Mae Czaky, conducted interviews with thirty-three "Booth girls" between the ages of fifteen and nineteen in 1963, which would later be incorporated into Konopka's book *The Adolescent Girl in Conflict* (Englewood Cliffs, NJ: Prentice-Hall, 1966).

17. Young, *Out of Wedlock,* 131–34; *The Unmarried Mother in Hennepin County,* 6–7, and "Unmarried Mother Services in Greater Minneapolis," June 1966, 12, box 19, folder 7—both in CHWCHC-SWHA.

18. Eric, "The Unwed Mother," 54–55; Rowan, "Increase in Unwed Mothers Is an Index of the Problem," 1, 13.

19. Wikstrom, "Greyhound," 15.

20. Scene based on account in Wikstrom, "Greyhound," 15–16.

21. Wikstrom, "Birth Rite," 7; Kim, email to author, December 9, 2018.

22. Mary, interview with author, July 19, 2017, BMHOH-SWHA. All further references to/about Mary come from this interview.

Notes to Chapter 4: "Booth Girl"

1. Wikstrom, "Greyhound," 16. Mom misremembered the specific date of her arrival at Booth. Records show that she checked in on December 31, 1960, though she writes that it was sometime in January. Her estimate, thirty-five years after the fact, is probably based on the intake/referral paperwork that an Anoka County caseworker completed on January 4, 1961, and that she had in her possession when writing "Greyhound."

2. Records in Gisela Konopka's papers at the University of Minnesota note that, of the thirty-two teenaged Booth girls she and her assistant interviewed in 1963, two were "Indian." Konopka noted that "Negroes were under care at Booth Memorial Hospital" at that time, but none of them participated in her project, which was focused on residents aged fourteen to nineteen. She did not note the specific number, however, so there's no way of telling how many Black women of any age, or Indigenous women age twenty or older, were at Booth at the time. "Final Tabulation," Adolescent Girl in

Conflict: Individual Interviews—Booth Memorial Hospital, 1963, folder 1 of 3, box 19, Konopka papers.

3. The idea of the "loyalty of the shared ordeal" comes from B. J. Phillips, "On Location with the WACs," *MS Magazine*, November 1972, 55.

4. Solinger, *Wake Up Little Susie*, 103–4, 114; Salvation Army, "Service to Unmarried Parents and Their Children, 1961," 1–6. The proportion of white women served in Salvation Army maternity homes in the Central Territory, of which Booth St. Paul was a part, was even higher, at 91.5 percent.

5. Kunzel, *Fallen Women, Problem Girls*, ch. 1; Edward H. McKinley, *Marching to Glory: The History of the Salvation Army in the United States, 1880–1992* (Grand Rapids, MI: Wm. B. Eerdmans Publishing Co.), ch. 1–2; Diane Winston, *Red-Hot and Righteous: The Urban Religion of the Salvation Army* (Cambridge, MA: Harvard University Press, 1999), 49–65, 76–82; Lt. Col. Edith A. MacLachlan, "Women's & Children's Social Services 1886–1978," in Women's Social Services—Rescue Homes (Unwed Mothers) file, SANA; Lillian Taiz, *Hallelujah Lads & Lasses: Remaking the Salvation Army in America, 1880–1930* (Chapel Hill: University of North Carolina Press, 2001).

6. "Rescue Home for Women; Work of the Salvation Army for Girls Who Have Gone Astray," *St. Paul Globe*, November 24, 1901; "Salvation Army Rescue Home Opened; Many Visitors Inspect New Building," *St. Paul Pioneer Press*, October 30, 1913; quotes from "The New Salvation Army Rescue Home," capital campaign booklet, 1913, Salvation Army Central Territory Museum, and "The Salvation Army Rescue Home and Maternity Hospital," annual report for year ending September 30, 1914, Louis W. Hill Papers, MNHS; "Booth Brown House History," ca 1976, in the historical records located at Booth Brown House in St. Paul (hereafter, BBH records). For a more detailed account of the origins of Booth Memorial Hospital on Como Avenue, including the Elsingers' role, see Heikkila, "Brighter and Better for Every Person."

7. Kunzel, *Fallen Women, Problem Girls*, ch. 2 and 5.

8. Laws of Minnesota 1917, chapter 194, section 2; Special Session Laws of Minnesota 1919, chapter 50, sections 1–12, and chapter 52, sections 1–10; MacGaffey, "A Pattern for Progress," 229; *Standards for Maternity Hospitals of Minnesota*, Children's Bureau, Minnesota State Board of Control, 1928, MNHS; for complaints about the home registered with the state board of control, see folder titled "St. Paul / Ramsey: Booth Memorial Hospital 1918–1957," box 162, Minnesota, Hospital Services Division, Health care facilities files, MNHS.

9. Report of Mrs. [Sally] Davis, social worker at Salvation Army Rescue Home, September 1934; letter from Salvation Army Central Territory Commissioner W. A. McIntyre to Dr. H. S. Lippman, Child Guidance Center, November 5, 1934; letter from Women's Social Service Secretary Brigadier Julia Thomas to C. R. Carlgren, State Board of Control, November 6, 1934; meeting minutes of Maternity Homes Committee, April 10, 1935; meeting minutes of St. Paul Community Chest, August 14, 1935; letter from William D. Schmidt, Chief of Child Welfare Unit of Department of Social Security, to Viktor O. Wilson, Division of Child Hygiene, Minnesota Department of

Health, March 14, 1942—all in box 162, Health care facilities files, MNHS. See Kunzel, *Fallen Women, Problem Girls*, 121, for link between community chests and state and federal child welfare agencies in exerting control over maternity home operations.

10. *Handbook of Information: Homes and Hospitals for Unmarried Mothers* (New York: The Salvation Army, 1952), 16, 21, 29–30, 32; effect of "differential diagnosis" in Kunzel, *Fallen Women, Problem Girls*, 126–28, 131–32.

11. Salvation Army, "Service to Unmarried Parents and Their Children, 1961," 2; Cara Kinzelman, "A Certain Kind of Girl: Social Workers and the Creation of the Pathological Unwed Mother, 1918–1940" (PhD diss., University of Minnesota, 2013), 221.

12. "The New Salvation Army Rescue Home," report for year ending September 27, 1912, Salvation Army Central Territory Museum; J. Arthur Myers, MD, *Masters of Medicine: An Historical Sketch of the College of Medical Sciences, University of Minnesota 1888–1966* (St. Louis, MO: Warren H. Green, Inc., 1968), 325; Proposed Agreement between the University of Minnesota School of Medicine and the Board of Trustees of the Salvation Army, September 22, 1957; letter from Dr. John McKelvey to Gertrude Gilman, Associate Director of University Hospitals, December 17, 1963; letter from Helen Knudsen, Minnesota Department of Health, to Brig. Gunborg Fugelsang, Booth Memorial Hospital, January 15, 1964—all in box 88, Health care facilities files, MNHS.

13. Anoka County Welfare Department intake form, completed by Patricia Peart, January 4, 1961. A copy of this form with all last names and other identifying information redacted was in my mother's possession. It also informs the preceding scene, pages 96–97.

14. Booth Memorial Hospital license application, December 1960, box 88; memo from Ethel McClure to J. W. Brower, November 30, 1955, box 162—both Health care facilities files, MNHS. "St. Paul Booth Memorial Hospital Percentage of Occupancy," box 47, folder 12; minutes of meeting between representatives of Community Chest, Salvation Army, and University of Minnesota, December 12, 1961, box 47, folder 4—both UWSP-MNHS.

15. Biographical information about Norberg taken from a brochure prepared in honor of Lieutenant Colonel Pearl Norberg's retirement in 1979 and a bulletin announcing Norberg's May 12, 2006, death, prepared by Major Karlene Lenz of the Retired Officers' Bureau, May 15, 2006. Both of these items were provided by Susan Mitchem, SANA, via email, July 31, 2019.

16. Biographical information and personal insights about Evelyn Headen from email communication with Evelyn A. Headen (the daughter-in-law of Booth social worker Evelyn Headen), July 5, 7, and 12, 2017, and August 12 and November 8, 2019. References to Headen's role in Konopka's research appear in memo minutes from presentation at Booth Memorial Hospital, November 6, 1963, prepared by Vernie-Mae L. Czaky, box 19, folder 1, and other records in Konopka papers. This research formed the basis of Gisela Konopka's book, *The Adolescent Girl in Conflict*.

17. Booth Memorial Hospital license application, December 1960.

18. Unless otherwise noted, this and all further information by or about June Wheeler is taken from June Wheeler, interview with author, October 11, 2017, BMHOH-SWHA.

19. United Way, "Worth of a Girl," presentation to United Fund, report staff listing, ca. 1961, box 224, folder 10, UWM-SWHA; anonymous, email correspondence with author, April 7, 2016. Initially, this woman had indicated a willingness to share more of her story with me. I invited her to do so on three separate subsequent occasions, however, and never received a reply. Fessler, *The Girls Who Went Away*, 149–53; Solinger, *Wake Up Little Susie*, ch. 5.

20. Information about the daily schedule at Booth comes from meeting minutes of the Committee on Services to Unmarried Mothers, June 6, 1956, box 19, folder 3, CHWCHC-SWHA; and from United Way, "Worth of a Girl."

21. Information about fees from meeting minutes, June 6, 1956; meeting minutes of the Committee on Services to Unmarried Mothers, March 3, 1960, box 47, folder 3, UWSP-MNHS. Quotes from "Worth of a Girl." Historical currency converter at https://futureboy.us/fsp/dollar.fsp. These sources cite $140 as the figure for (in 1956) five weeks' care plus $2/day if a girl stayed longer, or (in 1960) twenty days' residential care, delivery, and eight days in hospital. Some annual report figures from the mid- to late-1950s indicate that income from fees was slightly outmatched by income from the community chest. In a meeting in 1956, local social welfare experts noted that, despite some shortcomings in its program offerings, Booth appealed to girls who "shop[ped] around" because of its low cost: meeting minutes of the Committee on Services to Unmarried Mothers, May 2, 1956, box 19, folder 3, CHWCHS-SWHA.

22. Meeting minutes; United Way, "Worth of a Girl"; "The Salvation Army Booth Memorial Home and Hospital for Unwed Mothers," ca. 1964, box 37, Rejected Request Files of the Archie D. and Bertha H. Walker Foundation, in T. B. Walker Foundation and Relations Foundations Records, MNHS. Additional information about activities comes from an article about Booth St. Paul by Mrs. Major John Troutt, "The Forward Look," *The War Cry*, March 17, 1962, in Women's Social Services files, SANA.

23. For more on young women's experiences inside of maternity homes, and the social community amongst them, see, for example, Fessler, *The Girls Who Went Away*, ch. 6, esp. 138–42; Solinger, *Wake Up Little Susie*, ch. 4, esp. 134–44; Kunzel, *Fallen Women, Problem Girls*, ch. 3 and 4; Thompson, *The House of Tomorrow*; *Watermelon Hill*, by Lily Baber Coyle, dir. Anya Kremenetsky, History Theater, St. Paul, MN, March 19–April 10, 2016 (this play is based on Linda Back McKay's *Shadow Mothers*).

24. Vernie-Mae Czaky, "Memo for the Record," October 17, 1963, box 19, folder 1, Adolescent Girls in Conflict: Individual Interviews—Booth Memorial Hospital (Unwed Mothers), Konopka papers.

25. William F. McCool and Sara A. Simeone, "Birth in the United States: An Overview of Trends Past and Present," *Nursing Clinics of North America* 37, no. 4 (December 2002): 735–46; Tina Cassidy, *Birth: The Surprising History of How We Are Born* (New

York: Grove/Atlantic, 2006), esp. 90–94 on twilight sleep; Judith Lothian, "Childbirth Education at the Crossroads," *Journal of Perinatal Education* 17, no. 2 (2008): 45–49, available: https://www.ncbi.nlm.nih.gov/pmc/articles/PMC2409156/; observation about the crowded hallway from a report prepared by D. H. Tarlow and Company, Accountants and Auditors, March 26, 1959, box 47, folder: Agencies: Booth Memorial Hospital, 1952–1959, UWSP-MNHS.

26. Wikstrom, "Greyhound," 18.

27. Wikstrom, "Greyhound," 18. The young doctor who eventually arrived to help Mom deliver had to have been from the University of Minnesota, per the long-standing agreement between the two institutions.

28. Wikstrom, "Birth Rite," 8.

29. Quote and contents of this section from Gay, interview with author, June 12, 2017, BMHOH-SWHA.

Notes to Chapter 5: "Surrender"

1. First paragraph, Wikstrom, "Birth Rite," 8; second paragraph, Wikstrom, "Greyhound," 18–19.

2. Wikstrom, "Greyhound," 17.

3. Informal interview with Diane Pletcher, March 1, 2013, in my possession.

4. Solinger, *Wake Up Little Susie*, 164; Salvation Army, "Service to Unmarried Parents and Their Children, 1961," 7; "WCCO Television Reports: Unwed Mothers."

5. Solinger, *Wake Up Little Susie*, 148–54; Barbara Melosh, *Strangers and Kin: The American Way of Adoption* (Cambridge, MA: Harvard University Press, 2002), 105–22; Ellen Herman, *Kinship by Design: A History of Adoption in the Modern United States* (Chicago: University of Chicago Press, 2008), 106, 201; Julie Berebitsky, *Like Our Very Own: Adoption and the Changing Culture of Motherhood, 1851–1950* (Lawrence: University Press of Kansas, 2000), 16.

6. Wikstrom, "Birth Rite," 7.

7. Anoka County Welfare Department intake form, January 4, 1961, and Peart, Referral History Guide, January 4, 1961, 3. Both of these were in my mother's possession.

8. Melosh, *Strangers and Kin*, 105–7 and the rest of ch. 3; Solinger, *Wake Up Little Susie*, 152–56; Herman, *Kinship by Design*, 97–101, 201–2.

9. Salvation Army, "Service to Unmarried Parents and Their Children, 1961," 4, 7.

10. Kunzel, *Fallen Women, Problem Girls*; Kinzelman, "A Certain Kind of Girl," 131–32; "The New Salvation Army Rescue Home," 1912; Brigadier Annie Cowden in "200 Unwed Mothers Cared for Annually at Maternity Home," *Minneapolis Sunday Tribune*, January 23, 1921, 26; report about fundraising efforts prepared by Margaret Hughes, March 23, 1932, in box 162, Minnesota, Hospital Services Division, Health care facilities files, MNHS; Betty Marvin, "Christmas Collection One of 76 Salvation Army Projects," *Minneapolis Morning Tribune*, December 18, 1944, 8; "Booth Hospital Offers

Help—Haven for Unwed Girls," *St. Paul Pioneer Press*, September 25, 1950; "WCCO Television Reports: Unwed Mothers." The Salvation Army reported a 1961 surrender rate of 78.4 percent among its maternity home residents in the Central Territory, of which Booth St. Paul was a part, compared to a nationwide rate of 71.6 percent: Salvation Army, "Service to Unmarried Parents and Their Children, 1961," 7. Figures from public (state and county) agencies that worked with unmarried mothers show slightly different trends in the custody-release dynamic, likely because such agencies would have worked with women from more varied class and race backgrounds who were not necessarily maternity home residents. In 1952, for example, the Ramsey County Welfare Board indicated that 43 percent of unmarried mothers served by the agency surrendered their babies for adoption, implying that 57 percent of them kept their children: *All That Money! 1952 Annual Report of the County Welfare Board of the City of Saint Paul and the County of Ramsey*, Annual Reports, Ramsey County Welfare Department Annual Reports, MNHS.

11. For more on the evolution of views of illegitimacy and unwed mothers in the pre–World War II era, see Kunzel, *Fallen Women, Problem Girls*, ch. 2, 128–30; Solinger, *Wake Up Little Susie*, 152; Kinzelman, "A Certain Kind of Girl."

12. Solinger, *Wake Up Little Susie*, 154; Melosh, *Strangers and Kin*, 112; "Many Seek to Adopt Babies; Hard to Get as Mothers Won't Give Them Up, Authorities Say," *Minneapolis Daily Star*, July 29, 1921, 8.

13. Melosh, *Strangers and Kin*, 110; May, *Barren in the Promised Land*, 140–43; General Statutes of Minnesota, Supplement 1917, chapter 73, section 7152, https://www.revisor.mn.gov/statutes/; Solinger, *Wake Up Little Susie*, 156–61; Melosh, *Strangers and Kin*, ch. 1, esp. 21, 29–30, 38–40, and ch. 3; Young, *Out of Wedlock*, 160; Herman, *Kinship by Design*, 148–53.

14. Solinger *Wake Up Little Susie*, 157–64; Herman, *Kinship by Design*, 97–99; Helen Harris Perlman, "Unmarried Mothers," in *Social Work and Social Problems*, ed. Nathan E. Cohen (New York: National Association of Social Workers, 1964), 274, 301; E. Wayne Carp, *Family Matters: Secrecy and Closure in the History of Adoption* (Cambridge, MA: Harvard University Press, 1998), 116–17; Young, *Out of Wedlock*, 204, 210, 215, 217; Salvation Army, "Service to Unmarried Parents and Their Children, 1961," 7.

15. Fessler, *The Girls Who Went Away*, 148–53, 158, 170–71. In 1948 and 1953, Leontine Young herself had sounded warnings about the pressure the rising demand for adoption might put on unmarried mothers: see Solinger, *Wake Up Little Susie*, 154, 160. All material by and about Margaret is from Margaret Olson Seitz, interview with author, October 16, 2017, BMHOH-SWHA.

16. Melosh points out that social workers' ultimate influence on adoption was more limited than they'd have liked, with few states mandating social worker oversight of adoption and ultimate power over adoption decisions residing with the courts: Melosh, *Strangers and Kin*, 109, 203.

17. Herman, *Kinship by Design*, 113–17, 150–53, 202–3; Melosh, *Strangers and Kin*, 111–12; Berebitsky, *Like Our Very Own*, 152–53.

18. Melosh, *Strangers and Kin*, 154–56; Solinger, *Wake Up Little Susie*, 172–74; Fessler, *The Girls Who Went Away*, 181; Young, *Out of Wedlock*, 154; Sarah Evan, "The Unwed Mother's Indecision About Her Baby as a Defense Mechanism," in *Services to Unmarried Mothers*, Child Welfare League of America, February 1958, 18; Henry J. Meyer, Wyatt Jones, and Edgar F. Borgatta, "The Decision by Unmarried Mothers To Keep or Surrender Their Babies," *Social Work* 1, no. 2 (April 1956): 107. Roberta Rindfleisch quoted in meeting minutes of the Committee on Services to Unmarried Mothers, April 25, 1956, box 19, folder 3; Minnesota Council on Illegitimacy, "Report of Ad Hoc Committee on Unmarried Mothers Who Keep Their Babies," 1967, attached to MCI Annual Meeting minutes from February 10, 1967, box 19, folder 10—both CHWCHS-SWHA; Konopka, *The Adolescent Girl in Conflict*, 127–29.

19. Beatrice Bernhagen quoted in Beverly Mindrum, "The Unwed Mother: Her Portrait," *Minneapolis Star*, October 26, 1959, 9B; Marcel Heiman and Esther G. Levitt "The Role of Separation and Depression in Out-of-Wedlock Pregnancy," *American Journal of Orthopsychiatry* 30, no. 1 (January 1960): 172; Wyatt C. Jones, Henry J. Meyer, and Edgar F. Borgatta, "Social and Psychological Factors in Status Decisions of Unmarried Mothers," *Marriage and Family Living* 24, no. 3 (August 1962): 227, available: http://www.jstor.org/stable/349135.

20. Ann Landers, *Minneapolis Morning Tribune*, April 25, 1961, 10.

21. Ben Kaufman, "They Give Away 'Own Flesh and Blood'; Annual Event for Some," *Minneapolis Star*, August 19, 1965, 1; memo by T. O. Olson, August 31, 1965, and letter by T. O. Olson, August 24, 1965—both in box 19, folder 10, CHWCHS-SWHA.

22. Mrs. Kenneth Hill, letter to editor, *Minneapolis Star*, August 25, 1965, 12A; anonymous, letter to editor, *Minneapolis Star*, September 4, 1965, 6A; Grace C. Mayberg, supervisor, Family and Children's Service, letter to editor, *Minneapolis Star*, August 31, 1965, 4; Marlene Pinten, letter to editor, *Minneapolis Star*, September 9, 1965, 8A.

23. Solinger, *Wake Up Little Susie*, 187–99; Melosh, *Strangers and Kin*, 148–50.

24. Sam Newlund, "Wanted: Average American Families," *Minneapolis Tribune*, December 5, 1965, 1, 6.

25. Newlund, "Wanted," 6.

26. Solinger, *Wake Up Little Susie*, 42–50, 195–99, quotes on 78, 199; Briggs, *Somebody's Children*, 8–9, 29, 31–39.

27. Briggs, *Somebody's Children*, 41–42.

28. *Report of the 1957 Study of the Unmarried Mother*, 20. Information on PAMY from "PAMY's Progress," prepared by Parents-to-Adopt-Minority-Youngsters Project, 1963, 4, 6–7, quote on 7, figures on 9; Briggs, *Somebody's Children*, 36. PAMY was not an adoption agency; it was an information and referral source for families interested in adopting "minority" (or hard-to-place white) children. The report made no comment about the race of the families that adopted the white and Indian children; they were, presumably, white.

29. Eileen Chapman, "Unmarried Persons May Now Adopt," July 3, 1963, *Minneapolis Morning Tribune*, 15; Eileen Chapman, "10 White Families Adopt Negro Children," *Minneapolis Morning Tribune*, February 20, 1963, 14; "Placing Negro Children in White Adoptive Homes is Urged," *Minneapolis Star*, December 3, 1963, 1Y; Herman, *Kinship by Design*, 234, 243. See also Matine T. Spence, "Whose Stereotypes and Racial Myths? The National Urban League and the 1950s Roots of Color-Blind Adoption Policy," *Women, Gender, and Families of Color* 1, no. 2 (Fall 2013): 162; "Minority Adoption Plan Set," *Minneapolis Morning Tribune*, June 18, 1963, 11.

30. "PAMY's Progress," 27; Spence, "Whose Stereotypes and Racial Myths?" 159.

31. Numbers cited from Briggs, *Somebody's Children*, 37; Herman, *Kinship by Design*, 242; Roberts, *Shattered Bonds*, 246.

32. Jacobs, *A Generation Removed*, 8–19; Briggs, *Somebody's Children*, 7, 71–73. Jacobs points out that some boarding schools remained, even expanded, into the 1970s.

33. Jacobs, *A Generation Removed*, 20, 27–28, 31–32, 39–40, 50–53. As Jacobs points out, white adopters didn't necessarily share the goals of policy makers. "What may have been genuine acts of caring for and about Indian children among white adoptive couples," she writes, "became perverted by the IAP and other pro-Indian adoption groups as means to terminate Indian peoples": Jacobs, *A Generation Removed*, 64. On the other hand, some of those adopters certainly viewed themselves as heroic saviors trying to eradicate the "Indianness" from their adoptive children, as testimony from adoptees suggests: Jacobs, *A Generation Removed*, 251–64. Sandy White Hawk had been adopted from the Rosebud Sioux reservation and raised in an isolating and abusive white family. Her lingering sense of alienation prompted her to establish the First Nations Repatriation Institute, a Minnesota-based organization dedicated to helping Indigenous adoptees reconnect with their families, tribes, and culture: see Jacobs, *A Generation Removed*, 265–66; "About the First Nations Repatriation Institute," January 25, 2012, on the American Indian Adoptees Blog, http://blog.americanindianadoptees.com/2012/01/about-first-nations-repatriation.html; and letter from Sandy White Hawk, May 29, 2015, at turtletalk.files.wordpress.com.

34. Jacobs, *A Generation Removed*, 20, 60, 93; Briggs, *Somebody's Children*, 74.

35. Briggs, *Somebody's Children*, 29–30; Roberts, *Shattered Bonds*, 8; Jacobs, *A Generation Removed*, 76.

36. Solinger, *Wake Up Little Susie*, 18, 164; Penelope L. Maza, "Adoption Trends: 1944–1975," 1984, available: The Adoption History Project, http://pages.uoregon.edu/adoption/archive/MazaAT.htm; Melosh, *Strangers and Kin*, 105; Herman, *Kinship by Design*, 201; Solinger, *Beggars and Choosers*, 203; Fessler, *The Girls Who Went Away*, 8.

37. These interviews, along with interviews of residents at the two other local maternity homes and girls who had been adjudicated delinquent, form the basis of Konopka's 1966 book, *The Adolescent Girl in Conflict*. Interview and other study materials are housed at the University Archives, University of Minnesota Libraries. Quotes from interviews BH-233 and BH-242, Adolescent Girl in Conflict: Individual Interviews—Booth Memorial Hospital (Unwed Mothers) 1963, box 19, folder 2, Konopka

papers. For a more detailed discussion, see Heikkila, "Everybody Thinks It's Right to Give the Child Away."

38. BH-237 and BH-245, Konopka papers.

39. BH-222 and BH-223, Konopka papers.

40. BH-223, Konopka papers.

41. Wikstrom, "Birth Rite," 8.

42. Quote and contents of this section from Sandy #1, interview with author, June 29, 2017, BMHOH-SWHA.

43. Wikstrom, "Greyhound," 19.

Notes to Chapter 6: "Fresh Start"

1. Wikstrom, "Greyhound," 19. Despite Mom's writing that Lutheran Social Service had handled the adoption of her baby, LSS has no record of contact with her. MN Adopt indicated that, instead, Anoka County handled her adoption case (though my sister's adoptive parents may have gone through LSS for adoption on their end).

2. Wikstrom, "Birth Rite," 8–9.

3. Information about Mom's application to the International Cooperation Administration from a handwritten copy of an Application for Federal Employment that Mom signed and dated on February 18, 1961, and letters to Mom from Beulah Bean at the ICA, dated March 14, March 15, and April 4, 1961. "Office Secretary Turns Construction Worker," *Here We 'Grow' Again* (Gold Bond Stamp Company newsletter) 2, no. 2 (May 1962): 4–5. All of this material was in Mom's personal papers and is now in my possession.

4. This description of the nature of birthmothers' grief and bereavement comes from the following sources and studies: Fessler, *The Girls Who Went Away*, ch. 8; Kenneth J. Doka, ed., *Disenfranchised Grief: New Directions, Challenges, and Strategies for Practice* (Champaign, IL: Research Press, 2002); Evelyn Robinson, *Adoption and Loss: The Hidden Grief* (2000; reprint, Christies Beach, South Australia: Clova Publications, 2018); Evelyn Robinson, "Long Term Outcomes of Losing a Child Through Adoption: The Impact of Disenfranchised Grief," *Grief Matters: The Australian Journal of Grief and Bereavement* 10, no. 1 (Autumn 2007): 8–11; Sidney Zisook and Katherine Shear, "Grief and Bereavement: What Psychiatrists Need to Know," *World Psychiatry* 8 (2009): 67–74, available: https://onlinelibrary.wiley.com/doi/epdf/10.1002/j.2051-5545.2009.tb00217.x; Holli Ann Askren and Kathaleen C. Bloom, "Postadoptive Reactions of the Relinquishing Mother: A Review," *Journal of Obstetric, Gynecologic, & Neonatal Nursing* 28, no. 4 (July 1999): 395–400; Michael De Simone, "Birth Mother Loss: Contributing Factors to Unresolved Grief," *Clinical Social Work Journal* 24, no. 1 (Spring 1996): 65–76; J. A. Aloi, "Nursing the Disenfranchised: Women Who Have Relinquished an Infant for Adoption," *Journal of Psychiatric and Mental Health Nursing* 16, no. 1 (2009): 27–31; Carlie Dinwoodie, "Birth Mothers

[*sic*] Experiences with Grief after Placement of their Children in Adoptive Families" (master's thesis, City University of Seattle, 2015); Janet Fisher, "How Birth Mothers Fare: A Qualitative Study of Their Long-term Adjustment" (PhD thesis, New York University, 2010); Leverett Millen and Samuel Roll, "Solomon's Mothers: A Special Case of Pathological Bereavement," *American Journal of Orthopsychiatry* 55, no. 3 (July 1985): 411–18. This is just a sampling of studies; many blogs and online forums by and for birthmothers also detail their grieving processes (e.g., forthelove ofbirthmothers.com, adoptionbirthmothers.com, exiledmothers.com, confessions ofbirthmothers.tumblr.com).

5. Askren and Bloom, "Postadoptive Reactions of the Relinquishing Mother: A Review," identified Reuben Pannor, Annette Baran, and Arthur D. Sorosky's "Birth Parents Who Relinquished Babies for Adoption Revisited," *Family Process* 17, no. 3 (1978): 329–37, as the earliest study, with eleven more published in English-language journals available in the United States through 1994. Information from and quotes about the Adoption Research Project findings from Pannor, Baran, and Sorosky, "Birth Parents Who Relinquished Babies for Adoption Revisited," 331, 334. For a description of some birthmothers' experiences with therapy, see Fessler, *The Girls Who Went Away*, 222–25; Mary, interview with author, July 19, 2017, BMHOH-SWHA.

6. This account of events comes from my informal interview with Diane Pletcher, and from an email message from my cousin Kari, February 24, 2015.

7. Wikstrom, "Greyhound," 19.

8. Carp, *Family Matters*, 102–3; Ellen Herman, "Confidentiality and Sealed Records," Adoption History Project website, https://pages.uoregon.edu/adoption /topics/confidentiality.htm; Laws of Minnesota 1939, chapter 89, section 5356; Gregory D. Luce, "The Long and Costly Tail of Compromise," Adoptee Rights Law Center website, https://adopteerightslaw.com/costly-long-tail-compromise/. Gaining access to these closed birth records would become a major impetus for the adoptees' and birthmothers' rights movements.

9. Carp, *Family Matters*, 40–43; Minnesota Statutes 1917, section 7159; Minnesota Statutes 1945, section 259.09; Minnesota Statutes 1951, section 259.31, https://www .revisor.mn.gov/statutes/.

10. Carp, *Family Matters*, 43, 79–87, 103–12; Melosh, *Strangers and Kin*, 202–4, 215, 223; Herman, "Confidentiality and Sealed Records"; Minnesota Statutes 1982, section 259.46. In 1997, the law declared that confidential/secret adoption records would become public one hundred years after the adoption decree was granted: Minnesota Statutes 1997, section 259.79. For more information, see the Minnesota Coalition for Adoption Reform website, http://mnadoptreform.org/reform-efforts/.

11. Carp, *Family Matters*, 110–24; Fessler, *The Girls Who Went Away*, 182.

12. Quote from Sharon Wikstrom, "Life Stories—'Motz'—Matt Wikstrom," unpublished essay, September 1995, 1; letters from Matt Wikstrom to Sharon Moore, December 25 and 26, 1962. These were in Mom's papers and are now in my possession.

13. Pannor, Baran, and Sorosky, "Birth Parents Who Relinquished Babies for Adoption Revisited," found that 86 percent of the birthparents who were married at the time of the interview had told their spouses about their relinquished child (332).

14. Some studies have shown that mothers who have lost babies to miscarriage, stillbirth, or early infant death have difficulty forming attachments with their babies in utero. See, for example, Joann M. O'Leary, "Grief and Its Impact on Prenatal Attachment in the Subsequent Pregnancy," *Archives of Women's Mental Health* (2004): 1–12. I have been unable to find any literature about this phenomenon as it might relate to birthmothers' subsequent pregnancies, though some research has documented some initial hesitation about becoming pregnant again; see, for example, Fessler, *The Girls Who Went Away*, 215; Fisher, "How Birth Mothers Fare," 111–13; Eva Y. Deykin, Lee Campbell, and Patricia Patti, "The Postadoption Experience of Surrendering Parents," *American Journal of Orthopsychiatry* 54 (1984): 271–80; Mary Jo Carr, "Birthmothers and Subsequent Children: The Role of Personality Traits and Attachment History," *Journal of Social Distress and the Homeless* 9, no. 4 (2000): 339–49; Merry Bloch Jones, *Birthmothers: Women Who Have Relinquished Babies for Adoption Tell Their Stories* (Chicago: Chicago Review Press, 1993), 141–67. Still, most birthmothers of Mom's generation went on to have other children. See Fisher, "How Birth Mothers Fare"; Carr, "Birthmothers and Subsequent Children"; Pannor, Baran, and Sorosky, "Birth Parents Who Relinquished Babies for Adoption Revisited"; Fessler, *The Girls Who Went Away*; Edward K. Rynearson, "Relinquishment and Its Maternal Complications: A Preliminary Study," *American Journal of Psychiatry* 139, no. 3 (March 1982): 338–40.

15. Wikstrom, "Letter to Kim," 16. Mom's reference to having been "an independent person for 23 years" is either a mistake—she was twenty-eight when I was born—or a reference to her age at marriage.

16. Wikstrom, "Letter to Kim," 17.

17. Wikstrom, "Letter to Kim," 18.

18. Arlene Cardozo, *Woman at Home* (Garden City, NY: Doubleday & Company, Inc., 1976), 55–57.

19. The episode in which Lee Campbell appears on the Phil Donahue show for the first time can be viewed on the Concerned United Birthparents' YouTube channel at https://www.youtube.com/watch?v=qz8LV2_DsSM&t=1087s.

20. For a history of CUB and its deployment of the language and logic of *rights*, not *choice*, see Solinger, *Beggars and Choosers*, 70–138.

21. Solinger, *Beggars and Choosers*, 80–87, 103–13; Carp, *Family Matters*, ch. 5. Information on CUB's functions from CUB brochure, 1976, available in CUB History Channel, www.cubirthparents.org, and Nadine Brozan, "Natural Parents Seek Rights in Adoptions," *Minneapolis Tribune*, March 5, 1978, 2E.

22. Solinger, *Beggars and Choosers*, 110–11; Patty O'Gorman, "The Birth of M-CUB," February 19, 1978; minutes of CUB-M meeting, January 15, 1978; By-laws of Minnesota Concerned United Birthparents (M CUB), ca. 1978; M-CUB membership list,

December 26, 1978—all CUB-MN records, box 2, CUB-SWHA; informal telephone interview with Deanna Mramor, January 27, 2020. In its literature over the years, the Minnesota branch of CUB has referred to itself variously as M-CUB, M CUB, CUB Minnesota, CUB MN, and CUB Twin Cities Metro Area Branch. For the sake of ease and consistency, I will refer to the group as CUB-MN except when citing directly from its literature.

23. Suzanne Perry, "Adoption: The Pain of Surrender," *Minneapolis Star,* February 3, 1979, 9–11; "I Can't and I Don't Want to Forget," *Minneapolis Star,* February 3, 1979, 9–10; "The Joy of Discovery," *Minneapolis Star,* February 3, 1979, 11–12; "Are You Sorry You Gave Up Your Child for Adoption?" *Good Housekeeping,* June 1980; Claire Berman, "Love is Thicker Than Everything," *Woman's Day,* August 5, 1980, 40+; Pam Bolduc, "Giving Up a Child to the Agencies of Adoption Degrades All Involved," letter to editor, *Minneapolis Star,* November 20, 1980, 9A; Mr. and Mrs. Ralph Crowley, "Adoption Can Be a Happy Experience for All," and Pat DuFour, "Adopting Child Brings Joy to Frustrated Couple," letters to editor, *Minneapolis Star*, December 3, 1980, 7A; Priscilla Nelson (and two other unnamed birthmothers), "Birth-mother: Adoption Can Give Peace of Mind," letter to editor, *Minneapolis Star,* December 9, 1980, 7A; Gail Meyer, "Adoption Can Bring Happiness," letter to editor, *Minneapolis Star,* December 22, 1980, 8A; Pam Bolduc, "Loving Adoptive Parents Help Round Out Child's Family Circle," *Minneapolis Star,* January 5, 1981, 4A.

24. O'Gorman in Berman, "Love is Thicker Than Everything," 149; Gail Hanssen, CUB-MA, letter to Patty O'Gorman, CUB-MN, June 19, 1978; Governor Rudy Perpich, Birthparent Week Declaration, March 16, 1984—both in box 1, CUB-SWHA; ad for CUB open meeting, *Minneapolis Star and Tribune,* April 5, 1984, 9Y.

25. National Association of Black Social Workers, "Position Statement on Transracial Adoptions," September 1972, available at National Association of Black Social Workers website, https://www.nabsw.org/; Roberts, *Shattered Bonds,* 246–47; Briggs, *Somebody's Children,* 56–58.

26. Herman, *Kinship by Design,* 241; Jacobs, *A Generation Removed,* 98, 106, 115–16, 158–59. Jacobs points out that the Indian Child Welfare Act "was not an issue of race but of tribal sovereignty and survival. [Indian activists] were concerned that children grow up not to be 'Indian,' per se, but to be Standing Rock Sioux, Navajo (Diné), Zuni, or Winnebago (Ho-Chunk)": Jacobs, *A Generation Removed,* 151. See also Briggs, *Somebody's Children,* 61–64. Efforts to restore some degree of "race matching" in adoption, albeit for different ends than originally intended when it dominated adoption practice in the earlier postwar period, encountered a significant setback in 1994 when Congress passed the Multiethnic Placement Act (MEPA). Originating in an effort to find permanent homes for the many Black children in the foster care system, MEPA prevented adoption agencies that received federal funding from making placement decisions based solely on the race of the child or adoptive parents, though they were allowed to consider race as one of many factors and were obliged to recruit foster and adoptive parents of the same background(s) as children awaiting placement. Two

years later, however, Congress amended MEPA and eliminated race as a "permissible consideration" if it resulted in a delay or denial of placement. The effect, according to Dorothy Roberts, has been to "create a system that protects the rights of white adults to have access to the children of their choice": Roberts, *Shattered Bonds*, 167. ICWA placements, however, are exempt from MEPA and its subsequent amendments: see "Topic 19. Application of other federal laws," in the "ICWA Guide Online" at the National Indian Law Library, https://narf.org/nill/documents/icwa/faq/application2 .html#Q11.

27. Richard Meryman, "Adoption Part I: An Unwed Mother Gives Up Her Baby," *LIFE*, June 14, 1968, 88–98, and "Adoption Part II: Joan's Baby Gets a Final Home," *LIFE*, June 21, 1968, 72+.

28. Joe Blade, "Unwed, They'll Raise Baby as a 'Good Life Experience,'" *Minneapolis Star*, August 18, 1971, 1C; Joe Blade, "I Don't Think I Was Cut Out to Be a Mother," *Minneapolis Star*, August 19, 1971, 1C.

29. Ann Baker, "SA Hospital Wing Dedication Today," *St. Paul Pioneer Press*, December 7, 1969, 4; "Unwed Mother Study Committee—A Report to the Community Health and Welfare Planning Council of Greater St. Paul," June 1970, 13–14, box 47, folder 13, UWSP-MNHS; annual report of the Metropolitan St. Paul Hospital Planning Council, 1964, box 22, folder: MSPHPC Annual reports, 1963–1965, Metropolitan Health Board Records, 1960–1986, MNHS.

30. Major Mary White, letter to Robert Tucker, July 16, 1970, box 47, folder 13, UWSP-MNHS; Falsum Russell, "Booth Hospital Found Wanting After Study," *St. Paul Pioneer Press*, July 26, 1970, 2?.

31. "Report of the Booth Memorial Study Committee to the Board of Directors of the Community Health and Welfare Planning Council," September 1971, box 9, Community Planning Organization St. Paul Records, MNHS; Maj. Mary White letter to Benjamin Griggs, chair of the Greater St. Paul United Fund and Council, February 1, 1971, box 47, folder 15, UWSP-MNHS; Major Mary White in Ann Baker, "SA Home Helping Runaways 'Turn Themselves Around,'" *St. Paul Pioneer Press*, May 21, 1974, 10, in the BBH records.

32. "Historic Booth Hospital," on the Booth Brown House website, https:// centralusa.salvationarmy.org/northern/BoothBrownHouse/.

33. Deykin, Campbell, and Patti, "The Postadoption Experience of Surrendering Parents," 278; Laura Bloom, "Parenting Second First Children: What Early Childhood Professionals Need to Know About Mothers Who Have Relinquished a Child for Adoption" (PhD diss., University of Alabama at Birmingham, 2009), 79; Fessler, *The Girls Who Went Away*, 218–19; Jones, *Birthmothers*, 152–55, 158–61.

34. In her various writings, Mom cites both 1978 and 1980 as the year when Dad was diagnosed with Parkinson's. Her earlier writings most often refer to 1978, however, so that is the date I will assume here. This imagining is based on many of Mom's writings, including "Letter to Kim," which also inform the subsequent descriptions of my father's illness.

35. "Letter to Kim," 30.

36. Quote and contents of this section from Karen, interview with author, July 18, 2017, BMHOH-SWHA.

37. Wikstrom, "Greyhound," 19.

Notes to Chapter 7: "Reunited"

1. Wikstrom, "Greyhound," 20.

2. This account of the evolution of my father's illness comes from personal memory as well as a number of my mother's unpublished writings, including "Life Stories—'Motz'—Matt Wikstrom," 21–25, and ch. 2, "The Crisis," from "How to Survive Putting a Member of Your Family Into a Nursing Home," an incomplete draft of a self-help book manuscript my mother began in May 1995.

3. This account of the phone calls between Mom, Sandy, and Kim and Mom and Kim's first meeting comes from my informal interviews with my sister Kim (December 6, 2019) and my aunt Diane (March 1, 2013)—whom Sandy also contacted in search of Mom—as well as an entry in my own journal dated July 6, 1994. Mom must have recorded the details of these momentous events in her journal, but if so, that journal was among those she tossed out, either in her downsizing move from Crystal to St. Paul in 2006 or before she died in 2009. All further quotes attributed to Kim come from this interview unless otherwise noted.

4. Wikstrom, "Birth Rite," 9; account of Mom and Kim's first meeting from my interview with Kim.

5. Wikstrom, "Birth Rite," 9.

6. The following account of Kim's growing up and search for her birthparents comes from my interview with her as well as from a letter she wrote me on July 10, 2012, in my possession. Kim also provided me with copies of an undated (1989) letter she wrote to the Adoption Unit of the Minnesota Department of Human Services; a memo from DHS to her, dated January 9, 1989, confirming receipt of her letter; and a letter from her to DHS, dated February 22, 1994, with her updated contact information.

7. Peart, Referral History Guide, January 31, 1961, 3, 4.

8. Wikstrom, "Birth Rite," 9.

9. Michael Phillip Grand, *The Adoption Constellation: New Ways of Thinking About and Practicing Adoption* (CreateSpace Independent Publishing Platform, 2010).

10. Gail Rosenblum, "They Never Forgot," *Minneapolis Star Tribune,* July 8, 2007, E1; Kim Ode, "Opening the Books on Adoption," *Minneapolis Star Tribune,* February 27, 2011, E1; Memo from Sandy Sperrazza to CUB-MN members, November 20, 1984, box 1, folder: CUB MN Newsletters, CUB-SWHA; Sandy Louise (Longwell) Sperrazza obituary, November 22, 2019, https://cremationsocietyofmn.com/tribute/details/23514/Sandy-Sperrazza/obituary.html; Solinger, *Beggars and Choosers,* 118–24;

Arthur D. Sorosky, Annette Baran, and Reuben Pannor, *The Adoption Triangle: Sealed or Opened Records: How They Affect Adoptees, Birth Parents, and Adoptive Parents* (1978; reprint, Las Vegas, NV: Triadoption Publications, 2008); Carp, *Family Matters*, ch. 5 and 6, critique of Sorosky, Baran, and Pannor on 154–58.

11. Passive registries such as the ISRR functioned as an alternative, or supplement, to the adoption agency practice of holding "in search of" letters on file. Searching birthparents or adoptees would provide as much information about themselves as possible for the registry in hopes that it would align with information provided by their searching counterparts. Laws of Minnesota 1977, chapter 181, subd. 144.1761. This was the first confidential intermediary system in the country, according to Gregory Luce at the Adoptee Rights Law Center, https://adopteerightslaw.com/. In 1989, the minimum age for an adoptee to make a request was lowered to nineteen: Minnesota Statutes 1989, section 259.89, https://www.revisor.mn.gov/statutes/. See also Carp, *Family Matters*, 185–86; "Original Birth Certificates: New Law, New Rights, Adopted Persons, Birth Parents," CUB-MN brochure, November 1977, box 2, CUB-SWHA; Paul Klauda, "Seeking Out Birth Parents: Adoptees Unlock the Past" and "Law Allows Birth Parents to Maintain Privacy," *Minneapolis Tribune*, May 4, 1980, 1F, 11F.

12. See Melosh, *Strangers and Kin*, ch. 6, for a discussion of what she calls the "search narrative" advanced, in part, by adoptee and birthmother memoirs. Letters to Sperrazza and/or CUB-MN in box 4, CUB-SWHA.

13. If a birthparent wrote in hopes of locating children who were still under the age of eighteen, Sperrazza would advise them to attend a support group meeting until the adoptees became adults. A 1979 handbook discusses some of the records used by searchers: see Carol Anne Gray, "How to Find Your Past: A Search Handbook for Adoptee's [*sic*]," Pamphlet Publications, 1979, box 11, CUB-SWHA.

14. Letters to Sperrazza in box 4, CUB-SWHA.

15. Letter to Ann Landers, *Minneapolis Tribune,* April 28, 1978, 4C.

16. Open-records advocates and many CUB members argue that women uninterested in contact with their children constitute a small minority of the overall birthmother population. A pamphlet produced by the national CUB office, ca. 1978, claimed that "only a scant minority" of 5 to 18 percent of birthparents desired anonymity, noting that these figures came from "our experience—and [that] researchers and activist groups who effect reunions agree"—clearly a biased sample. Since these women's stories are, by definition, invisible in the literature by, and often about, birthmothers, we may never know their exact numbers. As vocal and visible as CUB is, however, we cannot assume that it represents the complete universe of birthmothers. For more on the dominance of the view that adoption inflicts psychological harm that can only be resolved through reunion, see Melosh, *Strangers and Kin*, 270–75. For more on development of birthmothers' rights claims, see Solinger, *Beggars and Choosers*, 118–24.

17. Melosh, *Strangers and Kin*, 248–53. One of the most cited works about the immutability of the biological bond between mother and child separated by adoption

is Nancy Verrier's *The Primal Wound: Understanding the Adopted Child* (Baltimore, MD: Gateway Press, 1993). Verrier, a psychotherapist and adoptive mother, is adored by the CUB community, and her book is described on Amazon.com as "the adoptees' bible." For a critique of the book, see Melosh, *Strangers and Kin*, 268–70.

18. This reimagining is based on events Mom described in "Greyhound."

19. Wikstrom, "Greyhound," 20.

20. Paul Sachdev, "Adoption Reunion and After: A Study of the Search Process and Experience of Adoptees," *Child Welfare* 71, no. 1 (January–February 1992): 53–68; Frances Pacheco and Robert Eme, "An Outcome Study of the Reunion Between Adoptees and Biological Parents," *Child Welfare* 72, no. 1 (January–February 1993): 53–64; Judith Modell, "'Where Do We Go Next?' Long-Term Reunion Relationships Between Adoptees and Birth Parents," *Marriage & Family Review* 25, no. 1–2 (September 2, 1997): 4–66; David Howe and Julia Feast, "The Long-term Outcome of Reunions Between Adult Adopted People and Their Birth Mothers," *British Journal of Social Work* 31 (2001): 351–68; Rae Goodwach, "Does Reunion Cure Adoption?" *Australian and New Zealand Journal of Family Therapy* 22, no. 2 (2001): 73–79; Julia Feast, "Adoption Search and Reunion: The Adoptive and Birth Parents' Perspective," *Adoption & Fostering* 26, no. 2 (2002): 64–65; Ulrich Muller, Peter Gibbs, and Sumi Gupta Ariely, "Adults Who Were Adopted Contacting Their Birthmothers," *Adoption Quarterly* 7, no. 1 (2003): 7–25; John Triseliotis, Julia Feast, and Fiona Kyle, "Summary: The Adoption Triangle Revisited: A Study of Adoption, Search, and Reunion Experiences" (London, England: BAAF, 2005); Karen March, "Birth Mother Grief and the Challenge of Adoption Reunion Contact," *American Journal of Orthopsychiatry* 84, no. 4 (2014): 409–19; Gary Clapton, "Close Relations? The Long-Term Outcomes of Adoption Reunions," *Genealogy* 2, no. 41 (2018).

21. Goodwach, "Does Reunion Cure Adoption?" 75, 77; quote from March, "Birth Mother Grief and the Challenge of Adoption Reunion Contact," 416.

22. Wikstrom, "Birth Rite," 10.

23. For more on the adoptees' reunions with birthmothers and birth siblings, see Sachdev, "Adoption Reunion and After," 65–66; Muller, Gibbs, and Ariely, "Adults Who Were Adopted Contacting Their Birthmothers," 10–11.

24. The Salvation Army Missing Persons service was first established in London in 1885 to help reunite families who had been separated as young people moved from rural areas to the cities to find work or by other economic, social, or health issues. In the 1990s, a woman named Astrid Steinsland from the Central Territory facilitated adoption reunions and published stories about them in a newsletter called "Booth Connection." Mom had thirteen copies of these newsletters in her possession. Though they are undated, it appears they were published between 1997 (volume 2) and 2001 (volume 6). Neither the Salvation Army Central Territories Museum nor the Salvation Army National Archives had any information about Astrid Steinsland or the adoption reunion service in their records. The Eastern Territory's Missing Persons Bureau no longer performs adoption-related searches: see https://easternusa .salvationarmy.org/use/missing-persons.

25. Quote and contents of this section from Sandy #2, interview with author, September 29, 2017, BMHOH-SWHA.

26. Some of these details from an email communication with Sandy's daughter, March 22, 2020.

27. Wikstrom, "Birth Rite," 10.

Notes to "Beginnings and Endings"

1. From "A Letter to Kim from Mom."

2. Tim O'Brien, *The Things They Carried* (Boston: Houghton Mifflin/Doubleday, 1990), 179–80.

3. Kim Heikkila, "A Child's Sorrow," in *Inside and Out: Women's Truths, Women's Stories: Essays from the Story Circle Network* (Georgetown, TX: Story Circle Network, 2017), 106-9.

4. For a tiny sampling of this work, see Trenka, *The Language of Blood*; Jane Jeong Trenka, Julia Chinyere Oparah, and Sun Yung Shin, eds., *Outsiders Within: Writing on Transracial Adoption* (Cambridge, MA: South End Press, 2006); Vilna Bashi Treitler, ed., *Race in Transnational and Transracial Adoption* (Basingstoke: Palgrave Macmillan, 2014); Barbara Yngvesson, *Belonging in an Adopted World: Race, Identity, and Transnational Adoption* (Chicago: University of Chicago Press, 2010); Toby Alice Volkman, *Cultures of Transnational Adoption* (Durham, NC: Duke University Press, 2005); Eleana J. Kim, *Adopted Territory: Transnational Korean Adoptees and the Politics of Belonging* (Durham, NC: Duke University Press, 2010); Kimberly D. McKee, *Disrupting Kinship: Transnational Politics of Korean Adoption in the United States* (Urbana: University of Illinois Press, 2019); Kim Park Nelson, *Invisible Asians: Korean American Adoptees, Asian American Experiences and Racial Exceptionalism* (New Brunswick, NJ: Rutgers University Press, 2016); and the work of Dr. Richard Lee, co-investigator of the University of Minnesota's International Adoption Project, https://innovation.umn.edu/international-adoption-project/team/faculty/. Statistics from Adoption Statistics, US Department of State—Bureau of Consular Affairs, https://travel.state.gov/content/travel/en/Intercountry-Adoption/adopt_ref/adoption-statistics1.html; "Child Adoption: Trends and Policies," Department of Economic and Social Affairs, Population Division, United Nations, 2009, 74–83; Intercountry Adoption & Global Child Welfare Statistics, Congressional Coalition on Adoption Institute, http://www.ccainstitute.org/resources; Shannon Prather, "Adoption Numbers Plummet in Minnesota and Nationwide," *Minneapolis Star Tribune,* June 23, 2018.

5. See, for example, Richard M. Lee, "The Transracial Adoption Paradox: History, Research, and Counseling Implications of Cultural Socialization," *Counseling Psychology* 31, no. 6 (November 2003): 711–44.

6. The following is from a blog I kept during the first year after Mom's death.

INDEX

Booth Girls was designed and set in type
by Judy Gilats in St. Paul, Minnesota. The text face
is Le Monde Livre Book and the display face is Futura.